Smart
Training

Smart Training

The Manager's Guide to Training for Improved Performance

Clay Carr

McGraw-Hill, Inc.

New York St. Louis San Francisco Auckland Bogotá
Caracas Lisbon London Madrid Mexico Milan
Montreal New Delhi Paris San Juan São Paulo
Singapore Sydney Tokyo Toronto

Library of Congress Cataloging-in-Publication Data

Carr, Clay.
   Smart training : the manager's guide to training for improved
performance / Clay Carr.
      p.   cm.
   Includes index.
   ISBN 0-07-010164-7
   1. Employees—Training of. I. Title.
HF5549.5.T7C29852 1992
658.3′124—dc20   92-7704
                                                    CIP

1 2 3 4 5 6 7 8 9 0 DOC/DOC 9 8 7 6 5 4 3 2

ISBN 0-07-010164-7

*The sponsoring editor for this book was Theodore C. Nardin, the editing supervisor
was Jane Palmieri, and the production supervisor was Donald Schmidt. It was set
in Baskerville by Carol Woolverton, Lexington, Massachusetts.*

Printed and bound by R. R. Donnelley & Sons Company.

*To the memories of
Elizabeth Hume Carr, my mother,
and Edward D. Myers, Ph.D.,
professor of philosophy at
Washington & Lee University,
the two people who more than any others
taught me that it was smart to think for myself*

Contents

Acknowledgments

The accounts of Preston Trucking, the Montreal Urban Community Transportation Commission, and numerous other examples of smart training have been adapted with permission from the National Society for Performance and Instruction journal *Performance & Instruction. P&I* also provided me my first opportunity to present some of these ideas in print. Thanks, Thiagi.

A sample job aid and several examples of smart training were furnished by Joe Harless of the Harless Performance Guild. Dr. Harless is well known for his pioneering work with job aids.

A job aid and example were also furnished by Jeff Nelson of Jeffrey Nelson Associates, another major source of job aid enthusiasm and training.

George Stybr, director of training for Caterpillar, Inc., contributed an example of that company's excellent job aids.

Valorie Beer has been kind enough to read a number of my writings, including the proposal for this book. You will find the book more helpful because of her. Thanks, Val.

Mike Snell, my literary agent, is one of my most valuable assets. Ted Nardin, the publisher of business books at McGraw-Hill and my editor for this book, was also extremely helpful. My thanks to you both.

Finally, my wife Gayle still remembered who I was and that she loved me even though she scarcely saw me for the summer of 1991. Thanks, darling—for this and so much more.

Clay Carr

Introduction: What Smart Training Will Do for You

$45.5 Billion—or Free?

How much is $45.5 billion? Well . . .

- Neither Chrysler nor Du Pont nor Boeing has assets or annual sales that high;
- Until 1945, the federal government didn't take in that much in taxes in a year; and
- Pakistan, with 114 million people, doesn't have a gross national product that high.

But in 1990, American business and industry spent $45.5 billion on formal training!

Knowing this, imagine my surprise when I sat in a conference recently and heard a speaker say, "Training doesn't cost anything."[1] At first hearing, this sounds foolish: Industry spent $45.5 billion for training, but training doesn't cost anything?

It was anything but foolish, though. The speaker was Robert W. Galvin, Chairman of the Executive Committee of Motorola, Inc. It was Galvin who has turned Motorola around from so-so performance to world class excellence. He's been there. He knows what he's talking about. When he says training doesn't cost anything, he's right.

What he means, and what this book is about, is smart training: training that pays back far more than its cost in improved performance. (Galvin was speaking specifically about training in Total Quality, but what he said is true of any training systematically designed to improve performance.) When you follow the principles in this book, it really doesn't matter how much money you spend for training because you will earn back much more in performance than the training costs.

Let me give you a quick example of why this is so. If American industry spent $45.5 billion for training, how much do you suppose it spent over and above that because it *didn't* do effective training? How much did it spend just

- To replace customers who were driven away by workers expected to provide effective customer service without proper training, *and*

- To reenter information that data entry people had entered incorrectly because they hadn't been trained properly on the new system, *and*

- To pay overtime for entire units to correct errors and catch up with their backlogs because no one had ever trained them in the most effective way to do the work, *and* . . .

The list goes on and on. Unfortunately, it touches only part of the problem. What about all the people who received ineffective training? What about

- The new workers who have to be retrained because their supervisors spend hours (lost to production) training them—but don't do it adequately, *and*

- The time that's spent resolving grievances caused by managers who deal poorly with performance problems because they have forgotten the training they received months before and have never used, *and*

- The time lost to production training workers and managers in new "flavors of the month" that are never implemented, *and* . . . ?

This list, too, goes on and on. The last decade has proven conclusively that American workers don't receive the training they need. Even worse, much of the training that's given isn't effective. Stop and think a moment about your own organization. How many crises, how much lost time, have you had in the past year because people weren't trained, or they forgot the details of the training they had, or they couldn't apply what they'd learned? How many times have you groaned to yourself because supervisors and specialists and secretaries came back from glitzy courses and then went back to doing their jobs the same old way? And how many hours have you and they lost getting trained in some fashionable new idea that never got applied in the organization?

In other words, the figure listed in your budget for formal training is nothing compared to the real costs of no training, poor training, and the wrong training. Firms need to do more training, but they need to do it far smarter than most do it now.

This book will show you how to do smart training—how to get the biggest bang for your training buck. It will do this by showing you how to increase the learning in your organization and, at the same time, significantly reduce the cost of that learning.

Please don't confuse effective training with high-tech, glitzy methods. The fancy techniques—computer-based training, multimedia—have their place. But so do very mundane, everyday techniques. Getting the greatest return for your training dollar means selecting just the right *type* of training for your needs. In Part 3, you'll get some very specific help on how exactly to do that.

Again, you can get very good, very effective training inexpensively. You only need to know what you're looking for—and insist on getting it. This book will help you do just that.

Where Smart Training Works

Let's leave the generalities for a moment, though, and look at the results some firms have achieved from smart training.

Everybody has orientation programs, or at least knows they should have them. But just what good do they do? When Corning installed their orientation program in 1980, they followed basic principles like those in this book. The first year the program was in effect was 1981. In follow-up studies, the company found that this one program reduced turnover enough to save the company $460,000 in that year alone.[2]

A major firm provided 30 days of conventional instruction to its new-hire service representatives. During the first week back on the job after this training, the representatives handled an average of three contacts an hour with a 20 percent error rate. The training was redesigned, based on the principles outlined in this book. The course time was reduced to *20* days—and during the first week on the job new representatives handled *four* contacts per hour with a *10 percent* error rate. (Sometimes less is more.)[3]

Federal Express measured the worth of its two-week basic training program for new couriers. It did a very careful study, comparing new workers with the training, new workers without the training, and veteran workers. The total cost to give the training was $1890 per individual, but an untrained new worker made errors costing $2341 more per year than a trained one. The $1890 training investment reduced first-year error costs by $451 more than it cost—for a one-year return on investment of 24 percent. (There was also an important but unanticipated outcome of the study: FEDEX discovered that veteran workers needed currency training because their own error rate was higher than that of the newly trained workers!)[4]

IBM moved thousands of student days out of classrooms into self-study or computer-based training. This resulted in savings in excess of $200 million each year. The enormous potential savings have led IBM to move more than 50 percent of its education in marketing and service to individualized learning centers in branch offices.[5]

Brace yourself for this one. Motorola embarked on an extensive campaign to train workers in Total Quality methods. Corporatewide, the training wasn't successful. A few plants, though, were dramatic exceptions. In those plants, the work force absorbed the whole curriculum of quality tools and process skills, and senior managers reinforced the training. The result? In the words of William Wiggenhorn, Motorola's vice president for training and education, "[We] were getting a $33 return for every dollar spent, including the cost of wages paid while people sat in class."[6]

A $33 return for a dollar spent is a return on investment (ROI) of 3300 percent. While this is truly impressive, it's not unique. CIGNA's training department, for instance, documented ROIs for its basic management training that ranged as high as 5900 percent for some courses.[7] Have you had a large number of investments with that return lately? Now you see why Robert Galvin is so emphatic that training costs nothing; he knows he's understating the case.

How You Can Profit from Their Ideas

The preceding examples aren't isolated, out-of-the-way incidents. Any firm, large or small, can use the methods these firms used to create smart training. IBM is a giant organization; Motorola's individual plants are relatively small. Size doesn't matter that much. The basic principles of smart training apply whether you're a manager in a firm with 100,000 employees, 1000 employees, or just 10 employees.

The ideas can be used in any size organization, but the way you use them may differ depending on the size. Because of this, most chapters in this book end with suggestions on how to apply the ideas.

- There's always a suggestion that you can use no matter what *the size of your organization* or *the source of your training*.
- Often there's a second suggestion, one you can use if you're in a large organization that has its own training department. This suggestion will help you deal with that department to get just the training you need. Don't worry—you won't have to become a training expert or learn training jargon. You just need to master and use a few basic principles.
- What if you don't have a training department? What if you have to send employees to canned courses or contract for training from a junior college or outside consultant? Many chapters have a third suggestion specifically for this situation. It shows you how to apply the principles in this book to get excellent results from outside training sources.
- Finally, suppose you have to do training yourself or have it done by one of your workgroups. You can't find anyone to do the training your people need, or they can't do it in time, or you can't afford it. This isn't a "how-to" book about training, but there's often a fourth suggestion to help you handle this situation. As you'll discover, you can use the two most cost-effective forms of training—job aids and structured on-the-job training—without any training experts around.

If all this sounds like a tall order, take a moment and turn to the end of a chapter that has a section headed "How to Use These Ideas." Take a quick look at the section. You'll see that there's nothing esoteric or technical about any of the ideas. In fact, they're just informed, intelligent common sense. That, in the long run, is exactly what smart training is.

Smart Training and the Learning Organization

You've heard about a "learning organization." Just what is it? And how does your organization become one? And what does it have to do with smart training? We'll get to those questions later on. For the moment, though, just keep in mind two of Peter Senge's descriptions of learning organizations. First, learning organizations are ones that "discover how to tap people's commitment and capacity to learn at *all* levels in an organization."[8] Second, a learning organization is one that is "continually expanding its capacity to create its future."[9] As you read through the book, keep these two characteristics in mind. In the last two chapters, you'll find that successful smart training is an effective way to transform your organization into a learning organization.

What You'll Find in This Book

Smart training has many aspects. In this book, the aspects are organized into four parts:

- *Part 1 gets to the basics of smart training.* Chapter 1 lays the groundwork: Smart training is always performance based. But, as Chapter 2 points out, this may be a bit more complex than it seems at first glance. Chapter 3 explains how critical an initial analysis is to effective training, while Chapter 4 very briefly describes the rest of the process experienced trainers go through to create training. Chapters 3 and 4 are very short; you need to understand the general ideas, but not the details.

- *Part 2 looks at the important topics of competence and mastery.* You may not use these words regularly, but the realities they describe are crucial to your firm's competitive success. Chapter 5 examines the benefit from spreading competence broadly and deeply through your work force. Chapter 6 builds on this with the idea of mastery—the necessary combination of competence with self-confidence. Chapter 7 looks at the basic strategic goal training: developing and maintaining the core competence of the firm. Chapter 8 suggests the kinds of competence that will be increasingly critical for success in the 1990s. Then Chapter 9 ends Part 2 by examining what has to happen for competence to actually get used.

- *Part 3 gets to the nitty-gritty of how you pick the most cost-effective training for your needs.* There are some bedrock principles of economical training; Chapter 10 shows you what they are. Chapter 11 looks at high-tech training methods, specifically video, computer-based training, and multimedia. Chapters 12 and 13 explain how to use just-in-time (JIT) training—in the form of job aids and structured on-the-job training. (Used properly, these are both very effective and very economical.) Chapter 12 also explores intelligent job aids, known as performance support systems. Chapter 14 looks at some other sources and methods of effective training.

- *Part 4 relates what you've read in the first three parts to the idea of the learning organization.* Smart training, with its emphasis on maximum learning at minimum cost, leads naturally to a learning organization.

Chapter 15 describes important characteristics of a learning organization and how smart training can help a firm develop these characteristics. Then Chapter 16 recaps the major ideas in the book and takes a final look at strategic and tactical learning.

- *The "Quick Guide to Media and Methods" summarizes the advantages and disadvantages of all the major training methods.* This Guide will help you get the best possible results from each method.

Throughout the book, you'll find repeated references to real organizations that practice smart training. Some of the firms are large (Corning, Inc., for instance), and some are much smaller (such as Preston Trucking or the Coast Guard). It doesn't matter; they've all discovered how to use smart training to improve performance and cut training costs at the same time.

I lead a group that furnishes training—as smart as we can make it—to an organization of some 65,000 individuals. There aren't many examples from this group because I want you to see how a variety of firms use smart training. Let me end this introduction, though, with a brief description of something the group has accomplished. It shows you how smart training looks in practice and what you can expect from it.

In the last half of 1988, we established a training program for an activity that pays several billion dollars a year to contractors and employees. We designed the overall curriculum and had the first courses ready to go in less than 6 months—a considerable accomplishment in itself. But then we started refining the training. By the summer of 1990, we had reduced training costs to a little under $13 per student hour (including the high up-front development costs). This meant that we were providing customized training for about what the organization would pay for the average canned course. Then we worked with the activity's managers to improve scheduling—and reduced the cost to just over $10 per student hour. Within the next few years, we intend, by further applying the approach described in this book, to reduce the cost even further.

Let me put this in perspective for you. Assume that there are 1000 employees, and each one needs 40 hours of training (in reality, there are more employees, and most receive far more training). By reducing the student-hour costs for those 1000 workers from $13 to $10, an organization saves *$120,000.* That's smart!

You have a right to expect this from your training department, or from anyone else who provides you with regular training. When you finish this book, you'll know how to deal with them to see that you get it.

PART 1

Just What Is Smart Training?

To cook a trout, first catch the trout. To get smart training, first get smart about what training can and should do for you.

We already know that the real goal of smart training isn't training but learning. In fact, smart training *means* the greatest amount of learning for the least cost. Unfortunately, this isn't what always happens. Any manager can tell stories of training that didn't work—of input clerks who kept making the same mistakes, salespeople who still refused to cold call, supervisors who still overappraised and undercounseled their workers. And any training manager can tell the same stories.

How can you avoid that? How can you get training that's more effective more often? Part 1 provides the basic answer to this question. The answer is simple and uncomplicated, but often overlooked. Here it is:

> The goal of smart training is learning that leads to improved performance.

That's it. It may not sound revolutionary, but it really is. As you go through the first part of this book, you'll see what's required to get training that really improves performance. This is what you'll find in it:

- Chapter 1 explains what has to happen for effective performance to occur and why training is only a part of what's needed. This doesn't mean that training is unimportant—but training won't necessarily improve performance by itself.

- Chapter 2 describes the different kinds of training that support performance. It also clarifies the difference between true performance-based training and education (the kind we got in school).

- Chapter 3 deals with a topic dear to the heart of every really good trainer—something called up-front analysis. Training is only smart when you know exactly what you want it to accomplish, and that's what up-front analysis is for. (Don't worry; the chapter doesn't get esoteric. And it isn't long. Front-end analysis is a very practical and basically a very simple step. You'll see.)

- Chapter 4 ends this part by presenting a very brief, nontechnical description of what has to happen to turn the analysis into an effective training course. It speaks to a frequent concern of managers: Why does training so often take so long to develop?

When you finish Part 1, you'll have the basic tools to ensure that the training your people get is smart training—training that provides the greatest performance improvement for the time and money spent.

1

Focusing on Performance

To use smart training, you need to understand what training cannot do. The introduction suggested that organizations may suffer as much from ineffective training as from lack of training. Training is smart not when it tries to improve performance by itself, but when it plays its part in a total approach to performance. In this chapter, we're going to examine the factors required for effective performance, and just how training fits in. We'll begin by looking at a trucking company that dramatically improved its performance in the 1980s by combining effective training with a total performance-focused approach.

The Preston Trucking Story

It was late in the 1970s, and the handwriting was on the wall: The trucking industry was going to be deregulated. Inefficient trucking companies would be swallowed up or simply forced out of business. Preston Trucking Company didn't intend to suffer either fate, but it knew it had to improve its operations sharply to be a survivor.

The problem was even more serious than it sounds. Preston's employees were, to put it euphemistically, unhappy. Since there were some 3000 of these employees, and many of them were paid 50 to 80 percent more than their nonunion counterparts, their unhappiness hurt! Preston might be the country's thirteenth largest freight carrier, but its future didn't look that rosy. In fact, it didn't look rosy at all.

Preston might have tried to improve just by developing training for everyone. Train customer-contact people in customer service and driv-

ers in safety (and in dealing with customers too). Train administrative
personnel to make sure they perform up to snuff. That's what many,
many companies do. It's not a bad approach, but it's far less effective
than the total approach Preston Trucking took.

Will Potter, CEO of Preston, implemented a total performance management system. It included training, but went beyond it. It dealt with
all the factors required for really effective performance. Here's a quick
summary of some of the steps the company took:

- Preston began to measure everything it could think of that affected
  costs and revenues. But these measurements weren't just for management, and they weren't just so poor workers could be identified. Everybody got to see the measurements. Everybody could see how many
  shipments were made per associate (Preston's new name for employees), how many miles trucks went without a breakdown, how many
  associates had perfect attendance, and many, many other measures.
  For the first time, each associate could see how he or she was doing.

- Once it could measure the critical factors, Preston could make its expectations for its associates very clear. Now that associates knew how
  long it took to ship freight, they could begin finding ways to ship it
  faster. Now that they knew how much they lost from damaged freight,
  they could begin reducing the damage.

- Preston established an official policy that each associate was an effective performer unless specific results indicated that he or she needed
  to improve. Then these specific results were used, working *with* the
  associate, to improve that performance. Despite the initial fears of
  some associates, poor performance never became a reason for criticizing or punishing the individual.

- Then the firm went even further. Managers began trying to praise at
  least four times for each time they pointed out deficient performance. They began to give informal recognition, too—plaques, and
  pens.

- There's one more point. If you want to praise your work force far
  more than you criticize it, your associates have to be very good at what
  they do. That's where training comes in. To Preston, the goal is simple and clear-cut: to build competent behavior. Put slightly differently, Preston used training combined with the total performance
  improvement program as the most effective way to improve performance.

What were the results of all this? Over the last decade, Preston has
been one of the most successful firms in the business. From 1978 to

1989, the number of terminals the company operated rose from 54 to 90, and the number of associates increased from about 3000 to just under 6000. The number of miles driven without a truck breakdown grew fourfold. Perhaps most indicative of all, Preston Trucking was described in the early 1980s as one of the best 100 companies in the United States to work for—and then 3 years later as one of the *10 best* to work for in the country.[10] When you can dramatically improve company performance *and* worker satisfaction that much, you've done a pretty good job.

What Does It *Make Sense* to Do? The Four Critical Factors of Performance

Why was Preston Trucking so successful? In a nutshell, it was because Preston considered *all* the factors required for effective performance and integrated training with a total approach. Let's look at these factors and at how training fits into the overall performance picture. We'll see that training is most effective when it's an integral part of a total performance improvement effort.

Why do you and I and other people perform as we do? Because that's what makes sense to us to do in the situation, based on what we know to do, have the means to do, know how to do, and have a motive to do—based on the feedback we've gotten from our past performance. Let's look at this in a little more detail.

If you want effective performance from your people, this is the most important single point to understand:

> *Everyone (you and I included) is constantly doing what makes sense to him or her in the situation.*

If your work force is performing efficiently and effectively right now, it's because that is what makes sense for them to do. If they're not— well, that's what makes sense to them.

Please note: I'm not saying that it's what would make the *most* sense to them in the *best* situation. Somewhere in your organization, right now, you have individuals who are taking actions they think are dumb. If things were different, they wouldn't do that. But things aren't different. They've been told to do it, because it's the way things are. So, in that situation, it makes the most sense to them just to go ahead and do it.

Why make a point of this? For two reasons. First, there are a lot of manipulative approaches to managing and supervising out there—approaches proposing that if you'll only push the right buttons you'll get the right responses. No question, you can do some of this some of the time. But people—like you and me—don't like to be manipulated. Any approach that deals with us as though we weren't thinking people who do what we do because it makes sense will backfire sooner or later. It's a lot easier just to recognize that people do what makes sense to them and deal with them that way.

There's a second reason, and it's this:

> *To change the performance of an individual, team, or organization, change what it makes sense to them to do.*

That's it in a nutshell. That's what it takes to manage performance effectively. Improve performance by changing what it makes sense for the worker (or supervisor or manager) to do.

The question, of course, is this: How do individuals decide what makes sense to them? They do it (often unconsciously) by asking and answering four questions.

What Do I Have the *Means* to Do?

This covers everything that an organization must provide individuals so that they can get their job done. It includes tools, equipment, and supplies. It also includes work scheduling and all the processes and procedures the work requires. Even the most expert secretary would have trouble performing well on a manual typewriter, and a unit of voucher examiners won't be very productive if its work comes in extreme peaks and valleys.

What Do I *Know* to Do?

Here's a critical point, and one that often causes performance to go wrong. How many frontline service people are there who think their job is protecting the company from its customers instead of serving them? And supervisors who think they should do all the challenging work themselves? And machinists who create mountains of scrap because they're going to make their production goals no matter what?

Organizations are full of individuals working hard to accomplish the wrong goals. Actually, there are two separate but related aspects to knowing what to do. The first is knowing just what output is important from my job. Do I do this or that? Make left-hand widgets or right-hand ones? Finish the Acme report or do market research for the new automated toaster? The basic idea of Total Quality, that an organization is a chain of customers and suppliers, is directed toward this single point: What's most important for me to do in my job?

The second aspect affects performance just as strongly: What standards am I expected to meet? How fast, how good, how much? Should I get the product out even though some of it is unusable, or make sure all of it is high quality even if it takes longer? Am I doing OK if I get office supplies quickly for a reasonable price, or should I take the extra time to make sure we get them for the lowest price?

What workers and managers understand to do and the standard to which it should be done put an absolute ceiling on performance. What we *know* to do limits our performance just as surely as does what we have the *means* to do.

What Do I *Know How* to Do?

All performance requires some degree of skill. Mail clerks need to know how to feed envelopes into the automatic opener, just as marketing managers need to know the steps to take to increase market share. All of us recognize how important it is for each worker to have the skills necessary to do the job.

The problem is that the skills workers need are changing rapidly and often becoming more complex. New computer systems, new software, new approaches to manufacturing, JIT delivery systems, Total Quality, self-managing teams—these and dozens of other competitive necessities change and increase what everyone involved must know how to do. And no matter how fancy my machinery is and no matter how well I know what I should do, if I lack the *know-how* to do it, it won't be done.

What *Motive* Do I Have for Doing It?

This is the final, and perhaps the most important, factor. We do what we have a sufficiently strong motive for doing; it's that simple. When Lee Iacocca took over Chrysler, few people could see the means for turning the company around, and fewer still knew what to do or had the know-how to do it. But, largely because of his motivation to succeed, Iacocca did it. The same thing happens less spectacularly every day; individuals with strong motivation overcome immense odds to accomplish their goals.

You, perhaps, can count on this motivation at times in your organization. Project teams (such as the one that designed the IBM personal computer) often have it. Really entrepreneurial self-managing teams sometimes have it. Day in and day out, though, it's terribly difficult for most people to sustain this level of motivation.

That's why all the factors—having the means, knowing what to do, knowing how to do it, and having a motive for doing it—are so important. Let me put that the other way around. The clearer you make your expectations and standards (knowing what), the better the supporting systems (means) you provide, and the greater the individual's competence (know-how), the less you will have to depend on a high level of motivation from the individual.

In other words, it's the balance of the factors that determines what makes sense to individuals and, therefore, what they will do. Preston Trucking concentrated on this balance; they created a total performance system. That's how they got such a dramatic improvement in the performance of their work force. They

- Made their goals and standards clear, so associates would *know* what was expected of them, and

- Worked constantly to improve safety, repair times, and equipment reliability so that associates would have the *means* to perform effectively, and

- Trained associates so that they would have the *know-how* to do their jobs well, and

- Recognized good performance and helped improve not-so-good performance so that associates would have a *motive* for performing well. Preston associates were also motivated by knowing what was expected of them and by being relied on to improve operations.

Remember the 3300 percent ROI that Motorola got from training in some of its plants? Motorola got it because the managers in those plants supported the goals of the training and integrated it into their overall operations. Wherever you find effective training, you'll find at a minimum that the training supports and is supported by the management practices of the organization.

Feedback: The Fifth Critical Factor

However, there's a final factor we haven't considered yet—one that's the linchpin of effective performance. Preston Trucking made it a vital part of its overall approach. Preston got the performance it wanted because everything else it did was supported by prompt, specific, direct, reliable, and useful *feedback*. Feedback is what powers the system and permits individuals to continually improve their performance.

Do you play bridge? Suppose you play one evening and the game goes like this: You and your partner bid the hand, then each of you is replaced by someone else who plays the hand for you. When the hand is over, you and your partner come back for the next round—but no one tells you what happened in the hand just ended. And then this repeats itself the entire evening. At the end, you're told that your play was fully satisfactory but could be improved, and the evening ends.

What a silly game that would be! How would you ever enjoy it, much less ever learn anything about the game? The answers to these questions are simple, of course: It wouldn't be satisfying and you wouldn't learn much. It would be a silly game indeed.

Yet this is the situation in which companies typically put workers—and even managers. Supervisors give workers basic information about the job, then workers learn the rest on their own or from other workers or managers—who may or may not know how to do the job well. If their supervisor tells them anything about their performance, it's once or twice a year, in general terms. If the supervisor talks with them in between times, it's usually because there's a problem with their performance.

Contrast that with what happens at Preston Trucking. Whatever counts for success or failure is measured, and everyone knows just how he or she is doing. Improving performance is easy because the information is

- *Prompt.* People find out about the results of their performance quickly, while it's easy to remember what they've done and they're able to change it.

- *Specific.* It contains the exact information that producers need to evaluate and, if necessary, change their performance.

- *Direct.* It comes from the individual or system that originates it directly to the worker, not through three or four supervisors or inspectors or other intermediaries.

- *Reliable.* The information is accurate, workers get it when they expect it, and it's in the form they expect.

- *Useful.* Workers can understand and use the information once they get it. (Information is most useful when it's presented objectively and nonjudgmentally.)

There's one other point about feedback that's critical: We only use feedback when it's about our performance on goals that matter to us.

Quantitative performance measures are a good example of this. Many firms make these quantitative measures primary: pack n number of boxes an hour, post n number of charges per hour, and so on. If that's the only standard, or clearly the primary one, information on the *quality* of performance will simply be ignored. If my goal is to pack 18 boxes an hour to meet my standard, I will. If I know that three of these boxes aren't sealed properly, I will ignore that data. It simply isn't related to my goal.

Now we have everything we need to understand how people, all of us—workers and managers and supervisors—perform as we do. We take actions that make sense to us, by taking account of what we *know* and *know how* to do, the *means* available to do it, and our *motives* for doing it. Then, when we act, we look for *feedback* from the results to tell us how effective what we did was—so we can change the way we perform in the future, if necessary.

How (and Where)
Training Fits In

What's the message in this discussion of performance? It's twofold. First, workers do what they do because that's what makes sense to them—and everything in their work environment affects their decision. Their work schedules affect their performance, as does the organization's pay plan, the informal "culture" where they work, the kind of equipment they use, the kind of supervision they get, and dozens of other considerations. What workers want from the job is also critically important; an individual who values a warm social environment at work will perform differently from someone who wants rapid promotion.

In other words, even the best training in the world is only a part of the performance equation. Depending on the other factors, training may dramatically alter performance, or have no visible effect at all. We'll pick this theme up again in Chapter 3 when we look at something called "up-front analysis."

The second point is this: Even though training is only part of the solution, it *can* help improve performance. In fact, as the introduction suggested, it can sometimes improve performance dramatically. Here is a short list of what it can and cannot do.

It Can Markedly Increase
Individuals' *Know-How*

Smart training can significantly increase the *know-how* of individuals. This is its strongest suit. It can help make workers much more competent at their jobs. Mazda spent some $11,000 to train each worker it hired for its new Flat Rock, Michigan, plant—*before* it opened the plant. At its plant in Blacksburg, Virginia, Corning took 25 percent of each worker's time the first year for training. Not all of this was for improved skills (know-how), but much of it was.

It Can Change What Individuals *Know* to Do

Smart training can make it clear what workers should do and the standards of quality, quantity, and timeliness expected from them. It can inform them of company policies and procedures that are important to them. It can help workers set realistic priorities. It can help them understand their roles in the organization, decide where to go for help with a problem, and appreciate what the product they help create will be used for. This is an important use of training, and training is very effective for it.

I have to pause here to make a most important point. It's this:

> *Training can provide workers with knowledge and know-how, but it will not make workers use them.*

Chapter 9 will examine in detail what has to happen for individuals to use the knowledge and know-how they gain in training. For now, just remember that workers won't use anything they get in training unless it's supported and reinforced back on the job. Now, let's return to our discussion of what training can and cannot do.

It Will Not Improve the *Means* Available to Do Their Job

This seems obvious. No amount of the smartest training can increase the means that workers have available to do their work back on the job. In fact, insufficient means *increase* the training that's necessary. Here's an all-too-common example. Every year training organizations all over the country (mine included) are called on to train data entry personnel of all kinds. Why do they need this training? Because the automated system doesn't have clear, easy-to-understand procedures for entering data. There's another, much worse but still common form of this: No amount of training will help because the automated system itself causes errors.

One of the smartest actions you can take is to ensure that the systems supporting your workers don't increase the training burden in the process. The best way to promote smart training is to make it unnecessary whenever possible. (Does this sound strange? Chapter 12, on job aids, will show you how you can often do just this.)

It Will Not Reliably *Motivate* Workers

Finally we come to one of the most frequent misuses of training: training to *motivate* workers. I'm sure you've been to that kind of training, since organizations often have training to motivate *managers* as well as workers. What's the usual pattern? You go, get motivated, leave the training—perhaps on a real high. Two weeks later, everything is the same as it was before.

The fact of the matter is that every individual's motivation is a product of *all* the performance factors—and of the individual's need structure as well. It's difficult to design a work environment that will motivate most workers effectively; it's all but impossible to produce this motivation with training.

It Will Never Substitute for Useful *Feedback*

Feedback is absolutely essential for improving performance. Even the best training in the world will flop if workers get no feedback on how effectively they're applying the training. This is so true, so obvious—and so often overlooked.

In short, train people extensively to *know* what's expected of them and *know how* to do it. Try to avoid training them because systems or schedules or equipment or some other *means* for performance are poorly done; correct the situation instead. Forget about training workers to *motivate* them; either the total job situation (including how you treat them) motivates them to perform as you want, or nothing will. Finally, even the best training in the absence of *feedback* will fail.

Three Points Worth Remembering

1. The primary goal isn't a lot of training; it's a lot of *learning* for the least amount of money.

2. The goal of this learning is *improved performance*, never anything less.

3. The performance of individuals depends on what *makes sense* to them to do in specific situations. What makes sense, in turn, is based

on what workers *know* and *know how* to do, what they have the *means* to do, what they have a *motive* to do, and the quality of the *feedback* they get. Improving their performance means changing one or more of these factors so that better performance is what makes sense to them. Smart training is a key part of this.

How to Use These Ideas

- Have a clear idea of what you want from any training. You may want an individual trained to type faster, create more complete budget models, or develop a team to manage a manufacturing plant. What goal you set is up to you—but you must have one. If you don't have a clear idea why you're sending an individual to training, the chances are excellent that you'll be wasting time and money. You're the key. Know the performance you want from training, see that the individual being trained knows what you want, and then check to see if you got it.

- Do you have a training department, or do you depend on external trainers? It makes no difference. Know the performance you want to improve by training and then make sure that your providers develop the training to produce this improvement.

- Do you have to provide some or all of the training for your workgroup? The performance focus is even more important. *Don't* begin by thinking, "Oh, I'll have to work out a course for this that will take everyone away from the job for at least all morning." Begin by concentrating on the performance improvement you want; be very, very specific about it. Then use the ideas presented in the rest of this book to choose how to develop the training.

2
What Do You Need: Training, Educating, Orienting, or . . . ?

The MUCTC Story

Montreal, Quebec, Canada, is like many American cities: It's multicultural and becoming more so. This raises problems, particularly for bus drivers who have to deal with people from different cultural backgrounds every day. Because the situation is new and strange, not all bus drivers handle it well.

The Montreal Urban Community Transportation Commission (MUCTC) decided to deal with this situation by developing a multicultural awareness program for the drivers. Stop for a moment and ask yourself how you'd expect this to be done. Perhaps a series of lectures on cultural differences, supplemented by videos and discussion. The instructor might have told everyone how important multicultural awareness was and tried to "motivate" the drivers to be more culturally aware. Predictably, everyone would have had their "awareness" raised and would have "understood" the problem better—and then there would have been little if any improvement in the drivers' performance.

This isn't what the commission did, though. Instead, it created a highly interactive program that involved the bus drivers from the beginning. It was presented by experienced bus drivers—people whom the participants knew understood their situation. The participants dealt with real-life situations, suggesting themselves what they could do to handle them effectively. And at the end of the one-day program, all participants made out Personal Action Plans detailing two to five specific actions that they would each take to improve their service to passengers from a variety of cultures. (A copy of the plan went to each participant's supervisor, so supervisor and driver could review it periodically together.)

Two goals of the training were to help individuals understand people from various cultures and to feel differently about them. The most important goal, though, was to get bus drivers to *act* appropriately. That's why the training focused from beginning to end on specific incidents and behaviors. By doing so, it concentrated on improving the *performance* of the bus drivers.[11]

This chapter will tell you more about the kind of training that results in improved performance, and how you tell it from training that doesn't.

Just What Should Training Do for You?

How many courses have you sent your people to, and attended yourself, that sounded like these?

- Quality Awareness Training
- An Overview of the Automated Payroll System
- New Employee Orientation
- Understanding Strategic Planning
- Safe Practices for All Employees

We get so used to this kind of course that we often just ignore it and let it happen. That's not the way to get smart training. Stop and ask yourself a question:

What job performance does each of these courses improve, or even support?

The answer, typically, is none. Courses that help attendees "understand" or "appreciate" something or provide an "overview" of something seldom provide them with either knowledge or know-how that they can use. Often, it's supposed by someone that these courses somehow "motivate" workers—but we've already seen that training doesn't do this well. Consequently, the net result is a few hours away from the job, with a break in the routine, some lost production, and little impact on anyone's performance.

I threw in the last sample course ("Safe Practices for All Employees") because it illustrates a different kind of wasted training. Safe practices are extremely important, but workers perform their duties in a wide variety of situations. The jobs of crane operator, stock picker, data entry clerk, and project manager all have very different hazards. Trying to lump them all into one course, as many firms do, produces a course that helps everybody a little bit and no one very much—and bores everyone in the process.

In reaction to this, many training designers and training departments have veered to the opposite extreme: The job of training is to train individuals to perform specific tasks, period. This is a clear improvement over the fuzzy kinds of training already listed. A course entitled "How to Enter Payroll Data and Correct Errors" is almost certainly going to improve performance more than an "overview" of the system.

As with so many reactions, this one can go too far. One trainer, obviously fed up with the approach, described such training disparagingly as "what we do to or for people. It does not involve a critical thinking process. Training only requires that we learn a specific thing and follow the directions precisely."[12]

I certainly share this trainer's dissatisfaction with training understood so narrowly; I suspect that you do too. But this kind of narrow training is no more smart training than is the fuzzy training we looked at a moment ago. Bouncing from one extreme to the other has an impressive-sounding name—*enantiodromia*—but it's a truly second-rate strategy for training. Let's see if we can find a better one.

Why Education Isn't Enough

As a way into this problem, reflect a moment on your own education. As you went through grade school, most of your courses involved two kinds of learning. First, you memorized rules (the multiplication table, subject-object agreement, "*i* before *e* except after *c*"). Second, you memorized facts (Cheyenne is the capital of Wyoming, George Washington was the first president).

Some of this continued into high school (as you learned the Pythagorean theorem and memorized the battles of the Civil War). But two new and closely related phenomena occurred. If you were lucky, you got a few teachers who dealt with ideas, not just facts. And you discovered that the "hands-on" courses like typing and auto mechanics were for the poor souls who weren't going to college. People on the college track took the "ideas" courses.

This got reinforced after high school. Individuals who went to technical schools or community colleges studied computer repair and bookkeeping. The ones who went to college took computer programming and accounting. The difference? Computer repair and bookkeeping are just "practical," while computer programming and accounting have lots of "theory." That makes the latter courses more important.

Most of us have soaked up three basic ideas from these experiences. First, what really matters is the theory; anyone can pick up the practice. Second, the best way to learn is to listen quietly and intently to an expert lecture. Third, the best place to do this listening is a classroom. We carry these ideas over to the workplace with us: If you want to get your people trained, put them in a classroom and have an expert come in and explain all the theory to them. This is where we get the "overviews" and courses that focus on "understanding" and "appreciating."

You've probably found this out for yourself. If you haven't I want to let you in on a secret: *None* of the three ideas is true. Theory is no more important than practice; listening to an expert lecture is a secondary way of learning at best; and none of this needs to happen in a classroom. Theory has its place, an important one. Classrooms have their place too. Lecture has its place as well, but only when it's held to a minimum and supports other learning methods.

At the end of Chapter 1, I made three important points about smart training. Here's a very brief summary of them, to which I've added a fourth point:

1. The primary goal of smart training isn't training but *learning*. Specifically, it's the most learning for the least expenditure of time, money, and effort.

2. The goal of this learning is *improved performance.*

3. The performance of individuals depends on what *makes sense* to them, based on what they *know* and *know how* to do, what they have the *means* to do, what they have a *motive* to do, and the quality of the *feedback* they get. Firms improve performance by changing one or more of these factors so that better performance is what makes sense to the individual.

4. The goal of training—improved performance—is the ability to *do* something effectively. *The way someone learns to do something is by doing it.*

Now you can see where the people who believe that training is only for specific skills get their ideas. We have to go beyond these ideas, though, and look at learning in a much broader context if we want it to be effective. This entire book is an attempt to do that; each chapter should help you increase your understanding of training in a broad, managerial context. For now, though, let's look at some of the specific ways that training can improve performance.

What It Means to Improve Performance

The question is simple and straightforward: What does an individual need to know and to know how to do to perform well?

Specific Job Skills

This is the place to begin, with the skills that an individual needs to perform the specific duties of the position. Training these skills is always the first priority. Here are some examples of it.

A data entry clerk needs to input data into the system rapidly and without errors. It's nice if the person knows how the data will be used and how the system functions. These knowledges probably won't affect performance, though. What the individual *must* have is the skill to read the data and punch it in without errors. That's what's necessary to support performance.

A computer technician needs to identify and repair malfunctions rapidly and without errors. It's probably interesting to the individual to know the history of the computer and of the computer system in the company, but it won't speed up the repair process. The technician *needs* to understand how the various chips and boards function, and how to use test equipment to track down their malfunctions.

A supervisor needs to discuss substandard performance with individual workers in a way that will help them improve. It's nice for the supervisor to understand Maslow's hierarchy or the company's rules for appraising performance, but none of that will provide the skills required in the face-to-face counseling situation. What the supervisor *requires* is basic skills training on providing objective feedback, helping workers set improvement goals, and following up effectively.

If you're starting to react that this is too rigid and too limiting, I understand. If it were all there were to performance-based training, I'd agree with you. Remember, though, we're just talking about the core of training—the training that has to happen or else. That's training in the specific skills required by the specific duties of specific positions. Nothing, absolutely nothing, substitutes for these.

Why am I dwelling on this? Because far too much training mixes long strings of background, overview, appreciation, and education in general with the skills needed for performance. As a result, training takes far longer than it needs to, and the emphasis on effective performance is diluted by the aspects of the training that have nothing to do with effective performance. Moreover, trainees often find the nonperformance parts of the training the most interesting, which completely reverses where their attention and effort should be. (After all, how fascinating did you find it to memorize the multiplication table?)

The moral is simple. If you want to do smart training, provide workers with training that supports the specific duties of their positions, and do it as soon as possible after they enter the position. (Later chapters contain specific details on how to do this.)

Acclimation

The term *acclimation* doubtless sounds a little strange. The other words I could use for it are even worse: acculturation, indoctrination, and inculcation. Despite its strangeness, acclimation has a simple meaning: Training people in "what we believe and how we do things around here."

The Japanese had to remind us that organizations function better when people can work closely together—and that working together requires everyone to understand what's important in *our* organization. Some American firms have learned the lesson. In one major computer firm, "employees are bound together in their common endeavor through extensive training and orientation programs that help them to develop common values and a sense of shared purpose.... The results have been spectacularly successful." [13]

Here are a few quick examples of the way that organizational values show up. None of the following statements ever appears in a job sheet, but think how a job is affected by them:

"We all work together here; we're one team. If you have a problem, I'll help you. If I have a problem I'll expect you to help me. No one will criticize you if you make a mistake, but everyone will expect you to learn from it."

"Our pay is good and we expect a good's day work for it. Be here on time, do what you're told, and get your day's quota done."

"The job you have to start with isn't the greatest, but it's where we start everyone. We expect you to learn it thoroughly and do it well. We promote from within, and we're always looking for people with the ability and motivation to move upward."

It takes little imagination to see that "good performance" means something different in each of these situations. That's the influence of the organization's culture, and it affects performance at all levels—from the day individuals enter the organization until the day they leave.

You won't want to play anthropologist and explain the culture to each worker in detail. That's back to education and the notion that ideas are what really count. But training should include substantial information on what's expected from the new worker who's now a member of your organization.

What do you cover? Here are two examples:

1. Does your firm have a working Total Quality program or use self-managing teams? New workers, even experienced ones, may not understand what this means for the way their job is organized and what's expected of them. Tell them, and tell them quickly. The general principle is this: Explain to new workers immediately how your organization is different from what they may be used to and, therefore, expect from you.

2. New workers need to understand how to treat others and how to expect to be treated themselves. Is your organization extremely informal, with everyone on a first-name basis and expected to communicate with everyone else? Or does it believe in more formal relationships, with contacts through the chain of command? Don't let a new worker find out this kind of information by making mistakes out of ignorance.

Hopefully, these two examples will get you thinking of exactly what new workers in your organization need to hear about who you are and how you operate. In addition, workers need to know how to really get things done in the organization. This involves very specific skills called "context skills," and Chapter 8 will deal with them in more detail.

What Else?

Haven't we left out a great deal? Sure—but perhaps not what you think.

For instance, take *orientation*. This is a big item in many companies. To the extent that it instills an initial pride in new workers, it may be useful and contribute to their performance. An orientation that shows new workers how what they do fits into the overall process of satisfying customers is even more useful. But a laundry list of facts about your company has little effect; neither does much of the traditional hype about how big and great the firm is. We've already looked at the importance of acclimating new workers to the firm's values. That's the best possible form of orientation.

There is more you can do. Instead of a traditional orientation, you can simply take time to see that new workers (and *all* your workers) know the importance of what your unit does, exactly what your customers need, how to give it to them, and how to find out if they're not getting it. This isn't just a training problem; all the training in the world won't create an effective production and feedback processes. But once you have these processes in place, see that your people are trained to understand and use them.

It's also possible to set specific performance goals and build orientation around them—as Corning did. We saw in the introduction that Corning saved some $460,000 in one year alone. This didn't happen accidentally. When Corning established the orientation program, its goals were (1) to reduce turnover in the first 3 years of employment by 17 percent; (2) to reduce the time needed to learn the job by 17 percent; (3) to improve the quality of the new person's contribution; (4) to impart a uniform understanding of Corning's principles, objectives, strategies, and expectations; and (5) to build a positive attitude toward the company and the communities in which it operates.[14]

Note that this approach to orientation combines a focus on performance with effective acclimation. The first two goals are specifically measurable; you can't get more focused on performance than this. The third goal is directly concerned with values; the fourth one also deals with values, though somewhat more indirectly. This is truly a smart way to orient new workers.

What about training in *problem solving and creativity*? It's great—if your organization values these and expects them. If it does, then problem solving and creativity are really part of people's jobs. Training people in them is just another form of performance-based training—smart training. If you don't expect and support problem solving and creativity in day-to-day work—well, training people in the skills is a simple waste of time. (And, in all probability, extremely frustrating for them.)

In the introduction I quoted Robert W. Galvin's comment that "training doesn't cost anything." This is generally true of smart, performance-based training. It's particularly true—and this is how Galvin meant it—of training that teaches workers the skills they need to constantly improve the company's processes and performance.

This use of training is one of the great strengths of Total Quality. When workers understand the basic process of which their jobs are a part, their ability to contribute to the company rises sharply. Take a simple example: clerks that examine requests for name changes on stock certificates. If the clerks have a checklist of the information that should be on the form, they can check the forms and route them. Explain to them *why* the information is needed and *what* it's used for, and the clerks' ability to process the requests will go up sharply. On top of that, they can look at the process in a new way and begin to find ways to improve it.

The best combination is to see that workers *know how* the process works, *know* that one of their responsibilities is to improve the process, and *know how* to use relevant problem-identifying and problem-solving methods. Whenever you train individuals to solve problems and be creative, though, remember that the training's all wasted if your firm doesn't expect workers to use these skills routinely on the job. (Initially Motorola's training was successful in only a few plants. In the rest, the major reason for failure was that managers didn't give workers the chance to use their learning on the job.)[15]

What about Development?

What about development? Don't you need to train workers and managers to be ready for the next step up? This isn't a book about development, as important as it is. We will look at it briefly a few chapters from now, but for the moment here are a few (even briefer) comments.

The best form of development in the world is giving workers and managers *significant freedom and responsibility on their current jobs*—and expecting them to continuously improve processes and performance. There is absolutely nothing that will substitute for this.

Amplify this by permitting individuals to *work for a time at each other's jobs* and, if possible, at higher-level jobs. This is particularly useful as a reward for effective current performance.

(I have to pause and tell you a quick true story about this. Data entry clerks—and their predecessors, keypunch operators—have terribly dull and boring jobs. Typically, data entry units have high turnover, high absenteeism, and low morale. But I know of one glaring exception. In one particular unit, turnover was high, but absenteeism was amongst the lowest in the organization, and morale was excellent. Why? Because the supervisor had made arrangements that individuals who completed their assigned work could train several hours a week for jobs that would be realistic promotion opportunities for them. All the classroom development in the world would be a pale substitute for this.)

This is the one point at which education can also be useful. Be sure you have an active *tuition-assistance program* that lets anyone in your organization take night courses relevant to his or her job. And interpret "relevant" broadly. The content of the courses may be useful to your organization—but the self-discipline and enhanced ability to learn the courses required will be even more useful.

Finally, each worker and manager should have an *individual development plan* of some sort. In many organizations these become rituals, just another layer of paper that weighs down the operation. That's wrong— but don't throw out the infant with the used cleansing liquid. Keep development plans simple and realistic. See that each worker and manager knows what these plans are really for and how to use them. It works for Motorola. Under its Annual Performance Appraisal and Career Plan, each employee meets with his or her supervisor at least annually to review career objectives and need for further training and development.[16]

By the way, you'll find that many of these practices (such as individual development plans) appear again in the book. The basic principles of smart training are simple; so are many of the organizational practices that reinforce and amplify this training. One of the basic problems most organizations have isn't that they don't adopt new practices, but that they aren't effective at implementing those they already have. You'll see again and again in this book that for training to work it and the organization's practices must constantly synchronize with one another.

How People—Like You and Me—Learn

There are volumes written on how people learn. There's probably a study somewhere of how left-handed redheads from eastern Nebraska learn best. You don't need to worry about all that. But there's one consistent characteristic of effective learning you do need to know. It's this:

People learn best when they actively participate in the learning. People learn the skills they need to perform only when they actually use these skills.

You recognize this as the restatement of a point I made near the beginning of this chapter. Just hearing or even seeing what should be done isn't enough. Someone once described the lecture method as a process by which certain information passes from the notes of the instructor to the notes of the student without affecting the minds of either in transit. That's more accurate than funny, and I expect your own experience bears it out. You and I simply aren't good at sitting passively and soaking up knowledge. And when the knowledge is how to do something (know-how), all the listening in the world won't give us the skills we need.

Some lecture can be useful, depending. It's a reasonably efficient way to transmit some information. People are used to it, so it's familiar. Used skillfully, it can get people thinking about a topic or explain what they are to do. None of this, though, is performance. Performance is doing something, not listening to someone else tell you how to do it.

Use this idea as a basic guideline. When someone proposes training for your people, check to see how the students will actually develop the skills. For instance, if it's a session on customer service, will they simply be told what customer service is and exhorted to do it, or will they actually practice key customer service skills? If managers are going to learn about performance coaching, will they just be told about it, with perhaps a case study or two, or will they have to role-play a counseling session that taxes their abilities and starts them learning how to really do it.

Don't forget this. See that any training course you send your people to actively involves them and gives them the chance to practice the skills they're supposed to be learning. But don't let their active involvement end there. What happens when they return to the job is critical, because

People learn when they put the skills they learn to work immediately on the job.

Look back at MUCTC's approach to training at the beginning of this chapter. All participants made Personal Action Plans, and copies of their plans went to their supervisors. That way, supervisors could make sure that bus drivers actually put to work what they'd learned. As good as the training was overall, this one factor probably made it twice as effective as it otherwise would have been.

What if workers can't put what they've learned to work immediately? Provide them with opportunities to practice the new skills until they can actually use them. Practice isn't as effective as actual use in developing and maintaining skills, but it's a thousand percent better than not using them at all.

Later in the book, we're going to look at just-in-time (JIT) training—training that's delivered just as the individual needs it. Even when training is performance oriented, it loses its effectiveness unless it's used immediately. To the greatest feasible extent, send people to training just before they need it, and then have them use the training as soon as they get back on the job. That's a unique contribution that you as a manager can make to see that the training your people get is effective.

Let me end this section with a solid-gold suggestion. Do you really want smart training, training that significantly improves performance? Identify the performance improvement you want. See that the training is well designed (which is what the next two chapters are about). Make it clear to the people who attend training why they're going. Have your people put their new skills to work—or at least practice them—as soon as they return to the job. Then take one more step:

Raise your performance standards (or at least your performance expectations), to reflect the increased performance you expect from the training.

Do this with the cooperation and participation of your work unit. Let them take as large a role as possible. At the minimum, be sure that the individuals involved know what you're doing and why; don't simply impose a higher standard on them. However the standard's developed, make it clear that they're taking the training so that they can use it to achieve this higher standard as the new norm. Tying well-designed training in with immediate use back on the job and a new standard that reflects the training is smart training indeed! Tennessee Eastman does this by comparing present performance with what the unit's standards should be, designing training to move workers to the new standards, and then expecting them to meet these standards after training.[17]

How to Use These Ideas

- See that individuals put any training they get to use as soon as possible after they get it. You're the manager; you can control this. If you know what you expect from training and then expect individuals to do it when they return, you'll get the maximum possible benefit from any training. It sounds simple, but it's critical.

- In this case, it doesn't matter whether the training is done by a training department or an outside source. Your part of the action is to see that it's put to work immediately. (You may think that this is often impractical; you can't get training for your people when they need it. There are ways to resolve this dilemma. Just keep reading.)

- Do you or one of your people have to provide the training? That has one advantage; you can time the training so that it can be put to work as soon as it's given.

3

The Gateway to Smart Training: Effective Analysis

Smart training happens when people learn what they need to improve their job performance—and only then. But how do you really know what they need? How do you know the way to create the greatest performance improvement for the time and money spent?

This and the next chapter speak to these questions. Each chapter is short, and between them they describe what trainers do to create effective, performance-based training. They're not written to make you a training designer, any more than a guide to cost accounting for managers would make you a cost accountant. Instead, they'll give you a compact overview of the process required to develop training that improves performance.

Why include them at all? Because a solid up-front analysis (described briefly in this chapter) and solid design and development (described just as briefly in the next chapter) are absolutely essential to smart training. If you need performance improved, you want training quickly; it's very easy to say, "I just can't afford the time—give me the training *now.*" But these steps take time to do. If you know what happens at each of the steps and how the process pays off in training effectiveness, you may be a little more patient and give your training folks time to do them right.

Think of it this way: Analysis, design, and development are really a problem-solving process. The problem is performance that falls below expectations. The solution is training that improves performance. Any problem-solving activity begins by framing the problem so that it can be most effectively solved. Then the problem solver decides what's needed to actually solve it and implements the solution. This is precisely what happens in training: The trainer frames the problem (analysis), decides how to solve it (design), and then solves it (development and delivery). The better the problem-solving process, the greater the performance improvement.

Let me give you an example of just how important an effective process is and just how great its payoff can be. Here's what happened at the U.S. Coast Guard Training Center in Petaluma, California.

The Petaluma Story

The Coast Guard Training Center provides training to more than 4000 students each year in some 25 countries. In 1983 the training provided by the center was much like that of many other training organizations. The courses weren't solidly linked to improved performance, and no one followed up to see whether student job performance improved after training. It took 2 years to lay a foundation for smart training at the center. Then, between 1985 and 1990, the center

- Reduced its staff and instructor positions by 24 percent (a recurring annual saving of $840,000), and

- Reduced the amount of time its students spent away from their jobs in training by 35 percent (a recurring annual savings of over $2 million in time returned to productive use), and

- At the same time increased the effectiveness of the training that was provided.[18]

For an organization that began the process with fewer than 125 positions, that accomplishment wasn't chopped liver. It was, in fact, the kind of savings that most managers only dream about where their training budget is concerned. If you're not using performance-based training, you can achieve savings like these—and get better training at the same time.

How can you do this? By seeing that your training providers follow the same kind of systematic process to develop training that Petaluma did. The next chapter will look briefly at the process of actually designing and developing training. This chapter concentrates on something called "up-front analysis" that begins the process.

What Is This Thing Called Up-Front Analysis?

You may have blanched a bit at the previous paragraph because it sounds like I'm getting technical on you. I'm really not. You don't need to learn or remember any details about the process. If you get a feel for what it takes to produce smart training, however, you greatly improve the chances that you'll get it. (Just for the record, by the way, what I'm calling up-front analysis is also called front-end analysis, needs analysis, training needs analysis, and so on. Don't let the name hang you up. If your organization uses a term different from up-front analysis, use that term.)

There are a lot of other areas in your business that you need to understand but not to know in detail. Consider what you know about what your accountants do. You don't need to know the details of their work, and you probably don't want to. If you want to benefit from what they do, though, you do need to grasp the basics of what they're up to. Once you have these basics down, you can make sure you get what you need from them—and leave the doing of it to them.

That's how it is with up-front analysis (and with training design and development). You don't need to know the details of any of it, unless you have to provide the training yourself. But you do need to know what an effective trainer does so that you can make sure the people who provide you training do it. And nothing they do is more important than a careful up-front analysis.

You shouldn't be surprised that training is more effective when careful analysis is done up front. Virtually every bit of evidence about corporate performance shows that the firms that do realistic, systematic data collection and analysis in the beginning produce a more successful result. This is true at every level in the organization, from the shop floor to the executive suite.

Good analysis is just as important for successful training as for any other successful corporate endeavor. And it's necessary for even the briefest training. (*Note:* In general, the more thorough the analysis and design, the briefer the training can be and still accomplish its goal.)

Robert Galvin of Motorola has made the same point repeatedly: Time and effort invested up front lead to far more efficient and effective performance later in the cycle. The reverse is also true: When the up-front work isn't done, problems plague the process the rest of the way. If the goal of smart training is to improve performance, you can't expect it to work unless you first find out exactly *what* performance needs to be improved and *how* it can be improved.

With that preparation, let me say this—as clearly and forcefully as I can:

If you want smart training, it must begin with an effective up-front analysis of the performance situation. There are no exceptions, period.

But won't this take time? Yes. Won't it delay the training? Yes. Can't I skip it so that I can get my people trained? No.

Let me give you an example. A major corporation, known for its success with Total Quality, began its program by providing some $7 million worth of training to its first-line supervisors and workers. When its director of training later described the situation, he said: "We would have accomplished more if we had given the $7 million to the United Fund." *Seven million dollars* wasted—and by a competent, effective corporation.

By the way, the corporation learned from its mistake. Its managers sat down, started over, and analyzed the situation. When they acted on the basis of this analysis, that program was immensely successful. They still provided a tremendous amount of training—but this time the training was integral to the program's success.

In other words, spend the time. A good up-front analysis lays the necessary groundwork for training that will produce the greatest performance improvement for the least expenditure. It will also do something more important; it will tell you *whether training will help you at all.* Many times, changes in work flow or compensation systems, or even being clear about what's important in a job, can produce far more performance improvement than training. When this is the case, you don't want to waste money and effort on training.

Training as Part of the Big Picture: The Superior Investments Story

We saw how Preston Trucking combined training with other performance improvement practices to increase its effectiveness dramatically. Let me give you another example of how up-front analysis produced a far more effective solution than training alone would have.

It began when a Canadian firm we'll call Superior Investment Services (a pseudonym)* wanted to improve its operations department. It

---

*In most cases, I am able to use the real names of the firms mentioned in this book. In some cases, and "Superior Investments" is one, I cannot. There are several reasons why firms don't want their real names used. One of them is simple: A major performance improvement project gives them a competitive advantage that they're not anxious to share with their competitors.

began by setting specific goals: Improve the overall accuracy of transactions, reduce the number of unresolved claims, and reduce the amount of dollars in uncollected claims. Instead of moving immediately from there to training its workers, Superior looked at the reasons why the discrepancy between goals and actual performance existed.

It was good that the firm did. Certainly training was necessary; lack of effective training was obviously part of the problems. But it certainly wasn't all of the problem. The analysis also showed that the work area was dirty, smoky, noisy, and generally completely inadequate; the expectations and standards for the workers were unclear; feedback on performance was delayed or nonexistent; and pay was low, there was no incentive for good performance, and looking busy was more important than producing.

In other words, poor performance resulted from lack of training and from (1) inadequate *means,* (2) inadequate *knowledge* of standards, (3) poor *feedback,* and (4) the lack of any *motive* for effective performance.

When Superior attacked the problem, it used training as part of the solution. It also simplified the work flow and procedures, developed structured on-the-job training for new workers, instituted a measurement and feedback system for all workers and managers, and took a number of other steps that affected the *entire* performance situation.

Because the firm took all these steps, the training it gave was effective. If Superior hadn't taken the steps—well, at best, the training might have produced the very limited improvements that generally happen when training is given without a careful up-front analysis. No matter how good it was at training, Superior couldn't have made up for the inadequate work area, the fuzzy standards, the undependable feedback, and the lack of reward for good performance. As part of the overall approach, though, training was a very powerful tool.[19] And the firm could fit it into the overall approach because it first did the up-front analysis.

How Do You Get
Good Analysis?

I hope that I've convinced you that up-front analysis is a necessity. The next questions are: Can you get it? Does your firm's training department have the ability to do it? Do consultants that do training for you know how to do it? And what if you use canned training or have to design your own?

Tough questions. Let's start with your training department, if you have one. The odds are good that they'd really like to do up-front analysis (though they probably call it "needs analysis"). But they may not be able to—and there could be several reasons for this.

Because training is often the first function cut when times get hard, they *may not have the staff* to do up-front analysis. There really is only one remedy for this problem. But before you advocate more staff for the department, make sure that neither of the following two problems is the real one.

The training department may *never have been asked* to do it. This is sad, but true. All too often, managers simply ask training people to produce such-and-such a course of such-and-such a length, period. If that's what's been going on in your organization, your training people may never have had the chance to learn or do up-front analysis. In this case, you need to support them in learning how to do it, then give them the opportunity to use it for you. (*Note:* It takes time to learn how, and then more time to learn how to do it well. Be patient.)

The training people may be so tied up in arranging and giving training that they *don't see any need* for up-front analysis. That's the worst problem of all; it's like your comptroller trying to keep the books without understanding double-entry bookkeeping. Perhaps the best approach is to find someone in training who's open to the idea and help him or her get training in analysis. Above all *don't* settle for the assurance that the analysis wouldn't make any difference.

Now, suppose you're dealing with consultants who don't understand up-front analysis. Or you're using canned courses by vendors who don't provide analysis in any form? Or you must provide the training yourself? What do you do?

The answer is simple but demanding: You find someone in your organization with good analytic skills and see that he or she learns and uses the rudiments of up-front analysis.

I thought a long time before I wrote that last sentence. Do you really want to disrupt your work not only to get up-front analysis done but to train someone to do it? Yes, you do. But you don't need to grow a full-blown professional analyst. Basically, this is the minimum that the person needs to be able to do:

1. He or she should deal well with others. Analysis isn't worth a darn if people won't level with the analyst. A good analyst should be someone who can make others comfortable and win their trust quickly.

2. The individual should understand the work that's being analyzed. Someone from the organization has a real advantage over even the most skilled outsider here.

3. The individual should also understand the five factors discussed in Chapter 1 that drive performance. These factors will give him or her a framework for the analysis so that the right questions get asked.

I'm not suggesting that it's desirable to train one of your people, only that it may be necessary. If this is what you have to do, I can provide you one more bit of help. Any individual (including yourself) can find out a great deal about what's needed for improved performance by finding the answers to these few questions (based on the five factors of performance):

- Do individuals understand exactly what they're supposed to do? Do they know the standard you expect them to attain and/or the goals you expect them to meet? (Don't assume the answer to either of these questions is "Yes"). If either or both of these are the problem, you can almost always improve performance significantly by fixing that situation.

- Are there glaring problems caused by the equipment; the way that inventory of materials, supplies, or tools is handled; or in the scheduling of the work load? If so, it's best to deal with these first, then go back and analyze the situation again.

- Do workers get prompt, direct, reliable, and usable feedback on how well they're doing? (Certainly don't assume on this one. Without knowing your organization, I'd give odds they don't). This situation is often harder to remedy, but it has a major impact on performance.

- Do workers get rewarded if they perform well? Or do they get the same rewards if their performance is mediocre? Rather than dwell on this anymore, let me suggest that you read a short, very readable book called *Analyzing Performance Problems* by Mager and Pipe (it's in the bibliography).

- When you rule out these four kinds of problems—or resolve them— then you know you need training. This is where it helps to have someone doing the analysis who really knows the work. He or she can identify where workers need more know-how—and then you can find (or, if necessary, develop) training that will provide this know-how.

The Performance Improvement Potential

Now, let me introduce you to a simple but powerful idea: the Performance Improvement Potential (PIP) in a situation.[20]

The idea of the PIP was developed based on the difference in performance among individuals performing the same job. There are generally several people performing basically the same work in most units—voucher examining, drafting, machining, and so forth. And generally one or two people who do the work are much better at it than the others. The more people, the more apt this is to be true. And that's good news.

We often explain this performance difference in terms of individual ability and motivation. Certainly, those are factors. Almost always, though, those one or two top performers *know how* to do the job better than others. They may have been better trained initially, or they may have experimented until they learned the best way. Whatever the reason, much of their skill can be taught to others. This is the PIP in the situation: the difference between the best performer and each other performer.

Let's take a fairly simple example. You have six purchasing agents. The best one can average about 30 purchases a day. The next one averages close to 25. The other four average about 17. If training improved those four so that they moved half way from their current performance to the top performer—from 17 to 23 purchases a day—you'd add the equivalent of *one full purchasing agent* to the capacity of the unit. This is quite a PIP—and it exists in many work situations where everyone supposedly knows how to do the job!

There are at least two other forms of PIP that you can make pay off for you. The first of these exists when no one in a particular kind of job is fully skilled at performing it. Such a PIP happens, for instance, when a data system changes and data entry clerks have to be trained in the way the new system works. It's also what happens when someone discovers a new and more effective way to do the job and everyone gets trained to do it that way. In both these cases, the PIP is the difference between what people produce now and what they can produce after effective training.

The final form of PIP is the potential for workers to understand and improve the processes with which they work. This is the core of Total Quality and constant process improvement, and its power to improve the overall performance of a process has been demonstrated over and over again. (*Example:* A team of maintenance workers in a GE plant learned the basic quality problem-solving methods. For their first project, they modified a machine plagued by downtime. The modification cost $30,000, saved $20,000 per year on a continuing basis, and increased the capacity of the machine by $655,000 worth of product per year. That's quite a PIP!)[21]

Keep the idea in mind as you go through your day-to-day business. Everywhere that a group, a system, or a process isn't producing as it might, there's Performance Improvement Potential. You may get it directly through training individuals to perform more effectively. Or you may get it through training them to identify and solve processes. But it's there. You (and they) can find it and use it to improve performance.

How to Use These Ideas

- Keep in mind why analysis is the first step. The performance you're getting is a result of what makes sense to the performers—and this results from what they know, what they have the means to do, what they know how to do, what they have a motive for doing, and the quality of the feedback that they get. Poor performance can result from any of these factors. Even if you know exactly what improvement you want, don't throw money away by jumping to the conclusion that training will give it to you. See that someone does a competent analysis, *then* decide how to improve performance.

- If you have a training department, insist that they do an up-front analysis for you. You've already read about why they may not be able to or want to. Those are problems; they have to be resolved. See that they are. One of the department's basic jobs is to provide you with effective analyses. See that they do.

- If you use one or more training consultants, which might include a local college, see that they do an analysis before you start talking about the training. It will cost you more, but if it's done properly it will save you even more. If you have to, hire someone just to do the analysis. But get the analysis done.

- Now, what if you only have access to canned training? Perhaps you can still hire someone to do an analysis so that you can choose the appropriate training. Or you or one of your people may need to do the analysis.

- What if you have to provide the training? Then you'll probably have to provide the analysis. Two short books will help you with this. The first is Mager and Pipe's *Analyzing Performance Problems* (in the bibliography). It's a great read and extremely useful; take the time to look at it even if you're going to delegate the analysis to someone in your organization. Whoever does the analysis should look at the first part of Rogoff's *The Training Wheel* (also in the bibliography). It presents a highly simplified but useful method for doing up-front analysis.

4
The Road to Smart Training: Design

The last chapter described effective up-front analysis—not so you could do it, but so you'd understand why trainers need to do it. This chapter carries the process from the analysis to the final training. It describes what trainers actually *do* when they design and develop training.

I suspect this isn't on your short list of things you want to know—so the chapter's very brief. And it includes a bribe for you. The chapter presents a set of principles that makes training effective. You can use these same principles to counsel and coach your employees more successfully. I'll show you how.

From Performance Need to Training to Performance Improvement

Most processes that reliably solve problems begin with analysis. Successful training design is no exception, as we saw in the last chapter. It begins with a competent up-front analysis. Then the process continues, through the following steps.

The trainer must *design* the training. In this stage, he or she identifies the objectives of the training—specifically, how it will produce the performance improvement you need. The trainer also decides how it's to be delivered. The method used might be a classroom course, computer-based training, a job aid, or any of a dozen other methods. No method is intrinsically superior to another; each is effective when used properly and wasteful when used inappropriately.

The next step is *development*. Here the trainer creates the actual training itself. This may be as short as outlining an hour's structured on-the-job training for a supervisor to deliver. Or it may be a lengthy project to create a flight simulator or complex management decision game.

When development is complete, the trainer *tests* the training. Will individuals be able to perform as intended when they finish the training? If they can, the training is ready to give. If not, it's revised and tested again.

Then the training is *delivered*.

Finally, the trainer will *evaluate* the effectiveness of the training in some way to make certain that it did achieve its goal. You also need to do your own evaluation, and we'll look at quick ways to do this later in this chapter.

That's the complete process for developing smart training. And here's the bottom line of the discussion:

> *You can't be confident that your training department or training consultants are delivering smart training to you unless they follow the process described in this chapter. Whether or not they use the process, and how well they use it, will determine the quality of the training you get from them.*

Let me suggest this analogy: Someone manages the budget for your organization. You know in general how the budget is managed. You know what to watch out for and how to use the budgeting process effectively. You don't need to know the details of the process—but you do need to know that whoever's managing the budget not only knows but uses an effective process to manage it. That's how it is with training. People who develop effective training use the basic process that this chapter describes. As a manager, you need to see that your trainers develop effective training by using the process.

The last chapter described the success that the U.S. Coast Guard Training Center at Petaluma, California, had with a systematic approach. It simultaneously reduced the cost of the training that it produced *and* made it more effective. (In the 1980s, IBM did the same thing on a much larger scale.) Petaluma began with up-front analysis—and then followed the analysis with a systematic design, development, and delivery process. It took the entire process to produce the savings Petaluma achieved.

It takes this process to convert the results of the analysis into effective training. If you play tennis, you might think of the relationship between analysis and design in terms of how you play an effective game of tennis. First, you watch your opponent, see how he or she hits the ball, and estimate where the ball will hit. That's analysis. Then you get into the best possible position, use the stroke that works best from that position, deliver the ball where you want it to go, and immediately prepare yourself for the return. That's design, development, delivery, and evaluation.

If you forget the analysis, you may be 20 feet from the ball when it lands in your court. If you ignore design, development, and delivery, your return may be a snap for your opponent to smash down your (hopefully figurative) throat. And if you don't prepare immediately for the next volley, you may be caught completely off balance. It's the same with smart training: It has to start with an effective up-front analysis, but it's not going to work unless the design, development, delivery, and evaluation process is just as effective.

How the Process Works

Very briefly, here's a little more detail on what happens at each stage of the process that turns effective up-front analysis into effective training. Let's assume that the up-front analysis shows that supervisors need to learn how to give prompt, accurate, useful feedback to their workers. Here's how that performance need might be translated into effective training.

Design

The trainer begins by developing clear, performance-oriented objectives for the training. He or she knows from the analysis that supervisors aren't giving effective feedback to their workers; this is the performance that needs to be improved. The question is: What does the training need to do to remedy the deficiency? After looking the data over, the trainer might come up with these objectives:

1. Supervisors need to *know* why it's important for them to provide objective performance feedback to workers. (If this is presented realistically as an avenue to success as a supervisor, it may also affect supervisors' *motive* for providing feedback.)

2. Supervisors need to *know how* to give performance feedback effectively.

The trainer must also know (or find out) the characteristics of the target audience. Will the training be given to beginning supervisors, experienced ones, or a mixture? Are there only two or three supervisors to be trained, or a large number? Are they all in the same area, or widely scattered?

Now that the trainer knows the objectives and the audience, he or she can select the proper method for the training. Perhaps only a few supervisors, located in the same area, need to be trained; in that case, an instructor-led classroom course might work best. Suppose there are hundreds of supervisors, though, and they're widely scattered. Computer-based training (perhaps using multimedia) might be the most practical choice. Whatever the final decision, the best method will be the one that will most effectively achieve the training objectives with the actual audience to which the training will be given.

By the way, it's important not to think of different methods as *either-or* propositions. Let's say the trainer decides to develop a short instructor-led course at two sites. He or she may still want to use a professional videotape demonstrating effective and ineffective ways of giving feedback and provide participants with a job aid to use back on the job. Then these supervisors might give structured on-the-job training to other supervisors back in their areas. The precise balance of methods doesn't matter that much. Choosing the methods—one or a dozen— that will work *for this training* is what counts.

Develop

When design is complete, the trainer moves to the development stage. (For simplicity, by the way, I've been talking as though a single individual is performing every step in the process. Sometimes this is the case. More often, a team goes through the process. For large projects, there may be a separate team at each step. No matter how many individuals are involved, though, they'll go through each of the steps in the process.)

The first development task is to find out just what knowledges and skills need to be taught. What does a supervisor need to learn to provide useful feedback? Library shelves are heavy with books on counseling and feedback, but these books are a secondary source at best. The real experts on giving feedback are supervisors who actually do it successfully—preferably in the organization that needs the training. So the developer may ask you to furnish one or more supervisors to serve as *subject-matter experts* (SMEs) for the course.

This often surprises managers. After all, shouldn't the training department (or contractor) take the up-front analysis and return with the completed course? Not usually. Finding one or more SMEs who can describe the best way to perform *in your organization* is absolutely critical to improving performance. In fact, it's so important that a later section of this chapter will deal with it at more length.

Back to the trainer. Working with SMEs, the trainer gets a clear picture of the skills used by real-world supervisors to give their workers feedback. Now it's time to produce the first draft of the training. The trainer sets the overall structure of the training and then finds or develops the videotapes, case studies, role plays, and other specific activities for the training.

Test

The next step is simple and straightforward: The trainer tests the effectiveness of the training. Let me warn you of a danger lurking here. Many times a manager wants the training tested on experienced workers or even on staff—to be sure that it follows established policy and practice. That's important, but it's part of the *development* step. A trainer can't be sure he or she has developed accurate training until subject-matter experts have looked at it and approved it.

But the experts don't belong in the testing step. Here, you want workers who represent the target group. Since you're training supervisors to provide objective feedback, you want a sample group of supervisors to serve as the test audience. And you don't want the ones who are easiest to train. Instead, you want those that clearly *aren't* displaying the performance you want. When the course is effective at changing their performance, it will be effective for almost everyone else as well.

The trainer presents the training to the target audience, exactly as though they were simply the first group. Using their feedback, the training is revised—and retested if necessary—until it will produce the performance the organization wants.

Deliver

Most of us at least think we understand this part of training. After all, we've been exposed to delivery in the educational system and in the training courses we've attended. Perhaps, though, we can usefully learn more about it.

Chapter 1 provided a quick overview of two of the principles of adult learning. Let's take a closer look at these two principles and at several others that go with them. By the way, this is the bribe I promised you; these are also the principles of effective change in general where adults are concerned.

1. Adults need to know *why they're learning* a particular topic. If it's how to review credit card receipts for accuracy, they can learn the "why" quickly. If it's why the firm is converting to self-managed teams—

well, that takes a little longer. In general, though, adults aren't interested in the what without the why.

2. Adults, when they're performing as adults, need to be *in control of their own learning.* Sure, you can get a group of adults in a training class that sit passively and wait for the instructor to pour knowledge into their waiting heads. But they're going to do a minimum amount of learning. When they get actively involved in the learning process, that's when learning really happens.

3. Adults have a *broad range of experience* that they can relate to the material they're learning. This may make them difficult to teach, because they can quickly spot someone who doesn't really know the topic. It's also a plus; if they can relate what they're supposed to learn to their experience, they'll learn the topic faster and better.

4. Adults are willing (sometimes even enthusiastic) to learn material they believe will make them *more effective and successful.* They are *not* willing to learn just because their boss or an instructor tells them they should. Adults keep asking: What will this do for me? How will it help me get ahead? What problem is this going to solve?

5. Given the proper support, most adults *want* to learn. Put another way, if they know why they're learning, have some control over the learning process, can relate the material to their experience, and see a direct benefit to them—they *will* learn.[22]

How can you benefit from this information? In two ways. First, you can ensure that whoever provides training knows and follows these principles. That isn't hard. Look over the course outline. Does it make clear why the training is necessary? Does it provide an active part for the trainees? Will they see how it can benefit them? These and similar questions will tell you quickly whether the training is apt to "take" for your people.

The second benefit is even more direct. These are the rules for adult learning—and since all change depends on learning, you can use them to help people change. Let's take performance counseling as a quick example. Your goal here is to change performance in a positive direction. Your coaching or counseling should:

1. Make it clear to workers why they need to change;

2. Involve them in planning the change and setting goals (so that they have some control over them);

3. Help them relate what they need to do to the experience they already have; and

4. Show them clearly how the new way of performing will make them more successful on their jobs (and perhaps contenders for bonuses or promotions).

When you do this, you significantly increase the chance that workers will *willingly* make the change you want.

Perhaps this training stuff isn't so technical and esoteric after all.

Evaluate

If the training is to be used repeatedly, the training department (or consultants) should perform a follow-up evaluation to see how effective it was. The evaluation begins with the final performance test that's part of the training. If every supervisor was able to give feedback in a realistic situation, you know that he or she possesses the basic skills.

After a few weeks or months, though, the training department or consultants should follow up to see exactly what's happening back on the job. They may send you and/or the supervisors who took the training a questionnaire about their use of what they learned. They may talk with you and/or the supervisors. Whatever they do, this is all part of the basic process.

That's how they evaluate training. How *you* evaluate it is a different subject, one that the last section of this chapter will analyze.

But This Takes Time!

That's probably your first reaction when you see the complete process. And, unfortunately, you're right. The time it takes to produce effective training is the single greatest drawback of a systematic training design process. In language current in manufacturing today, the process has a long cycle time.

Of course, training designers can take some steps to shorten the process. Four people can design and deliver training much faster than two people. Classroom training takes much less time (and expense) to develop than computer-based training. If the training *must* be done in a short time, some corners can be cut.

Putting more people on the job is a legitimate way to cut training design time. Picking a delivery method because it shortens design time and other methods for cutting corners generally aren't. They get the training done faster, but at a great loss in effectiveness. The result is a lot like introducing a new software product before it's been completely tested: If you don't get a lot of luck, it doesn't work.

All good trainers are constantly trying to shorten the cycle time. That's one of the major goals of my own group. But it's not the number one goal, or even the number two goal. The number one goal is to produce training that accomplishes its intended purpose—improved performance. The number two goal is to take workers away from the job for the shortest possible time. Only then do we get to number three, designing the training as quickly as possible.

Of course, good trainers will also use common sense in the process. If the course is a very short one, for few individuals, they may hold the analysis, design, and development to a minimum. On the other hand, if the training is critically important, even these few individuals may be worth taking more time for analysis, design, and development.

There's no easy solution. Sometimes effective training can be produced quickly, by using job aids and on-the-job training (see Chapters 12 and 13). Other times, it can't. Training design and development shouldn't ever take longer than absolutely necessary, but you and I can't afford for it to take less.

If Trainers Are So Smart, Why Can't They Do It by Themselves?

We looked briefly at the whole topic of subject-matter experts a few pages back. Now we need to visit the topic again, and particularly the question of what you gain from giving up the time of your best people.

Let's begin with the question most managers ask: *Now that you know what to train my people in, why can't you just develop the training and give it to them?* That's a sensible question. After all, it's the job of the training department (or consultants) to develop the training. Why should they have to depend on your workers—and your best workers at that—to get their job done? It's disruptive, and it takes the workers away from their jobs.

All that's true. But, disruptive as it is to use your best people as SMEs, you wouldn't want it any other way. Here's why:

> *Only the people who actually perform the work that's being trained are true experts on it. If you want training that really improves performance, it has to be designed around the real-world skills of your best performers.*

Let me give you an example where this is always true, one where it's somewhat true, and two where it's not true. As you'll see, the situations where it's not true are the ones *least* likely to improve performance in your organization.

- Your voucher examiner section is making too many errors. When an up-front analysis is done, you find that two of the examiners make almost no mistakes—while the other seven examiners average a mistake every 12 documents. It's almost certain that the way to improve the performance of the unit is to find out how the two "experts" do it and teach the rest to do it that way. [Remember, that's finding and using the Performance Improvement Potential (PIP) between the best performers and the others.] Clearly, you want one or both of those two to serve as SMEs.

- Your supervisors need training in providing objective feedback to their workers (the example already used). Why not develop training based on a good textbook and teach it to the supervisors? That certainly sounds neat and simple, and whoever designs the training may want to use a text for part of the training. But it's not enough. To be realistic, the training has to fit the way *your* organization operates. How often do supervisors get performance information to pass on to workers? Do they see their workers regularly or infrequently? Are workers particularly defensive in this organization? Only supervisors in the organization know the answers to these and dozens of questions like them. If you want really good training, supervisors need to serve as SMEs.

- They've just released the new version of your accounting software and your clerks and bookkeepers need to be trained in it. Clearly, they're not the SMEs—because all they know is the old way. In this case, the analysts who created the revision are the SMEs; the trainers must find out from them how the job should be performed. This sounds fine, but what gets taught is someone's *idea* of effective performance. The "experts" have never done the job. If you go back in 90 days, you'll probably find a wide variation in how well your people use the system—because some of them have discovered really effective methods that weren't part of the training. This puts you back in the situation in the two preceding paragraphs: More training, based on the real SMEs, can use the PIP to improve overall performance.

- Corporate has decided that all supervisors need to be trained in Total Quality methods. They've contracted the training to an outside consulting firm. The firm comes in and teaches the best and most current ideas and practices. Your people don't have to be SMEs at all. When it's over, how effective is the training? The most probable answer is "Not very." All the consulting firm can teach is the way that it's done in other places; that may or may not work where you are. It's a crap shoot.

Do these last two examples mean that "outsiders" won't ever provide effective training? If training is *all* that happens, it probably does. But if the same training is given as part of an overall performance improvement initiative—as Preston Trucking or Superior Investments did—it can be very effective. Remember, too, the training MUCTC gave in dealing with cultural differences (Chapter 2)? It was designed by outsiders—but they worked closely with the commission, drew their examples from the real experiences of bus drivers, and used bus drivers to lead the course.

Even if I gave another dozen examples, I doubt that I could make you anxious to give trainers your best people as SMEs. I hope, though, that you can see the benefit that comes from doing just that. If the goal of training is improved performance, the best way to achieve the goal is to build it on the best performers you have. It may not be convenient, but it is the most effective way.

Now, How Do You Tell It Worked?

I mentioned evaluation briefly as part of the overall training design and development process and promised we'd talk about it here.

How do you effectively evaluate training? That's an important question, and a difficult one to answer. Why difficult? What about those evaluations that instructors (my own included) pass out at the end of courses? "Did the training meet your expectations?" "Will it be helpful to you on the job?" And so on. Don't they tell how good the training was? No, not really. The truth of the matter is that they're not much use. They make trainers feel good (which is why we call them "smile sheets"), and they'll help spot a really bad trainer or really bad training. They don't help much, though, if your goal is to get a balanced and useful assessment. The books in the bibliography by Brinkerhoff and Phillips deal with evaluation—though I don't recommend you read them.

Instead, let me suggest several practical ways to ensure that the training accomplishes what it's designed to do. Here's the first one:

If training is designed after a thorough up-front analysis, and if an effective design and development process is carefully followed, the training will accomplish its purpose.

Does that sound almost too simple? If it does, think for a moment of one of the powerful discoveries of the Total Quality movement. It's the simple discovery that if you design an effective process and follow it carefully, you'll get a satisfactory product every time. It's exactly the same way with training: If you use an effective process to create the training and follow it carefully, the training will do exactly what you intended for it to do.

That's a good start, but there are one or two more steps you can take. First, remember one of the points originally made in Chapter 2: If you want training to be effective, trainees must put it to work immediately. That's a basic key to training effectiveness, and only you and I—the managers—can see that it happens. Doing that won't guarantee that the training is effective, only that your people will get the greatest possible benefit from it. However, it also gives you an insight into how good the training was. If your workers put it to work right away and still can't do the job, it wasn't very good training. You can have a heart-to-heart talk with whomever designed and developed the training.

Second, as Chapter 2 also suggested, you can improve performance if you raise performance standards to incorporate the new training. Many times, this isn't realistic or practical. That's OK; let it be. Sometimes, though, it's both realistic and a helpful message to your workers when you explain that the training will enable them to produce more—and you expect them to do so.

What if there's not an existing standard to raise? Let's use the example of supervisors and feedback again. You almost certainly don't have an existing target for the number of times supervisors give feedback to their workers. But you can still set a target you expect them to meet after the course. What kind of a target might you set? Well, you might say that when supervisors complete the training all of them will create at least 10 instances a month for 3 months where they provide objective feedback to a worker. (Note that this combines having them put the training to work *and* setting a new standard based on the training.)

Ask the supervisors to keep a diary, and then have a conference with each one at the end of the month. If they do provide feedback, you'll have your evidence that the course was effective. If they don't? Then someone needs to look at the situation again to see why training wasn't enough.

Notice how important *you* are to successful training. One of the greatest determinants of training effectiveness is whether the results of the training matter to you. If they do, and the trainees know they do—that in itself will increase the effectiveness of the training. You and I, the managers, are the last step in the process that delivers effective training.

Let me give you one final way to evaluate training. This one is from

Walt Thurn, manager of employee development for Florida Power Corporation in St. Petersburg. According to him, there's a relatively simple way to tell a successful course. If a senior executive suggests that the course should be cut, the training department shouldn't have to say a word—because some line manager should be in the executive's office "banging on the desk and raising hell."[23] That's the ultimate test of effective training!

How to Use These Ideas

- I can only repeat: If you possibly can, give your training provider time to do the design and development job right. Just keep remembering that what you're doing is spending time here so that you can save it when the training is given. If there are many people to train, your ROI from this will easily be 1000 percent or more.

- This is true whether your provider is your training department or an external source. Side by side with giving them time, though, goes their obligation to do a competent job as quickly as possible.

- Now, suppose you have to provide the training yourself. You can get a good though simplified idea of the process to follow from *The Training Wheel* (mentioned at the end of the last chapter). You should probably look at *Active Training* by Mel Silberman. Don't try to read it in detail; just skim it to get his basic points about good training. Then, if you can use job aids and/or structured on-the-job training, read it in more detail. It's an excellent guide.

PART 2

Building the Firm's Competence with Smart Training

Part 1 dealt with the essentials of smart training: increasing the performance of workers and managers. Part 2 moves further along the road to economical, effective training by looking at the fundamental goals of smart training from the organization's point of view.

Chapter 5 leads off with the key concept of *competence*. Competence simply means the ability to do a job, whether as a janitor or as a CEO. In traditional organizations, competence often requires nothing more than the ability to do a simple job with reasonable productivity at an acceptable level of quality. The firms that are competing successfully in the 1990s, though, are developing a far higher level of competence in their workers. Chapter 5 explains what this competence is, and why it's paying off for the companies that use it.

Competence is the potential to perform effectively; *mastery* is the ability to use this competence and build on it. Mastery is produced when competence is combined with confidence and provided the opportunity for use. When competence, confidence, and opportunity increase, mastery spirals upward. When one or more of the three factors are missing, mastery begins to slip away. Chapter 6 looks at the idea of mastery and its importance to both the individual and the firm.

In recent years, the idea has emerged that in addition to its core market and core technology, a firm must develop and maintain its *core competence* to succeed. It doesn't take a lot of explaining to see how important this is to smart training (and vice versa). Chapter 7 discusses this relationship.

Chapter 8 deals with an eminently practical question: What types of competence will be required to do a job in the 1990s? Ten years ago, this would have been of interest only to trainers; even five years ago, that might have been the case. But not today—and certainly not tomorrow. Job competence is only part of the picture, and smart training must deal with the total competence picture—or else.

However we look at it, competence doesn't exist in a vacuum. It's not enough to decide in the executive suite that such and such competence is important and needs to be developed. Very specific events have to occur if competence is to be gained, used, and turned into mastery. These events are the subject of Chapter 9, the last chapter in Part 2.

5

Gaining the
Competence Edge

The basic meaning of *competence* is a simple one: the ability to do a job successfully. Competence is most obvious in an executive who successfully rescues a floundering company, an experimental machinist who finishes a piece to microscopic tolerances, a computer programmer whose complex program runs successfully on the first try. But an individual at any level can have a competence. Assembly-line workers who only tighten three screws but always tighten them well are competent at what they do. So are data entry clerks who input shareholder name changes without error. Unfortunately, these last two represent a very *limited* level of competence.

Competent? Well, Sort Of

For a very long time, this limited meaning of competence has been the one most common in American industry. Reduced to its essentials, it's part of this job-design sequence:

- Simplify the job so that it can be performed without a great deal of training by a lost-cost worker.
- Work out the procedures for the job in detail and teach them to the worker.
- Expect the worker to perform them at an acceptable speed with an acceptable error rate.
- If the job changes, retrain the worker and return to the previous step.

This is essentially the approach that Frederick W. Taylor developed in the 1880s and 1890s. Because they have such a low level of competence, these workers cost very little to hire, train, or replace. As a result, they contribute very little value to the final product. That was, and is, an acceptable way to do business. Its most publicized examples are the American automakers, though they form only the tip of the iceberg of low-paid, low-competence workers in America.

The evidence is growing that in the highly competitive 1990s this kind of competence won't be enough.

Another Vision of Competence

There's another approach, one that appears consistently to produce a clear competitive advantage. In this approach, the competence required by the worker is *increased*—on the assumption that a more competent worker will add considerably more value than a less competent one. The difference in value more than pays back any increased cost to hire, train, and pay the worker. This is the real payoff from competence, and many companies are already profiting from it. Here's a very small sampling of them.

The Corning Company

Corning has a plant in Blacksburg, Virginia, where employees work in teams with minimal supervision (three "supervisors" for 150 workers) assembling air filters. All the workers on a team know all the jobs on the team, not just individual narrow slices of the pie. This represents a level of competence well above the traditional assembly line. And it pays off. A Corning team can retool a line for a different product in a sixth of the time it takes a conventional plant of the same kind to do so. This is a basic reason why the plant returned a profit of $2.3 million its first 8 months of operation. (This is more impressive than it may sound; start-ups aren't expected to make money the first year.)

As you might expect, training played a major part in this. The first year, 25 percent of the workers' time was spent in training, at a lost-time cost of $750,000. With the payoff it got from this training—remember the $2.3 million—Corning has now decided that each and every worker in the whole corporation should spend at least 5 percent of his or her time in training year in and year out. Corning has proof that increasing the competence of the "average" worker returns a value much greater than its cost.[24]

The GM Saturn Plant

So much has been written about this start-up that I hardly need mention it. There, teams hire their own members, even develop their own budgets. This requires competence at least a level of magnitude above that of the traditional assembly-line worker.

Toyota's Plants

No Toyota plant gives workers as much freedom as Corning or Saturn. But Toyota was a pioneer in expecting employees to continuously improve the processes with which they worked. Toyota's success at penetrating the American automotive market testifies to the payoff they get from this approach.[25]

American Transtech

This subsidiary of AT&T was created to handle the colossal number of stock transfers created by the divestiture of AT&T. From this beginning, it has become a major player in the stock transfer business and has expanded into several related endeavors. This is pure white-collar work, but Transtech's use of teams in which workers share all the tasks and assume most of the functions associated with supervision resulted in productivity increases of as much as *500 percent* from 1983 to 1991.

Procter and Gamble

Procter and Gamble, one of the world's great consumer-products companies, began experimenting with self-directing work teams in the 1970s. P&G was one of the first U.S. companies to do so. It gave the company such a competitive edge that it was very coy about mentioning it for years. Now the firm has committed itself to adopt companywide this highly competent way of organizing.

Federal Express

Federal Express is one of the premier American companies at empowering its workers individually and in teams. It's famous for the initiative and competence that everyone in the firm shows. FedEx is also famous for its dominance of its market.[26]

The list goes on and on and on. A wide variety of firms have broadly increased the competence of their production workers (both blue- and white-collar), with a dramatic payoff in quality and productivity. Don't think, by the way, that this kind of payoff is limited to large companies. Individual plants of Corning and Procter and Gamble aren't that large. Litel Telecommunications, which we'll look at in a few paragraphs, is a small company by any standard. Most of the firms that make the headlines are large—but every principle in this chapter can be applied no matter what the size of the organization. In fact, because they don't have layers of bureaucracy to contend with, small firms can often increase their workers' competence more easily than large firms can.

I think it's time, by the way, to clarify my language. You may be a little uncomfortable with the word *competence*, and more used to using *skill*. Competence began as a trainer's word, but it's passing rapidly into common management use—for a very good reason. When we talk of skills, we tend to concentrate just on what the person *does*. Skills form part of competence, but are never all of it. Competence always includes a knowledge aspect. We may admire a carpenter's skill with tools, but the individual's ability to plan and lay out work—a very conceptual ability— is at least as important. A general manager's sense of timing is at least as important as the more visible skills of communication and decision making. By using *competence*, we can include both the knowledge and the know-how that successful performance requires.

Firms trying to increase worker competence throughout the organization are practicing what many economists are preaching these days. These economists are suggesting that the only real competitive advantage during the 1990s is going to be a highly competent work force whose competence is regularly used. Robert Reich of Harvard is a major spokesperson for this point of view. In his book *The Work of Nations*, Reich underlines the stark contrast between the prospects of educated and broadly competent individuals and those in traditional, low-competence production and personal-service jobs.[27] This contrast exists because highly competent individuals contribute high value and thus can command high salaries. On a different level—primarily blue-collar work—the report by the National Center on Education and the Economy, *America's Choice: High Skills or Low Wages!*, makes the same point.[28]

Because it takes highly skilled and competent individuals to make our increasingly high-tech society work, their abilities are worth a higher and higher price tag. The watchword isn't what human resources cost but *the value they add in relation to their cost*. Put most simply, highly competitive firms can no longer afford to hire low-cost, low-skilled, low-value-adding workers. They need highly competent workers who can add significant value to their products and services. This was the challenge Motorola faced when it found that many of its workers lacked basic reading and arithmetic skills. The firm had to set a standard of seventh-grade performance as the minimum—and then it trained workers until they reached this standard. Now Motorola is raising the standard to the eighth-grade level. And, remember, this is the *minimum* level.

(Time for another quick note. You may have noticed that *skill* keeps creeping back in. I use it both to provide a little variety and because it's commonly used. Just remember that I use it as synonymous with *competence*—to include a healthy dose of knowledge along with the visible know-how. Even the simplest skill requires some knowledge, and any significant skills require a great deal of it.)

Chapter 7 looks at the critical idea of a firm's *core competence*—its ability to develop and retain the specialized competence required to compete effectively in its chosen market. Here, we need to look more closely at competence in general—and what firms must do to develop and maintain it.

Increasing Base-Level Competence

Like so much else that supports smart training, increasing the overall competence of the firm is a strategic choice. It can be done piecemeal; sometimes that's the only way to get started. For maximum impact, though, it needs to be carried out as part of an overall strategic vision. Since it's strategic, this increasing competence needs to support the business goals of the firm directly. That may sound a little abstract at the moment. As we continue through this part, however, you'll see more and more clearly what the strategy involves and what you can do to implement it.

Now, back to the practicalities of increased competence. The way to increase worker competence is to create jobs that are challenging and provide control to workers—and then train them as necessary to perform these jobs. In turn, there are three basic ways to create these jobs:

1. Give the individual or team responsibility for most or all of the full job cycle.

2. Give the individual or team direct responsibility for satisfying a customer (internal or external).

3. Give the individual or team responsibility for using problem-solving skills on the job.

Let's look at these three approaches in more detail.

The Full Job Cycle

This is one of the oldest "job enrichment" methods around. Practiced for its own sake, just to give the worker a more interesting job, it's probably worthwhile. Practiced as a way of removing non-value-added tasks from jobs, it's immensely effective. Here are two quick examples.

I've already mentioned American Transtech's successful use of teams. Let me add some detail on what Transtech does. Its most effective teams are in its customer service operations, where multiskilled teams respond to customer requests. This used to be a serial process, but now each team handles all five functions required to respond to an order and prepare it for computer processing. Each member of the team is trained to handle all the team's functions, so they all share responsibility for (and commitment to) the effectiveness of the whole process.

Remember my statement that you don't have to be a large firm to profit from this? Consider Litel Telecommunications of Columbus, Ohio. This small but growing company started by dividing order processing among five separate groups: the first sorted the orders; the second screened them for proper information; the third screened them again, this time for credit information; the fourth keyed the orders into the computer system; and then the fifth and final group set the new customers up in the billing system. A typical order took 14 days to work its way through the system.

Litel's response was to set up three teams of five or six people each, with all necessary functions on each team. When it did, time to process an order plummeted to *1* day. Quality shot up. And the team members were much happier than they had been. Each team could see each order through to completion; this gave them a new sense of responsibility—and a new sense of satisfaction in what they were doing.

For Transtech and Litel, the competence of individual team members rose sharply. From performing a fraction of the total processing, each worker became directly involved in the whole process. He or she knew much more about the process than before and applied that knowledge daily. Teams could train new members and integrate them rapidly because they had this competence. Workers were much happier because they knew they were more highly skilled. This same pattern has repeated itself, time after time, in Shenandoah Life, the Lutheran Aid Association, and hundreds of other large and small white-collar firms.

There's another reason why these teams are so much more effective. When work flows from one function to another in a single process, anywhere from 50 to 99 percent (and normally much closer to the latter than the former) of the total time is spent moving paper to someone and then waiting for that individual to take an action. The process also generates other non-value-adding activities, like making multiple copies and returning paperwork to a function that has already worked on it once.

When all the skills are combined into a single work team, based on carefully reengineered processes, most of the non-value-adding parts of the processes simply vanish. The product is either being worked on or is gone. Transportation and waiting times drop sharply, and copies become unnecessary. This same basic process occurs whether the team is in a manufacturing environment or in a white-collar one.

In short, the effectiveness of the processes increases in tandem with the increased competence of the workers.

All of the preceding examples involved teams. There's a good reason for this: To be completed effectively, most processes require more than one person. This isn't always the case, though. Where workers can do individually all of a process previously divided among several employees, the performance improvement can be just as great. Either way, developing individual or team competence to the point that the individual or the team can perform an entire process will normally pay back far more than the training time it takes to learn this competence.

Serving a Customer

Does serving a customer really matter so much? After all, how much difference can it make for an individual just to have a customer?

If you ask companies like Federal Express or SAS, they'll tell you: plenty! Both companies are expert at empowering their frontline people to take care of customers. WordPerfect Corporation, though not as well known, has the same philosophy: Give customer-service people the freedom and authority they need to solve customers' problems, then let them do it.

In many firms, customer service is a low-paying, low-skilled, highly dissatisfying occupation. The people who deal with customers have little authority; if anything happens that isn't specifically covered in the rule book, they have to go to senior workers or supervisors. They're expected to handle so many customers per hour, no matter what. And heaven help them if they exceed their authority in trying to satisfy a customer.

What kind of performance do you get in a situation like that? You know the answer, because you deal every day with firms that organize their customer-service people this way. The service is *pro forma*. If you have a problem that's at all out of the ordinary, you have to wait until someone can be found who knows an answer. All too often you're treated as though *you're* the problem, an irritating disturbance between coffee breaks.

Smart training can help in this situation; even customer-service people with limited responsibilities need to be competent. They can be trained to perform even these tightly bounded duties more effectively. But the incremental improvement is small.

Firms get really improved customer-service performance when they empower workers to serve their customers and then train them so that they can do it well. Here's what one of Federal Express's customers has said about the consequences of that for him: "In an age when most attempts at customer service raise my blood pressure, the mere sighting of a Federal Express truck calms me down. The drivers treat my problems as *their* problems." [29]

SAS's customer-service people have just as strong an impact on their customers. WordPerfect Corporation markets a word processor by the same name. It's an excellent word processor (I'm writing this on it). WordPerfect's reputation for customer service, though, sets it apart just as surely as the quality of its software. The company is a leader in the personal computer market, and it's hard to tell whether the software or the customer service is the more responsible for WordPerfect's success.

I'm sure that you've dealt with a few—probably all too few—customer-service people who *know* down to the tips of their toes that their job is to satisfy you. Just one contact with them can make your day. And the range of competence they display is impressive.

Almost the same commitment and competence can characterize individuals who truly serve their customers *within* the company. Units that get to know their internal customers, understand their needs, and meet their needs normally perform at a level of competence significantly greater than those that simply produce the product as required by following the procedures imposed on them. They just know more about satisfying their customers, and they put this competence to work on a daily basis. Once again, they represent a significant competence payoff for you and the firm.

Turning Jobs into Problem Solving

This is the approach characteristic of Total Quality programs. It gives workers ownership for a process and then makes them responsible for constantly improving that process. The ways for expanding competence that we just looked at give workers responsibility for *performing* a whole process. This approach expands their competence by giving them responsibility for *troubleshooting* and *improving* the process.

The heart of this approach is contained in the Shewhart or PDCA cycle. If your organization has an active Total Quality program, you're familiar with the cycle—which takes an individual or group through the entire problem-solving process. If you're not familiar with the PDCA cycle, here's a quick summary of it.

- First, the individuals concerned *plan* what to do to correct a problem or improve a process.
- Then they *do* it; they implement the planned improvement.
- Once the improvement is in place, they *check* the results of doing it to see what happened.
- Finally, they *act* to learn from the results and begin another PDCA cycle.

Other ways exist to structure problem solving. Any of several approaches can be used. The important point is that individuals and teams are given responsibility for solving problems and for constantly improving their process. This kind of responsibility increases markedly the competence used by these individuals.

Stories about the improvements produced by quality teams are legion and growing constantly. Some improvements, as simple as tearing down a wall between machines, barely pay for themselves. Others, such as restoring troublesome machines to full operation, pay off in thousands and millions of dollars in savings.

Two aspects of the PDCA strategy stand out. First, giving workers problem-solving responsibilities results in significant process improvements, which means quality improvements, which means productivity improvements, which means profits and enhanced competitiveness. Second, meaningful problem solving changes workers' jobs and enhances their competence. This is one reason why quality teams require significant up-front training; they need a boost in their skills just to start the process. This boost in skills is nothing, though, compared to the competence level they reach in a year or two of constant process improvement.

Why does the workers' competence level keep increasing? Because the kind of systematic problem solving represented by the PDCA cycle is a tremendous *learning experience*. Taking an action, evaluating its results, and then using these results to plan the next action forms the basic learning cycle. We've already seen that smart training is really about learning, not training. The smartest training of all, though, is the training that prepares individuals to learn through what they do on the job. Hold that thought; we'll be back to it in spades in Part 4.

Compounding the Payoff

Each of the three ways of increasing worker competence and value to the firm is important by itself. I'm sure you've noticed already, though, that the three ways overlap. It's more than that: The three ways reinforce and support each other synergistically. If you really want to kickstart competence in your firm, begin making organizational changes that will organize teams of workers around processes. Then put the team in direct contact with its customers and make it responsible for satisfying those customers. Finally, make the team responsible for both operating and *improving* the process.

You can't do this quickly. It takes a minimum of several months to plan this kind of change, even if you're just doing it as a pilot (which I strongly recommend). Then it takes several months to a number of years to fully implement. American Transtech, successful by anyone's standard, has been continuously improving its use of teams for 8 years. The firm is still working on it, as it probably will be a decade from now. But the competence of its workers has increased continuously throughout the period. You can do the same. You don't need to do it all at once, or complete it in a specific time. As the Chinese proverb says, the important step is the first one.

By the way, there's a payoff to this that may not yet have occurred to you. Many firms that increase their base-level competence in these ways find that their turnover rate drops. Stop and think for a moment. Put yourself in the shoes of one of these increasingly competent individuals. If you're used to working in a team that's responsible for operating and improving its process and satisfying its customers—just where else are you going to go for a better job? From your point of view, most traditional jobs (even higher-paying ones) will be terminally boring.

If you're thinking it can't all be this good, that there have to be problems—you're right. You will have individuals who resist the change, problems with teams cooperating with one another, quite possibly problems developing an effective compensation system. But you'll always have problems. What's different about these is they'll be happening in a more competent, productive, and committed organization.

A Quick Summary

Before we leave this discussion, let me remind you again why we began it. We wanted to take a close look at the whole idea of competence in a firm. Traditional organizational theory descended from Frederick Taylor looks at workers as production costs. Improving productivity, in this view, means cutting the cost of labor. To the extent that this means making full use of sophisticated technology, it's often a good strategy. The assumption that sophisticated technology can be combined with low-cost, low-competence workers, however, is a dangerous one.

In a world where implementing rapidly changing technology is necessary for survival, these workers simply are not flexible and adaptable enough. Increasingly, new technologies require workers not only to have greater skill, but to have different and more demanding skills. Let me give you two examples.

General Motors has what may be the world's most automated plant in Saginaw, Michigan. It's not an operating plant, but one designed to test and provide new automated methods. It has far fewer workers than a traditional plant: 24 systems attendants and 18 skilled maintenance people. But the systems attendants require 1000 hours of training to prepare for their jobs, while the maintenance workers require 1700 hours. That's astronomically more training than traditional production workers require.[30]

I've already mentioned Motorola's push to upgrade the educational level of its production workers. Ingersoll-Rand had the same experience when it set out to modernize its Athens, Pennsylvania, plant. The new technology created similarly increased demands on workers as Motorola's changes did, and Ingersoll-Rand had to provide training in basic reading, writing, and arithmetic skills, as well as in subjects more related to the technology itself.[31]

These two stories barely depict the tip of the iceberg. In 1987, Walton and Susman pointed out in the *Harvard Business Review* that many newer technologies demand much higher and different competence from workers.[32] Even before that, in 1986, *Business Week* was warning that "through the rest of this decade [the 1980s] 400,000 workers a year may need extensive retraining to find new jobs. This includes people who must acquire higher technical skills, as well as those who will need remedial training in basic English and mathematics."[33]

Much of this discussion, and many of my examples, has centered on firms that have increased the competence of low-skilled blue- and white-collar workers. That's been the easiest to do, so companies have concentrated on it. Ultimately, though, competence has to increase at every level in the organization. Everyone, bottom to top, from one side of the organization to the other, will simply have to work smarter and add greater value.

In the 1990s, competitive success will go to those firms that hire, train, retain, and use individuals with a far greater range of competence than those of the traditional organization. While these workers cost more, they add more value than their cost to the company's final product. In simple economic terms, the incremental value of increased competence far outweighs its incremental cost.

How to Use These Ideas

- It doesn't matter who does your training; the way you use these ideas only secondarily involves training. This chapter was about empowering workers, giving them ownership of their processes. You do that by *managing* differently. Using quality teams in a Total Quality environment is one way to do this. Creating self-managing teams is another way. If your organization is thoroughly traditional and not open to these alternatives yet, at least see that you delegate as fully as possible to your workers (and any managers who report to you). This isn't easy or quick. It will get your people developing and using far more competence than they presently do. And that's the bottom line.

6

The Mastery Spiral

Federal Express and Mastery

In the last chapter, we looked briefly at what everyone knows: Federal Express is famous for customer service. One reason for this reputation is the extraordinary lengths to which its people go to deliver packages as promised. One of the most famous stories in the organization is about the agent who chartered a helicopter because that was the only way he could make sure a package would arrive on time.

We look at this performance and we say, "Wow, what initiative!" or "That's great—as long as it doesn't happen very frequently!" We don't often stop and ask: "What makes these people go to such lengths to keep their service commitment? What leads an agent to take the responsibility on his own to *hire a helicopter* to get the firm's job done?" It's training and a high level of competence, of course. It's the company culture. It's initiative on the part of its people. But it's something more. Companies like Federal Express are so good at what they do because their people experience and display a strong sense of *mastery* in their jobs.

Mastery and Competence

The last chapter looked at the broad goal of smart training as the development of competence in the organization. In the narrow sense, whenever anyone can do the job right he or she is competent. From the point of view of the overall success of the firm, though, competence needs to be developed at all levels. The message of Chapter 5 was that the more

71

competent individuals are at every level and the more their competence is used, the more competitive the firm will be.

So the first goal of smart training is the development of a broadly competent firm. If a firm focuses on competence alone, though, it doesn't go far enough. It can fall into the trap of looking at building competence in the organization the same way we look at filling our car's gas tank: "Put two gallons worth of competence in my work force, please." This point of view makes competence something static. You get it, and then forever after you have it.

That's not the real world. Competence is the raw material, the potential to excel. It gets transformed into actual effective performance only when competent individuals have both the opportunity to perform and the *confidence* that they can perform well. Chapter 5 delineated some of the ways that firms can organize work to give individuals the chance to gain and use competence. This chapter deals with the critical combination of opportunity with competence and confidence. This combination creates *mastery,* and it's what the game is all about. Whether or not you've ever thought of it in that way, what your organization needs in its human resources is this mastery.

This concern with mastery is very, very practical. It may take you months or years to spread competence through your organization. However, you need mastery *today.* Look around you, at the individuals in demanding jobs that require high competence day after day: product designers, programmers, salespeople, actuarians, supervisors, managers, and all. How many of them come to work every morning with a glint in their eyes, anxious to see what challenges they can conquer today? Every one of them who doesn't cheats you of his or her full potential. If they have truly mastered their jobs, the mastery has gotten lost in boredom or frustration.

You don't have to reorganize the company for them to exercise mastery and become stars in their jobs (though it might help). You do have to understand what mastery is and then provide them with the opportunity to exercise it. This chapter will help you do just that.

What Is Mastery, Anyway?

When individuals acquire competence, they have the skills to do specific tasks. In terms of the factors of performance, they have the *knowledge* and the *know-how* to perform. As we've seen, simply possessing the competence isn't enough. Individuals must have the *means* to perform effectively (including the opportunity), as well as at least one *motive* to perform. They also must *know* they have the competence, and *know* that they can use it successfully. When they do, they possess mastery, and the competence will be used.

There's more at stake here than you may think. Individuals who have mastery, who possess both competence and the confidence to use it, behave quite differently from those who may or may not possess the competence but lack the confidence. Here are some of the differences.

Individuals who possess mastery are far more willing to aim high, even if they may not make it. Individuals without mastery doubt their ability, so they often choose low, easily met goals. Where an individual with mastery may commit himself or herself to a 10 percent increase in quality, one without mastery may well settle for 1 or 2 percent. An individual with mastery may avidly try a new technique that may work more effectively, while one without this mastery will hang back, staying with safe and familiar techniques.

Individuals with mastery will stick with a difficult project far longer than those who lack this mastery. In this day and age, when constant innovation is a competitive necessity, perseverance is still a requirement for innovation. An engineer with mastery will persevere through tough times, while one without will give it a try and then quit because it seems too difficult.

Because of these two characteristics, *individuals with mastery constantly increase their competence.* Because they will try difficult tasks and stick with them, they learn at a far greater rate than individuals without mastery.

> Picture two production workers, each with the same initial competence. The first lacks confidence in his competence, so he operates his part of the process carefully. If something goes wrong, he's cautious about what he tries, and he calls for help if the repair appears difficult. He maintains his competence, but increases it only slightly if at all. Now look at the second worker. She's confident of her competence, so she keeps trying to find ways to improve her process, to get just a little more performance from the process. If something goes wrong with it, she tries aggressively to fix it. She'll make mistakes—but she'll understand and operate the process far better than the first worker. Mastery keeps building on itself, continuously increasing the competence on which it's based.[34]

The last point is the most critical of all. Competence is never stagnant. When combined with confidence and opportunity, it becomes increasing mastery. When either the confidence or the opportunity is missing, mastery begins to slip away. In other words, competence in the real world is always part of an ascending or descending spiral of mastery, as seen in Fig. 6-1.

When you look at the highly competent workers of Chaparral Steel, for instance, it's really mastery that you're seeing. The founder of Chaparral, Gordon Forward, refers to the "lab" in his plant—because work-

Mastery

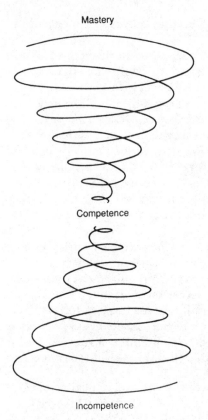

Competence

Incompetence

Figure 6-1

ers are forever trying new ways to improve production in what is already one of the most productive steel companies in the world.[35] Chaparral's success would never have happened, and Chaparral would never enjoy the competitive edge it does, if the workers didn't combine a high degree of competence with equally high confidence. You see the same combination in Procter and Gamble's plants and American Transtech's customer-service teams. Their workers are continually increasing their competence, demonstrating their *mastery* of their jobs and the processes for which they're responsible.

Mismatching Competence and Confidence

Unfortunately, no law requires that competence and confidence be well matched, that all competent individuals be confident and vice versa. Because they can be separated, either confidence without competence or competence without confidence will harm the organization. One of the goals of smart training is to see that as far as possible, the two are always combined. This may sound self-evident, even a little trite. In the real world of organizational performance, it isn't. It's far more of a problem than it seems at first blush. Let me illustrate this with the simple chart that appears as Fig. 6-2.

This chart oversimplifies the situation, of course. What it suggests, though, is that there are four different kinds of workers and managers in your (and every) organization.

Many individuals are stuck at the level of *incompetence.* They don't know how to do much (at least on the job), and they don't have much confidence in their ability to do much. These are the people who, when asked what they do, respond with, "Oh, I'm just a . . . " They're data entry clerks chained to one or two fixed formats and a tight production standard; assembly-line workers on a traditional assembly line; supervisors who simply carry out the policies and directions from higher levels without using judgment or initiative in the process.

A second group is made up of those who actually have acquired competence, but who don't have the confidence to apply it. They have competence, but it's *unusable.* These are the workers who at least occasionally use judgment and creativity, but who don't get credit for it—and thus don't realize that they're actually competent. Many blue-collar and clerical employees fall into this group; they often must develop innovative procedures on the fly, but get credit only for following the firm's standard procedures. If a crisis comes up, they don't have the confidence to tackle it; either someone else tackles it or it doesn't get tackled.

The third group, the most dangerous, have the high confidence in themselves that goes with competence, but lack the competence itself. These are the people who believe they can do jobs for which they're unprepared. They have a "can do" attitude, but their compe-

High Confidence	False Competence	Mastery
Low Confidence	Incompetence	Unusable Competence
	Low Competence	High Competence

Figure 6-2

tence is *false*, and they can get themselves and the firm into trouble quickly.

Finally, the productive heart of any organization is made up of the individuals who are *masters* of what they do. They can be found at any level: a skilled machinist or engineer, freight specialist or designer, recruiter or packer. They're the people who create and maintain the *core competence* of the firm that the next chapter examines. The real training and development task in every organization is how to move as many people as possible to this level of performance. The endeavor is successful whenever individuals with competence have confidence in their competence and the opportunity to exercise and increase it.

The Costs of Deadweight, Waste, and Risk

Figure 6-3 is the same chart as in Fig. 6-2, relabeled to make its impact on your firm more evident.

If you look at it this way, everyone in your organization who doesn't possess mastery—competence plus confidence and the opportunity to use it—is either Deadweight, Unnecessary Waste, or an Unnecessary Risk to your organization. Here's why.

The Incompetent

Incompetent is a harsh word, but it's an all-too-accurate description of the individuals who perform minimally skilled, repetitive jobs day after day. They may not cost you much in direct labor, but they're adding minimal value to your organization. (We saw that in the last chapter.) Unfortunately, the situation is worse than that. Because they haven't had to

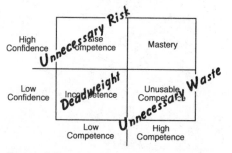

Figure 6-3

learn any new skills for years, perhaps even decades, they don't learn or change rapidly. If you need to implement new technology, they can't adapt to it easily. Their jobs have trained them not to look for mastery, so their motivation for it is limited.

One of your first priorities is to move as many workers as possible in this category out of it, as quickly as possible. If they don't add value to your customers, consider contracting their jobs out. If they do add value, or if you decide to keep them in-house, use Total Quality Management (TQM) or self-managing teams or some similar approach to add definite, meaningful competence to their jobs. Retrain them; find ways to motivate them—do whatever you have to do to move as many of them as possible out of the incompetence box. Does this sound difficult? It probably will be, because uncomplaining incompetence is what many firms have expected from their workers (and even their supervisors and managers) for years. But it can be done. For the competitive health of the firm, it must be done.

The Wasted

The second group, the one with the greatest potential to help you compete, is composed of those with unusable competence—the ones who're unnecessarily wasted. They don't lack competence, because their jobs as accounting clerks, tool crib attendants, warehouse workers, bookkeepers, personnel clerks, customer-service persons, or whatever have actually required more skill and inventiveness than you know. The problem is that the organization doesn't believe they're particularly competent; after all, they're nothing but (fill in the title of your favorite low-skilled job). There aren't any provisions for them to move up in the firm or even to expand their competence where they are, so they don't try. But the potential is there.

These people comprise a real reservoir of available talent. They may not have all the skills you need for higher-level performance, but they're well on the way. They can be given more responsibility and authority and brought along quickly. Because their problem is lack of confidence, management support and encouragement will work wonders with them.

The Risky

The individuals in the third group, with confidence but insufficient competence, are the most dangerous. They create an unnecessary risk for the firm. They don't hesitate to tackle projects they're unequipped to handle. These individuals may be very competent engineers, supervisors, accountants, managers. They have real mastery in their fields. They have a "can do" attitude and often strong ambition. They'll volunteer for any project and throw themselves into it, sure that they have the raw ability to succeed.

This group also contains the individuals who want a promotion at any price. They may be in any occupation, at any level. These are the individuals who've never really evaluated their strengths and weaknesses or set realistic goals for themselves. They jump at any opportunity that drifts by.

Why are the individuals in this group an unnecessary risk? It's simple—once they get outside their areas of competence, they can't tell when they're getting in over their heads. Fully competent workers know where their competence ends; not so with falsely competent ones. They continue struggling on—remember, individuals with confidence persevere—not realizing that the path they've chosen leads to a dead end. When they get selected for projects, the firm can never trust the results they produce.

These individuals often go unrecognized. Even more, they may be widely appreciated for their "can do" attitude. But they take a significant toll on the organization. Do any of these examples sound familiar?

- Marilyn, the branch secretary, has been recognized as a master of her job for several years. Her mastery is so evident that when the branch picks up responsibility for its own budget, Marilyn's boss gets her position upgraded to handle the budget. In preparation for her new responsibilities, he sends her to a three-day budget course. Five months later, the branch can't account for $50,000 of its expenditures. Marilyn didn't do anything underhanded. In fact, she worked extremely hard. She just didn't understand what she needed to do to manage dollars effectively.

- Roger runs the maintenance engineering function with real mastery. He has preventive maintenance organized so well that significant breakdowns in the equipment are rare. His boss picks him to head a project team to select a new heating system. Two months later, the team has accomplished virtually nothing and Roger has to be replaced. His mastery of a stable administrative situation didn't carry over to organizing a tightly time-bound project.

- Marie is clearly the technician with the greatest mastery in the whole fabrication branch. When a supervisory position comes open, she's a shoo-in for it. Three months later, her boss is trying to resolve three grievances filed against her, and several other technicians have asked for transfers out. You know the answer to this one: Her mastery as a technician is of almost no use to her as a supervisor.

■ Finally, Robert is a master at controlling costs and running a "tight ship." He gets promoted to CEO, heading an organization that's under significant pressure for market share from a German company with exceptional quality. He tries to meet the challenge by doing what he knows how to do: cutting costs. Two years later, having lost 25 percent market share, he takes early retirement.

Note the similar thread in each case. An individual with obvious mastery of one job is moved into another, different job. Because the individual was so effective at the first job, his or her boss assumed that the mastery would carry over. But it didn't because mastery is always based on specific competence, and these individuals didn't have the specific competence they needed in the new jobs. In each case, a job that could have been handled well by an individual with the right competence was done badly. That's the unnecessary risk that individuals with false competence create.

The costs of wasted competence are just as real, but much harder to spot. Perhaps there was a bookkeeper in Marilyn's branch who could have done the budget job—but neither she nor anyone else realized that she had the necessary competence. As good a technician as Marie was, perhaps another technician was better at the people skills a supervisor needs.

Cutting Waste and Reducing Risk

When you look out over your organization, how many incompetents, how many wasted talents, how many unnecessary risks do you see? More important, how many individuals—workers and managers alike—do you see exercising mastery day after day? If your firm is like most, there are too many in the first three groups and far too few in the last group. And you pay some price, large or small, for each person who contributes less than true mastery to your firm.

Now that we've identified the problem, where do we find the solution?

There are several solutions, most of them tried and true. The problem isn't that no one knows them—it's that so few firms practice them. They all come under the general heading of "development," and that's what the rest of the chapter examines.

Good Job Analyses

This may surprise you. Why do we talk about job analysis first when we're supposed to be talking about development? The answer is a simple one. Orderly development depends on knowing what skills your jobs require, and then preparing individuals with these skills.

Here's a brief example. At the very minimum, a firm should know the basic competencies that its supervisory, managerial, and executive positions require. In a large firm, these competencies should be systematically documented and updated every few years. A small firm won't normally have the time to do this formally. But it can track the competencies of its supervisors and managers informally and review them every year or so to make sure they're up to date. That makes it easy to identify the skills that a worker needs, for instance, to move up to a supervisory position. If Marie is selected to be a supervisor, at least she and her boss will know what she needs to do to succeed in the job.

Formally gathering information on supervisory, managerial, and executive competencies requires time and skill. The same individuals who design training have the skill to do the analysis. Once the analysis is done and the competencies are identified, though, there's a very simple way to present the information in a useful form. Create a matrix with representative jobs across the top and the various competencies down the left column. Table 6-1 shows a highly oversimplified example. Using just these three symbols, look at the information this simple matrix provides.

First- and second-level supervisors and managers normally have the *technical skills* they need. However, senior managers, division chiefs, and vice presidents—who have responsibility for very broad operations—may or may not have the skills. A well-designed development program

Table 6-1

	Position			
Skill	1st- & 2nd-Level Supv.	Operating Manager	Senior Manager	Division Chief, Vice President
Technical	+	+	0	0
Listening	–	+	+	+
Planning	–	–	–	–
Presentation	–	+	–	+

Key:
+ means that most individuals will already have this skill and will not need to be trained in it.
– means that most individuals will *not* have the level of skill they need for this level. This is an identified training need.
0 means that an individual may or may not have the skill, depending on background and career path.

will provide rotational assignments for individuals hoping to move into the two top levels.

Virtually all first- and second-level supervisors need to be trained in *listening skills*. After that, if the individuals continue to practice these skills, they will possess the necessary competence for each higher level without further training.

Because the nature of *planning* changes so dramatically as an individual rises in the organization, training (or other development) in new planning skills is a requirement for each level.

Finally, supervisors need training in *presentation skills*. These basic skills will then carry them through operational management. An individual aspiring to or already in a senior management position needs further development because the type of presentation and audience changes sharply at that level.

Remember, the matrix is just an example. Your supervisors, managers, and executives will require many more skills, and the requirements at each level may be quite different from those shown in Table 6-1. You can see, though, how economically and concisely the matrix presents the requirements.

You should have a clear focus on the skills required in the jobs that report to you, particularly the supervisory and managerial ones. If you don't, it's time to ask your training department (or a consultant) to help you identify the skills.

Individual Developmental Plans

This isn't the first time I've mentioned individual developmental plans, and it may not be the last—because simple developmental plans can yield such a large payoff for a small investment. I'm sure that your organization has at least tried them in the past, perhaps several times. It's all too easy for supervisors to see them as a paperwork exercise and employees to look on them as guarantees of training. They're neither. Instead, properly used they can be a powerful device for promoting mastery and doing away with false competence and wasted competence.

Properly done individual developmental plans enable individual to focus on exactly what their career aspirations are. Particularly at lower levels, many workers simply want to get promoted. What they get promoted *to* is much less important. That's a recipe for disappointment— for the worker and the firm. Employees need the discipline of deciding *what* they would like to be promoted to and then of preparing themselves for it. Supervisors who work with employees to prepare the plans can help them develop realistic expectations and map out realistic development activities. Then they can work together to see that the employees follows through.

Don't let it deteriorate into a *pro forma* annual ritual. Here are some suggestions for keeping the program alive and well.

1. *Don't make a detailed plan mandatory.* When individuals are happy where they are, let it be. Even if they have definite career goals, they may still be quite happy with last year's developmental plan. Let that be too.

2. *Require developmental plans of employees who want to be promoted.* If the selecting supervisor interviews candidates for promotion, one of the first questions should be: What have you done to prepare for this job? The supervisor should ask to see the employee's developmental plan and discuss it with the individual.

3. *Review them periodically.* Employees who really want to advance should be pursuing their advancement continuously. When this is the case, the individual and the supervisor should review the developmental plan every few months; it may even need updating that often.

4. *Keep them as simple as possible.* I haven't enclosed a sample because firms vary so widely in the formats they use. Your firm may already have a format. If it doesn't, either an in-house trainer or external consultant should be able to provide you with one. But make sure it's simple. Here, as in so many other places, less is more.

Developmental Assignments

A developmental assignment is another traditional developmental method, one that was first mentioned in Chapter 2. When you're trying to prevent the danger of false competence or the waste of unusable competence, this is the best method of all. Let me explain.

All true mastery is based on actual experience at the work. If you look back at the ascending spiral in Fig. 6-1, you'll see how individuals with mastery continually do more and more demanding work. Developmental assignments further this upward spiral.

And what about those with false competence? Developmental assignments make clear quickly where the gaps are in their experience. Once the gaps are apparent, individuals can begin converting false competence to true mastery.

Look back at the example of Roger, an excellent routine manager. He was put in charge of a project for which he lacked mastery. The result was a disappointment to everyone. Now suppose that Roger hadn't been put in charge of the team, but had served as assistant to an experienced project manager. Everyone understood that he was to understudy the manager with the mastery and that he was to assume as much of a leadership role as his competence permitted.

What would have happened? Roger would have found out quickly that he lacked the competence to manage a project. It wouldn't have been a disaster, though, because the experienced manager would have been there to keep the project running. He and Roger could have worked together to identify the skills that Roger lacked and begun to remedy them. Roger probably wouldn't have been able to run that project before it was done, and quite possibly not the next one he was on. With just a little more experience, though, he could have had the necessary competence. Then when he was assigned to head a team, he'd have been ready. Instead of failing, he would have begun developing mastery at project management.

The same logic would apply if Marilyn's boss had let her try her hand at budgeting on a developmental assignment, or Marie's supervisor had let her understudy him for a few weeks. This would have given individuals the opportunity to find out how much real competence they possessed for the new position. The result? They would have made a far more realistic assessment of their competence for the position—*and begun planning what they needed to do to gain the competence they lacked.*

In short, an excellent cure for false competence is a temporary assignment to a new line of work. At the same time that the false competence vanishes, the individual begins to acquire the rudiments of honest competence in the new field. That's a really potent twofer.

Putting Skills to Work

I've said this before. I'll say it again and again before the book is done. But that's because it's so very important. One of the great contributions you can make to individual mastery (and the defeat of false competence) is to see that employees who get training put it to work immediately after they receive it.

I've stressed this as a key to real performance improvement. Here, I'm stressing it because it's so critical for the development of mastery. Let me give you a quick example. Tom joins the budget branch as an analyst. The branch uses spreadsheets on personal computers to do both projections and budget tracking. Since Tom isn't experienced with spreadsheets, he attends a three-day course. When he returns, he's enlisted into a special task force to review budgeting processes at a district office. There's only one portable computer for the three people on the task force, and a more experienced analyst uses it.

When Tom returns two weeks later, he begins using a spreadsheet.

Since he's forgotten most of the training he received, he has to look up many of the commands. This is time-consuming, so he sticks to the simpler commands; they do the job adequately. A few months later, as he's now "experienced" at using spreadsheets, he's sent to an advanced class. This class assumes that everyone has all the skills from the first class and goes from there. Tom can't follow many of the steps; if he takes time to look back at the basic material, he falls behind even further.

When Tom returns from class, he possesses neither solid basic knowledge nor a significant portion of the advanced knowledge he's supposed to have. He's not at the level of competence that's expected. Worse, his experience in the second class and back on the job have convinced him that he doesn't understand spreadsheets very well—and that he's not very good with them. He remains with the limited knowledge he has and doesn't experiment. He has neither the competence that's expected nor the mastery that could have been built on this competence (another example of the downward spiral illustrated in Fig. 6-1).

This is one more reason why the most important step you can take to see that training is effective is seeing that workers put it to use immediately.

Mastering the Discontinuities

Every firm has steps in its promotion paths that lead to positions quite unlike those that individuals have held before. In this section, we look more closely at some of these *discontinuities*. They occur when individuals leave jobs in which they possessed genuine mastery for promotion into ones for which they lack competence. Actually, it can be even worse; the competence they have may mislead them in the new position—as when new supervisors try to do all the most difficult work themselves.

You can't anticipate all the discontinuities, but there are four situations where the firm should prepare individuals in advance or immediately after selection to perform very different work. These situations are (1) when individuals are promoted from clerical or assistant-type positions to administrative, technical, or analytical positions; (2) when they're promoted from nonsupervisory to supervisory positions; (3) when they're promoted from supervisory to full-fledged managerial positions; and (4) when they're promoted from managerial to executive positions.

You want to be prepared for each of these situations, so what do you do? The temporary assignment we discussed earlier is a good solution, but it often isn't feasible. Mentoring, another solution, is discussed in a few paragraphs. There's something else you can do: present succinct, clear training in the *role* that the new work requires.

Training for New Roles

Take the transition from a nonsupervisory to a supervisory position. Typically, individuals selected for these jobs are skilled workers, used to getting results from their own efforts. You want them to stop that the moment they become supervisors and learn instead how to get work done through others. That's not an easy transition. It requires a whole new group of skills that will take time to acquire.

What can be acquired immediately—perhaps even before the individual becomes a supervisor—is training in the new role. Even in a training situation, an individual can learn what it means to get work done through others and experience simulations of it (through role plays and so forth).

You might think of this as a new and higher level of *orientation*. Chapter 2 looked at how new workers could be acclimated to their roles as producing workers. Whenever individuals make each of the four jumps previously described, they need to acclimate themselves to a different kind of role. This training doesn't equip them with the skills they need. Instead, they learn the different expectations that the organization has of them in their new job. New supervisors learn that they will need to become good at delegation to succeed, and that "if you want the job done right do it yourself" is a recipe for failure.

This won't work wonders, but it will help individuals catch themselves before they unthinkingly act in familiar ways. Then, as quickly as possible, the firm should follow this training with training in the specific skills of supervision.

A final suggestion. If you can do it, it's a good idea to provide individuals with experience and or training designed to experience the new role *before* they move into it. For instance, you might offer all potential candidates for supervisory positions the opportunity for this experience or training. You normally want to hold off on skills training, though, until *after* individuals have been selected for the job. Remember, you want them to apply the skills they've learned as soon as possible.

Mentoring

Mentoring has been around for a very long time. Seasoned performers or managers who take neophytes under their wings and help them develop mastery have always been a feature of effective organizations. The popularity of mentoring *programs,* however, ebbs and flows.

Popularity isn't the point. It doesn't matter whether other firms are hot on mentoring or not. It does matter whether and how you use it to develop mastery in your firm. An effective mentor can smooth the way and accelerate the learning curve in any circumstance. Perhaps it's most useful, though, when an experienced individual can mentor someone who has just moved into a new and unfamiliar line of work. In other words, mentors can be most helpful when individuals move from clerical to specialist, nonsupervisory to supervisory, supervisory to managerial, and managerial to executive work.

There are many ways that mentoring can be used, and many books to tell you how. Let me simply suggest that your firm establish a formal mentoring process for individuals who make each of the four jumps listed at the end of the last paragraph. Yes, this probably does happen often without a formal program. No, putting in a formal program doesn't guarantee it will happen. But if you make it a responsibility of supervisors, managers, and executives to see that the individuals who make these jumps are effectively mentored, it will be done more often and more effectively.

Don't Forget Why
You're Doing It

Let me remind you quickly of what this chapter is *really* about: the mastery spiral. The usable competence of your organization never stands still; it's constantly increasing or decreasing in comparison with your competitors and your market. When competence is supported by confidence and given opportunity, your firm's mastery spirals upward. When competence, confidence, or opportunity is missing, the spiral heads toward the basement.

This is important in any situation. It's crucial, though, for a learning organization—because a learning organization is one that commits itself to and achieves an unending upward spiral of mastery. It's also critical when we talk about the *core competence* of your firm. This core competence is what keeps you in business. The next chapter is devoted to it.

How to Use These Ideas

- Here, again, it doesn't matter who does the training. This is a *management* issue. You want as much mastery as possible, as widely spread as possible in the organization. Where do you start? You can build the demand for competence that the last chapter described, then see that it leads to mastery. You can make sure that you're organized to produce high-quality work, not just quantity. Workers always feel a greater sense of mastery and pride when they know they've helped create a quality product. You can also offer opportunities for individuals with actual or potential competence to turn it into mastery.

- I have another suggestion, just as important as these. Don't fall into believing that because an individual does very well in one area that he or she will excel in a different one. Give individuals the experience of a different kind of work, but provide them a mentor to see that they're successful.

7

Core Competence: The Name of the Game

In many ways, this is the pivotal chapter of the book. Up to this point, we've gradually broadened our focus—from the results of individual training courses to the organization's need for mastery. The first part of this chapter takes one more broadening step; we look at the strategic core competence that a firm must have. I've hinted that smart training must be linked to the basic strategy of the firm; this chapter describes just how that link is made.

After that, the focus becomes more specific again. The chapter ends with some of the tactical considerations required to maintain and increase core competence. Chapters 8 and 9 tackle some very practical aspects of getting and using competence. Chapters 10 through 14 deal with the equally practical questions involved in selecting the training methods to support smart training. Chapters 15 and 16, which complete the book, broaden the focus again. They deal explicitly with the relationship between smart training and the learning organization.

What Core Competence Is

In Chapter 5, I mentioned the opinion of numerous economists that the decisive competitive factor in the 1990s and beyond will be the skill not only of the work force of a firm but of a nation. Here's what economist Robert Reich, one of the strongest proponents of this view, said in an article in the *Harvard Business Review:*

> American ownership of the corporation is profoundly less relevant to America's economic future than the skills, training, and knowledge commanded by American workers.
>   . . . If we hope to revitalize the competitive performance of the United States economy, we must invest in people, not in nationally defined corporations.[36]

Chapter 5 used this basic idea to describe how competence needs to be spread throughout the organization. That's only the beginning, though. Every firm needs to develop not just competence in general but its *core competence.* Using the term *intellectual capital, Fortune* magazine described a firm's core competence as "the sum of everything everybody in your company knows that gives you a competitive edge in the marketplace."[37]

The essence of the idea is simple: A firm's core competence is the mastery it must have to compete successfully in its chosen markets, now and in the future.

The core competence of 3M is the totality of its people's mastery of all the skills it takes to innovate constantly and successfully. Rubbermaid isn't as famous for its innovative competence, but it's used it to drive remarkable growth in the last few years.

Emerson Electric's core competence is all the skills it takes to be a successful low-cost producer in the crowded consumer electric and electronics market.

Worthington Steel's core competence is the accumulated and accumulating mastery it takes to produce very high quality steel that meets the very precise needs of its customers.

Just what a firm's core competence is depends on how the firm sees itself. The length and breadth of its strategic vision determine what mastery it will develop.

In the May–June 1990 issue of the *Harvard Business Review,* C. K. Prahalad and Gary Hamel compared the core competence developed by NEC, a leading Japanese electronics firm, with that of GTE. In 1980, the American firm had net sales of $9.98 billion, nearly three times as high as those of NEC. By 1988, GTE's sales had risen to $16.46 billion— but NEC's sales were at $21.89 billion. GTE had retrenched significantly from its 1980 position, while NEC had become a world player. Why?

There probably is no single explanation. Part of the answer, though, is related to the core competence each firm developed. In Prahalad and Hamel's words, GTE conceived itself in terms of a "portfolio of businesses," while NEC saw itself as a "portfolio of competencies."[38]

Just what does this mean? According to Prahalad and Hamel:

> The survivors of the first wave of global competition, Western and Japanese alike, are all converging on similar and formidable standards for product cost and quality—minimum hurdles for continued competition, but less and less important as sources of differential advantage. In the long run, competitiveness derives from an ability to build, at lower cost and more speedily than competitors, the core competencies that spawn unanticipated products. The real sources of advantage are to be found in management's ability to consolidate corporatewide technologies and production skills into competencies that empower individual businesses to adapt quickly to changing opportunities.[39]

These authors are focusing on large, multinational corporations, suggesting that competitive advantage lies in the synergy between the different technologies and markets they pursue. It doesn't take a lot of imagination, though, to apply their basic idea to even the smallest firm. It's this:

> *The ability of any firm to compete in today's dynamic economy stems from its ability to develop, maintain, and increase the competence necessary not only to preserve its current position but to identify and respond successfully to the new opportunities the market presents.*

Note that this is a very forward-looking definition. Trying to preserve the core competencies of the past isn't enough. In fact, it's an almost sure ticket to corporate oblivion. Core competence has to grow continually, concentrated on the evolving business strategy of the organization.

I've used the term *core competence* because it's a commonly used one. If you read the last chapter carefully, though, you know we're really talking about *core mastery*. What powers a competitive firm isn't a collection of competencies it has accumulated—it's the ability and confidence not only to use these competencies but to increase them. I'll continue to use *core competence* as the term; please remember that either this competence is demonstrated in mastery or it isn't demonstrated at all.

In many ways, it's even harder but more important for a small firm to develop and enlarge its core competence. One advantage of large organizations is that they can afford a dozen or a hundred or even a thousand individuals with the same basic competence. Look how many automotive engineers GM or Ford or Chrysler employs, or how many sales personnel IBM has. This makes it easy for them to bring new workers along in an orderly progression until they accumulate the necessary mastery.

But what if you only have one or two or a half dozen individuals with this basic mastery? Suppose you're a small machine shop, or a regional department store chain, or a medical electronics firm with a limited product line? You don't have the luxury of redundant experts in your competencies. This isn't all negative; just a few people can work together far more effectively than hundreds or thousands. You need to be very clear, however, just what your core competencies are—and constantly reinforcing these competencies.

(Time for a quick note. I've been using not only competence but competencies—and this may have been confusing. *Competence* refers to the broad ability of an individual or organization to accomplish tasks. *Competencies* are the specific skills they need to support this broad ability. An insurance adjuster must be *competent* at pricing repairs accurately. This competence requires the *competencies* of accurate observation, effective use of reference manuals, and so forth. I don't like to burden you with this new terminology. However, it's beginning to become common language, so we may as well use it.)

What *Your* Core Competence Is

Clearly, I can't tell you what your core competence should be. I can tell you about three of its characteristics, though.

It's Strategic

The core competence that your firm develops must derive from its deepest strategic understanding of itself and its market. Here are some examples of the difference this strategic vision can make.

Most firms that make automobiles think of themselves as car manufacturers. For many of them, just diversifying into trucks is a major strategic initiative. Their core competence, then, is in automotive design, manufacture, and marketing. It's designed to serve a strategic goal with a 5- to 10-year horizon. At least one Japanese automotive manufacturer, though, sees itself in the transportation business, with a planning horizon of 100 years plus. What it considers core competencies will be quite different—because its strategic vision is different.

Suppose your firm is small and only serves a local or regional market. Let's say you're a wholesaler serving office supply stores in a large metropolitan area. Is your fundamental job stocking and delivering your products, or is it enabling your customers to operate with the smallest possible investment in inventory? How you answer that—your basic strategy—will determine the core competence of your firm.

This kind of strategic decision is applicable over a broad range of firms. Is your basic mastery the ability to deliver something to your customers at a reasonable cost for them and a reasonable profit for you? Or is it to support them and make them more successful by providing a product or service more effectively than they could provide it for themselves? This choice has dozens of variations, but all of them ultimately boil down to the same choice. Public agencies and nonprofit organizations have to make it just as surely as profit-making firms do.

Why do I stress this so? After all these strategic choices don't directly concern training. Whatever choice you make, you can still train your firm to mastery in the competencies it requires. That's true—but your strategic decisions will put formidable limitations on what your people can learn effectively. What people learn well, they stick with. Trying to get them to do something very different very quickly is somewhere between difficult and impossible. Let me give you some examples.

American automakers a decade ago were very competent in designing, manufacturing, and selling a mass-produced, standardized automobile with high style and low quality. Then the Japanese manufacturers began to capture market share. The American firms changed their strategy and decided that (in Ford's words) "Quality Is Job One." We're now into the second decade of this improvement, and the American firms are still playing catch-up. I'm not criticizing them—just pointing out how difficult it is to change core competence.

Compaq Computers began as a firm with one competency: building durable, portable IBM-compatible computers. They expanded that competency into the ability to build a range of high-quality portable and desktop computers. Then they added the competence required to remain innovators in their market. Because the company was highly selective in its competencies, it could build them on one another to serve a changing market.

The core competence of Polaroid Corporation has been in chemistry, since that's what it takes to make conventional instant film. Now, as digital photography becomes more significant, Polaroid needs individuals with electronics competence. It is building its strategic hiring plans around this need, and offering significant incentives to current workers who acquire electronics know-how.[40]

The need to change strategy and support it with new core competence isn't confined to the Fortune 500. Suppose you're a local supermarket chain that has been competing against mom-and-pop grocery stores. That takes one set of core competencies. Now a nationwide chain with much greater floor space per store moves in. You need a new strategy, quickly, to compete against it. And then you need to get the competence to support this strategy propagated through the firm as quickly as possible. You may decide that you'll compete by providing the friendliest and most responsive service possible—but you can't change the skills and attitudes of two hundred front-line people and their managers overnight. The question is: Can you do it soon enough to survive?

In other words, you can change aspects of your strategy far easier than you can change the competence that undergirds the strategy. Nonetheless, your strategy must drive your core competence. Once that happens that same core competence will limit the strategic changes you can make. A firm's ability to select, master, and evolve essential competencies is one of the basic determinants of its success in every dimension.

It's Limited

As the preceding paragraphs suggest, there's a limit on how many core competencies a firm can master. One of the firms that Prahalad and Hamel describe in their article is Canon, an extremely large firm that competes worldwide. In the authors' view, though, Canon has only three basic competencies: precision mechanics, fine optics, and micro-electronics.[41] A firm that tries to develop a variety of competencies is skating on thin ice—and most firms fall through. Kentucky Fried Chicken understands this clearly. Their ads of a few years back stressed that all they did was chicken, and that "we do chicken right." They have a clear focus on their core competence.

What does "limited" mean for your operation? I don't know. I do know, though, that Xerox wasn't able to develop core competence in computers and AT&T hasn't been able to do so yet (though the merger with NCR may change that). IBM is still trying to master communications as a core competence.

Looking at companies that have been successful, though, I have a suggestion that may help. You will derive the greatest benefit from limited competencies when they are related to one another and when they can be used not only independently but in combination with one another. In other words, your core competencies should be synergistic. Canon is a large and diversified company, but almost all of their core products use two and even three of the company's core competencies. Xerox is attempting to remold and focus all of its core competencies around document processing.

It's Your Business's Ability to Add Value

This should go without saying. Your firm's competitiveness is its ability to add value in a way that other firms can't. There are dozens of effective companies that build computers, but for years Digital Equipment

Corporation was able to add value that other computer firms couldn't by offering a broad line of computers that all ran the same software. Nordstrom has built its success on an extraordinary level of customer service. Even in a market that has increased quality dramatically, part of Toyota's success is its ability to build the highest quality car in most of its niches.

These companies, and thousands of others, succeed because they add value in a way that their competitors can't. Their core competence is their ability to do this year after year. It isn't their mastery of a particular technology, or the breadth of their distribution system, or even their ability to reduce cycle time in isolation. Instead, true core competence is the ability to use whatever it takes to add more value to their products or services for their customers than their competitors can. Core competence links directly to customer satisfaction.

Smart Training Is Strategy-Driven Training

This section heading says it all. The strategic basis of all smart training has been lurking in the shadows from the beginning—and now it steps into the limelight. You can follow every other recommendation in this book, but if your training isn't driven by your firm's strategy it will never achieve its potential. And, in Robert Galvin's words, it will never cost nothing. It will, in fact, be extremely expensive, because it will help you create and maintain the wrong competencies.

Please pause a moment and think about that last sentence. The phrase *core competence* is new. The concept behind it isn't. Once-mighty railroads fell on hard times with the rise of the trucking industry—because their strategy and their core competence was running railroads, not providing transportation. IBM has seen its core competence for years as the ability to provide exceptional service to customers; today, personal computers are virtually commodities—and it's not at all clear what "exceptional service" means in this circumstance. United Airlines tried to change its core competence from running an airline to providing a range of travel services—and took a bloodbath before it gave up the attempt. Over and over, firms rise, fall, go bankrupt, and dominate their market because of their understanding of their basic strategy and the core competence that supports it.

The worst situation of all, of course, occurs when a firm has no clear strategy or no understanding of the core competence that supports it. When this happens, the company falls prey to the popular ideas of the time—which always provide the *least* effective competitive advantage. Even a poor strategy can be examined and improved if it's explicit. A strategy by default just lies there and slowly withers away. The smartest training in the world can delay its demise, but never prevent it. Strategy drives core competence which drives smart training. This is Plan A. There is no Plan B.

Don't think that the need for a clear strategy applies only to large firms. In my part of the world, there's a small restaurant chain called Cookers. It began a few years ago and has been expanding gradually. Just over a year ago, a competing restaurant opened across from a Cookers. At first, the new restaurant was packed. Gradually, though, the crowds have thinned; now you don't need to wait as long to get a table.

Cookers is still crowded. Why? The new restaurant is targeted at the young-adult crowd, as are dozens of other restaurants in town. They don't really do anything distinctively. Not so Cookers. Its goal, in the words of one of its founders, is "to provide customers with the same level of satisfaction from an $8 meal that they expect from a $50 meal." This is Cookers' core competence, and it works hard to develop and maintain it. That's why Cookers' parking lot stays full.

Keeping this requirement for a clear strategy in mind, we now make the turn described at the start of this chapter—from the increasingly broad to the increasingly specific. Beginning with a short section on the tactical approach to core competence, we'll move further and further into the nitty-gritty of smart training.

Core Competence in the Trenches

It's easy to take this broad, strategic view. It's much harder to implement it effectively. And it's devilishly hard to see that the day-to-day decisions that affect training are consistent with it. Regardless of the strategy, these day-to-day decisions added together are the ones that will make or break the firm's core competence.

Remember the examples of Ingersoll-Rand's Pennsylvania plant and Motorola as a whole, two firms that decided to make major changes in their way of doing business. Before they could implement the new technology their business plans required, they had to commit themselves to dramatic training programs in basic skills. These programs were hardly exciting, and what you'd expect to find in a community college rather than a major corporation. Without them, though, neither firm could have implemented its strategy.

In many ways, those are the easy choices. They're so obvious that they virtually cry out to be attended to. Other choices, just as important, aren't necessarily as obvious. What will be the impact of a new automated system? Should this kind of work be contracted out or done in-house? What kind of new machinery should we buy? What training should we develop and give next? These dozens and hundreds of small decisions support and increase or gradually erode the firm's core competence.

How do you ensure that these decisions get made in a way that creates and maintains the core competence that you must have? One way of answering the questions begins with the relationship between competence and added value in the firm. We've become very conscious these days of the value-adding process in firms. We've realized that one of the basic tasks of management is finding and rooting out the non-value-adding work that keeps creeping in. It may help to look at a firm's value-creating activities in relation to its competence. Fig. 7-1 shows one way the relationship can be diagramed. To summarize the points that will be made in detail in the next few paragraphs, this is what Fig. 7-1 suggests:

- Activities that add little value and require little competence are, at best, *minor distractions* to the firm. They are prime candidates for contracting out.

- On the other hand, activities that add significant value but require little competence create only a *marginal advantage* for the firm. Because the required competence is low, other companies can easily copy these processes.

- Perhaps less obviously, the activities that require considerable competence but add little value are *dangerous distractions*. They are expensive and generally interesting, but take attention away from satisfying the customer.

- Finally, the heart of a company's competitive ability is in the individuals that deliver high value with high competence. They constitute the true *core mastery* on which competitive advantage depends.

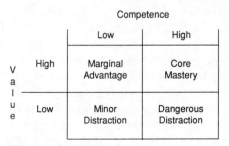

Figure 7-1

Before we look at the four quadrants in more detail, let me make a general comment on the chart. Most orthodox approaches to job design aim at reducing the competence required to operate a firm. We've seen that jobs are typically engineered so that they're simple and repetitive. They can then be filled with low-paid individuals who require little training and are easily replaced. If this chart in Fig. 7-1 is correct, however, *this is precisely the wrong way to create competitive advantage.* By reducing worker competence, the approach hamstrings the organization's ability to create the necessary core competence or mastery.

This will become clearer as we go through the four quadrants.

Low Value/Low Competence

Every organization requires low value/low competence activities. Typical workers in this group are janitors, food service workers, data entry personnel, stock clerks, and so on. Many organizations recognize the small contribution individuals in these activities make by contracting them out.

This is the appropriate way to deal with these activities. Companies simply don't need the distraction. Further, it's easy; there are dozens of firms even in smaller cities that will perform the activities. The first moral for preserving core competence in day-to-day management, then, is to let others do the activities that don't require this competence—leaving the firm free to concentrate on high-value-adding activities.

High Value/Low Competence

The consistent trend in American organization from World War I into at least the 1960s was to move as many activities as possible into this quadrant. Perhaps the best known of these activities is the assembly line and its white-collar equivalents. Typically, the high value/low competence equation is achieved by capital investment; every assembly-line worker is supported by thousands of dollars of machinery.

For years, this seemed to be a winning combination. Lately, though, it hasn't won so many races. There appear to be several reasons for this.

In an era when capital flows easily from one country to another, duplicating the equipment required for a high value/low competence activity is relatively easy. Korean and Brazilian workers earn far less than their American (and Japanese) counterparts, yet have access to the same machinery. Input for data entry can be flown to Barbados, entered there, and transmitted back to the United States by satellite for less than it costs to enter it in the United States.

Perhaps even worse, such activities are extremely brittle. By that I mean that individuals accustomed to this kind of activity don't change easily to adapt to newer technology. Unfortunately, the problem is compounded because newer technologies are consistently more demanding than the ones they replace. Workers with limited and stable competence must suddenly develop not only different but greater competence. They don't do it easily or well. Remember the experience of Motorola and Ingersoll-Rand in retraining their workers, and GM's Saginaw, Michigan, plant—where semiskilled line workers are replaced by attendants and maintenance people requiring 1000 to 1700 hours of training.

This quadrant also locks a firm into the technology it uses because the technology is key to creating the value. If the technology is changing rapidly, as more and more is these days, the organization repeatedly faces the choice of whether to invest heavily in new (and many times unproven) technology or stick with a known but increasingly obsolete one. Even when this is a "soft" technology, like expert systems, it raises the problem of constant updating.

Finally, the humans often form the weakest link in the system. Since they typically perform functions that machines could do better but can't do yet, they often perform them poorly. The recruiting, retention, and attendance problems of routine workers is all too well known.

I mentioned before that traditional organizational and job design moves activities into this quadrant. For instance, virtually every conventional ADP application takes the skills of semiskilled or skilled clerks and off-loads them onto machines. Formerly skilled billing clerks, for example, become data input clerks. The systems they tend are efficient. Because automated systems are notoriously hard to reprogram, however, the systems are far more rigid than the manual one they replace. These rigidities then cause problems for both the firm and its customers. In the pursuit of the chimera of low labor cost, firms deprive themselves of the highly competent use of automation that could be an effective competitive weapon. (If you doubt that automation can be an effective competitive weapon, just ask the airlines that compete with American or the firms that compete with American Hospital Supply. They'll tell you just what an advantage it can create.)

The methods we focused on in Chapter 5, to use challenge and worker control to spread competence throughout the firm, are largely focused on workers in this quadrant. When Chaparral Steel makes its factory its lab, it dramatically increases the human competence involved. As a result, workers are able to update machinery constantly—which largely blunts the choice between existing and new technology. (Many leading Japanese firms also possess high competence at upgrading machinery on the floor.) And highly competent production workers enable GM Saturn to build a highly competitive car using only "medium-tech" methods.[42]

These approaches are attempts to move workers from this quadrant into the upper right quadrant—using high competence to contribute high value. We'll look at this process again soon. For the moment, though, we need to look at what happens when low contribution to value is combined with high competence.

Low Value/High Competence

I think the low value/high competence component of organizational activities is largely overlooked. And that presents a problem.

The movement of industrialization in the United States from 1910 to 1960 didn't just create low-competence workers supporting increasingly sophisticated technology. It also created whole occupations of high-competence workers that only indirectly—at best—added value to the final product or service. Neither accounting nor personnel add value to customers directly. Nor does a legal staff. Perhaps the most glaring example, though, is provided by financial experts. From a strictly second-tier support role, individuals in this field rose to largely rule American industry during the 1970s and 1980s.

As these occupations rise in prestige and pay, they draw both human and other resources away from direct value-adding activities. Staff jobs become much more "important" than line jobs. The trend becomes particularly dangerous as this secondary competence becomes so attractive that it begins to starve the value-adding part of the organization.

This happens as the really sharp MBA graduates go into finance, where the action is. They put their very considerable talents to work at mergers, acquisitions, leveraged buyouts, and the other exciting activities. Meanwhile, manufacturing and sales settle for whomever they can get from technical and liberal arts schools. Their problems aren't interesting, so the firm doesn't pay attention to them.

This works as long as everyone plays by these same rules. As long as every firm in the market has the same distorted competence, none of them can significantly outperform the others. Everyone, except of course for the customer, prospers. As soon as firms center that focus on their value-adding processes, though, all hell breaks loose.

GM has become the national scapegoat for this kind of problem. In the 1960s and 1970s, GM progressively turned its attention away from building vehicles effectively. In part, it concentrated on technology for technology's sake. (Remember the Cadillac engine that could operate as a 4-, 6-, or 8-cylinder engine? If you do, you're one of the few.) It also concentrated considerable energy on persuading the American public that what they wanted was what GM was prepared to build and on "strategic" acquisitions. Its manufacturing processes stagnated, waiting for the technological miracles of robots and broad-scale automation.

Then the Japanese jumped into the market. Unfortunately, the low-value-adding, highly competent people who had been running GM remained in control. For instance, GM entered into a joint venture with Toyota in Fremont, California; rotated managers through it; and then completely ignored what these managers had learned because their ideas didn't fit the established molds. It took most of the 1980s for GM to concentrate more of its energies on the high-value-adding activity of building a durable car.

In GM's case (and that of Ford and Chrysler), competitors entered the market who were concentrating on their value-adding activities. The same problem can be created, however, when a market change moves former high-competence, high-value-adding functions to the high-competence, *low*-value-adding quadrant. This happened, for instance, when banks were deregulated. For years, the ability of skilled loan officers to make loans with acceptable risks was the banks' core competence. Suddenly these banks found themselves in a competitive situation that required developed marketing competence. Most of them responded slowly to the new situation; they were still concentrating their attention on the competence of loan officers who had ceased to be the major value-adding activity. Even when they understood the marketing imperative, it took years for them to develop the competence it required.

This emphasis on high-competence, low-value-adding activities is most obvious in public agencies. In them the process of bureaucratization gradually transfers the expertise of the organization from accomplishing its mission to maintaining itself. Don't relax because you're in a private firm, though; all of the same processes are at work in *all* organizations. Where competition is limited, or limited to other staff-heavy firms, the same transfer of attention to this quadrant occurs. Unfortunately, it's encouraged in even the most value-focused firms by the current tendency of government to pass detailed rules that must be followed, litigated, interpreted, and, when possible, avoided. It's not that the rules themselves are wrong (though they well may be). It's that they tempt firms to develop high competence in areas only tangentially related to their value-adding activities.

Let me make a prediction here, one that you can check for yourself. At the moment, with only a handful of exceptions, local cable companies are monopolies. Their services are expensive, and they often have the arrogance associated with monopolists. If the move to multiple providers of cable services succeeds, you should expect a major change in core competence of these companies from public relations with their public clientele and snappy marketing to the basic skills of providing inexpensive, quality service to customers. As I say, you can check me on that one.

I hope the point is clear: If you really want to starve the core competence of your firm, force it to compete with activities that require high competence but contribute low value to the customer. Just as you need to add competence to production workers and clerks who add value, you also need to reorganize highly competent "support" activities to provide far more direct value to the firm—or else significantly downgrade the competence they require.

High Value/High Competence

All of the paragraphs in this section have been tending toward one conclusion. Contract out, automate, or otherwise take care of low competence, low value work so that it doesn't distract your firm from its basic mission. Then, by increasing either competence or value-adding activities, move all the other activities to the high competence/high value quadrant.

The Practicalities of Core Competence

Here are a few specific suggestions on how to increase both competence and value-adding activities.

1. The first suggestion is unabashedly strategic: Be sure you know what value you offer your customers—where your competitive advantage lies. And know this not just for now but for 10 years from now. Once you know it, you know just what core competence you need. Then you can take the steps to create and preserve it.

2. Identify all the activities in your firm that don't add value and require low competence. If you're satisfied they don't take management time and attention away from value-adding activities, leave them alone. If they are distractions, take steps to contract them out or otherwise get them off your plate. You have better things to do.

3. Now comes the hard part. Identify all the activities in the firm that appear to combine high competence and low value. This is where the greatest potential is for waste. Do you get rid of the activities? Not most of them; I suspect you're going to want to keep your accounting and personnel departments and legal office. Instead, get some individuals or task forces working to identify how these activities can actively sup-

port the firm's creation of value. They don't? Look at the situation again—because if the activity genuinely doesn't support the creation of value you don't need it.

That may sound harsh, naive, simplistic, or even worse. Stop and think for a moment, though. You're paying good money for a lot of competence that isn't helping your competitive position. Is that really wise? (It may be a difficult political problem, but that's another matter.) Unless you have a safely sheltered market (which probably won't last long anyway), you can't afford this kind of drain.

The fact is that any activity worth doing *does* support the creation of value for customers—if it's properly understood. How does your legal office see themselves? Are they committed to avoiding litigation at all costs? Do they specialize in legal hair splitting? Does every new proposal have to undergo their detailed scrutiny? This orientation doesn't support the creation of value worth a damn. But if they're aligned with the firm's mission and understand that their responsibility is to shelter the legal flank so that the firm can achieve that mission—*voilà*, they're helping to create value. If all this sounds like a play on words, it isn't. Any worthwhile functions can be performed in complete alignment with the organization's mission—or as an independent function, responsible for its narrow specialty. Which way the function sees itself is critical for its contribution to the firm.

4. At the same time, begin to evaluate the high value/low competence activities to see how you can create even greater value by raising the competence level. Total quality management is one way of doing this. (When Robert Galvin said that training was free, remember, he was specifically speaking of training in TQM.) Another way is the creation of self-managing work teams built around a process, product, or customer. (If this seems difficult, here's a motivator. The Gaines Dog Food Plant in Topeka was built around self-directing work teams in 1971; Proctor and Gamble began using self-directing work teams in its Paper Products Division at about the same time. For more than 20 years, these plants have consistently outproduced conventional plants of the same kind by at least 20 percent. What more encouragement do you need to investigate whether you can get the same improvements in your firm?) Remember, the goal is to move as many activities as possible from the high value/low competence quadrant to the high value/high competence quadrant.

5. Finally, track what's happening in the high value/high competence quadrant constantly. Make sure everyone in that quadrant is getting every bit of training and support he or she needs. Whenever you implement new technology, make sure it doesn't diminish the skills of

your highly competent people. The same with new automated systems. And don't even think of contracting out any of these activities, no matter how much trouble you may have with them. Expert systems are quite fashionable now; if you use them in core competence areas, make sure they support your human competence, not replace it. If Reich and others are right, the more you can strengthen this quadrant, the more competitive you will be.

How to Use These Ideas

- The first serve is yours. All this talk of strategy is empty until your firm actually has a real strategy. When you have a strategy, your training can support it. It's up to you, and other managers, to develop a clear vision of why the firm is in business, who its customers are, and where it's going. Until you do this, no one can know what your core competence is.

- Once the strategy is done, your training department gets into the action with both feet. Once you know why you're in business, their job is to determine the competencies that the strategy requires. Then they can devise the training required for your work force to acquire and maintain these competencies. (Reminder: Your training department needs to concentrate on the jobs that require high competence *and* add high value.)

- If you don't have a training department, you may be able to find an outside contractor with good job analysis skills to help you recognize your core competence. Be careful, though. If all a contractor (or your training department) does is look at the skills in your current jobs it won't be enough. You need to see these competencies as a group, not as individual items. And you need to see them in light of where the firm is going, not just where it is now.

- You have no training department and no contractors? No one is more familiar with your organization than you and the others who work in it. Put a team together to identify what *really* earns your bread and butter. Then have them identify the competencies needed to do that.

8
Competence for the 1990s—and Beyond

Like the proverbial five men and the elephant, we've examined the competence an organization needs from a variety of angles. To this point, we haven't looked at what the competencies themselves need to be. Now we're going to stare at the beast from that angle.

Of course, there are hundreds and hundreds of different competencies. If you manage a job-order printing establishment, the competencies you need are dramatically different from those of a worldwide automotive manufacturer or a department store. Or are they? The answer, unsurprisingly enough, is "yes and no." This chapter will explain just what that answer means.

The next few pages suggest that firms in the 1990s use four basic kinds of jobs—and many of these jobs, no matter where they're located, increasingly require three specific job competencies and one global "metacompetency." Most of the jobs also require interpersonal, background, contextual (organizational), and self-management competencies. In the past, we've assumed that we didn't need to worry about these latter competencies. Those days are gone, at least for the next decade or two.

The basic point is a simple one: The scope of training is expanding—and many companies are already beginning to feel that it's expanding to their breaking point. Smart training must deal with this new challenge effectively, or else.

Doing a Job in the 1990s

The first set of competencies required in the 1990s is the most familiar of all: the skills needed to do a specific job. While new jobs come into existence, old jobs vanish, and existing jobs change, every job has a set of skills that must be mastered. These may be the minimal skills of a McDonald's hamburger flipper or the demanding knowledge of a global corporation's CEO. But they are skills, and the individuals performing the jobs must master them.

This, of course, is hardly news. What is news is a group of competencies that the workers of the 1990s will increasingly require. To put these competencies in context, we need to take a quick look at the types of workers that organizations are employing in the 1990s. From where I sit now, these workers appear to fall into one of four very different groups.

Unskilled and Minimally Skilled Workers, Both White Collar and Blue Collar

These are the individuals working in jobs that are almost completely programmed, leaving them responsible only for following simple instructions. Their jobs are found in fast-food chains, corporate data entry departments, the back offices of stock brokers, banks, and insurance companies, and on dozens of different kinds of assembly lines. They're designed to require the least possible skill, and will increasingly serve as tenders of robots, expert systems, and other computerized processes. They will be significantly less skilled and challenging than the next two groups of jobs, will receive little training, and will add minimum value to the firm.[43]

Increasingly Skilled Production Workers

More and more formerly unskilled and semiskilled production workers are now responsible for improving and upgrading processes (TQM) and even for taking full responsibility for these processes (self-managing teams). Many of these workers are blue-collar; because of the prevalence of white-collar "production lines" in many offices, however, an increasing number of them perform clerical work. Whether their work processes are blue- or white-collar, these workers are characterized by increasing levels of competence, especially problem-solving skills, and increased responsibility for their own product. Whether they're making filters at a Corning plant, processing insurance claims at Shenandoah

Life, or making paint at Sherwin-Williams, the skills these workers require and the responsibility they exercise are more like skilled craftsmen than traditional production workers.

Highly Skilled Blue-Collar Workers

The number of traditional skilled craftsmen is shrinking. Many of the jobs created by automation and robotization will be minimally skilled (to be filled by workers in the first group). But another group of jobs, most of them "blue-collar," will serve as highly skilled operators of and attendants to automated processes. Compared to the first and second groups, there will be far fewer of these jobs. Their importance, however, will be out of all proportion to their numbers.

The jobs range from those in established fields such as machining and tool-and-die making to those of attendants and maintenance persons operating highly automated nuclear and chemical plants, assembly lines, and other complex systems. Many of these individuals will require the same abilities to deal with information that we associate with white-collar jobs. More and more of their positions will require both broad and deep knowledge, combined with the ability to deal quickly and effectively with sudden crises. And the jobs will require significantly more formal schooling and training than traditional ones.

Highly Skilled White-Collar Workers

The ranks of these workers are increasing, though it's not clear how fast. A bachelor's degree is nothing more than a gate ticket to this part of the field; more and more practitioners have master's degrees and doctorates. They are the brains behind the worldwide economic boom, and range from molecular biologists and design engineers to computer programmers, playwrights, and financial planners.

I'm sure you can recognize at least two or three of these kinds of positions in your own organization. For our purposes, we can omit group number one, the unskilled production workers. These low-skilled, low-paid, low-value-adding workers require little training, smart or otherwise. And, as I've already suggested, they're too expensive for most firms that compete globally to afford.

The other three groups of workers are significantly different from one another. Nonetheless, I believe significant numbers of jobs in each group will have to acquire and use three competencies that haven't been widely required before. These competencies are (1) the ability to deal with abstraction; (2) the ability to be creative in everyday work; and (3) the ability to learn rapidly and continuously. Let's look at each in turn.

Microchips and Abstract Jobs

The atomic revolution produced few visible changes in our jobs. The revolution in molecular biology produces mind-boggling results weekly—but few of the results affect us at work. Not so with the microchip revolution.

Computers are taking over or assisting more processes daily. Many process industries, such as petrochemicals and papermaking, are essentially run by computer, with humans serving as general overseers and maintainers. Virtually all production processes are becoming more and more automated, as computer-controlled robots develop sight and manual dexterity.

As microchips penetrate more and more of our processes, the processes require fewer humans. Workers who remain often find that their jobs require significantly more skill than before. And, whatever else, they find that their work processes become *more and more abstract.* The abstraction of work is one of the defining characteristics of work in the 1990s and beyond.

What does it mean to say that work is more abstract? This is how Lund and Hansen described it in *Keeping America at Work: Strategies for Employing the New Technologies:*

> The direction of manufacturing skills changes is from physically involved, manipulative, tactile, "hands on" type of work to that which is conceptual, cognitive, and based on an abstract understanding of the process. Instead of maintaining close physical contact with the product and with the process through touch, sight, sound, and smell, the production worker stands aside while the integrated combination of computers and machines proceeds with minimal direct human intervention.
>
> . . . The worker is *monitoring* the process rather than being a part of it.[44]

To say that workers are monitoring the process only scratches the surface. They're responsible for an operation that is fundamentally invisible, except through dials, computer screens, and printouts. Workers have to visualize how the process is working; they can't see it. Breakdowns may occur less frequently than before the processes were automated—but they're harder to anticipate, harder to understand, and harder to fix quickly. On top of that, most routine problems can be programmed into the machine's controllers; by definition, the problems that occur are the less routine, more difficult ones. The more serious ones have the potential to be Bhopals and Chernobyls.[45]

This is a very different kind of work, one that requires very different competencies from most traditional jobs. And none of the other competencies work unless they're grounded in the ability to respond to increasingly abstract signals. The responses themselves must be both rapid and imaginative—and that leads us to the next skill increasingly characteristic of jobs in the 1990s and beyond.

Applied Creativity

Courses in creativity have sold well for the last decade. Their results, however, have often been disappointing. In the real world, creativity just hasn't been that highly valued. And matters are made worse by the tendency to view creativity as something "special," possessed by a relatively few lucky people and hidden from the rest of us.

Cut! It's time to end that scenario. Jobs in all three of the groups we're analyzing have become far more creative than they were a decade or two ago—but the creativity has been integrated into the work itself. Far from the sort of off-the-wall creativity we expect from artists, this creativity is grounded in established principles and methods. In many jobs, it appears as systematic, data-driven problem solving. In others, it emerges as the ability to innovate ever more rapidly. Virtually all jobs require more creativity, and they require it in practical, everyday ways.

As formerly unskilled/semiskilled production workers take responsibilities for their processes (through TQM, self-managed teams, and similar programs), they become problem solvers. The structured problem-solving methods they learn may not appear too exciting, but these methods help them develop and focus significant creativity. Production workers in the GM Saturn plant or Corning (Blacksburg, Virginia) plant do their jobs very differently from their counterparts in traditional production operations. In fact, because of the applied problem solving required, they have fundamentally different jobs.

Because we generally didn't think to look for it there, we seldom found creativity in skilled blue-collar jobs. But it's been there. Expert machinists, cabinetmakers, and plumbers have used it all along. The new skilled attendants and maintenance personnel supporting automated and robotic processes are also creative—perhaps an order of magnitude more so. We've seen how abstract these jobs are becoming. Because of this, it takes creativity just to envision what's happening when the process is going right. Problems may be signaled by no more than a dial reading, a funny sound, the wrong figures dancing across a screen. It often takes considerable creativity to translate these cues into a coherent picture of what's happening—or even to know where to start looking for some cues.

The creativity required in highly conceptual jobs has climbed just as dramatically; the sheer speed of scientific and engineering research makes sure of that. Thirty years ago, microchips didn't exist. Today, thousands of engineers create ways to embed them in ordinary products daily. Twenty years ago, genetic engineering was a small research field. Today, its developments (including a mouse patented for its ability to develop cancer!) are brought to market in a constant stream. Engineers have even found ways to make bearings "smart."[46]

Perhaps nothing drives creativity in today's competitive world as much as reduced cycle time. As life cycles shrink to less than the *development* times of just a few years ago, enhanced creativity becomes the price of survival. We see this most clearly in high-tech equipment, such as computers, printers, and cellular phones. Because intelligence can be added to any product, however, any product can become part of this innovative spiral. Services are also becoming part of this creative explosion; just look at the dramatic changes made or envisioned in American stock and commodity markets.

There's always been more creativity in the work force than most of us imagined. Even clerks, supposedly tied to rigid procedures, have had to be creative just to keep routine systems running.[47] But we could separate the few dozen people who did the "real" creative work from the thousands who routinely embodied their ideas in products and moved them to market. In many businesses and industries, this structure has vanished forever; in others, it's beginning to fade into the proverbial sunset. When General Motors can announce that it will introduce more new models in one model year than it's three main competitors combined, the world has surely changed.[48]

So, do you rush out and get creativity training for all your people? Only if you have a driving need to reduce your profits for this year. Applied creativity is a very specific activity, not some general set of principles that can be sprinkled throughout the organization like fairy dust. Here are a few ideas, though, that might help you keep profits up and fairy dust down:

1. Don't expect training to drive creativity in your organization. You can't increase creativity without effective training, but training by itself isn't enough. (I expect that you know this already. However, the myth has been so widespread that something miraculous will happen if you just train people to be creative that I thought the caution was worth repeating.)

2. Start by changing the way you do work so that it requires more creativity. Whenever you change work so that it's more challenging and more under the control of workers, the more it will demand creativity.

3. This need for creativity will show up first as an increased demand for problem solving. For individuals accustomed to nothing more creative than following detailed instructions, this is a good beginning. Expect problem solving, reward it, and train to get it.

Continuous Learning

Workers in the 1990s will deal with abstractions and routinely exercise creativity. They will also need to learn continuously.

Learning organization isn't just a catch phrase; the ability to learn effectively may be the single most important characteristic of effectively competitive organizations in the 1990s and early 2000s. As Russo and Schoemaker put it in *Decision Traps,* "slow learning can ruin you or your organization in a rapidly changing environment."[49] That means that everyone in these organizations—everyone—will be highly skilled at learning. The world is changing too fast for *anyone's* knowledge to safely remain where it is. This is true for Ph.D.s, and equally true for production workers. As Michael Rothschild remarks, "the best protection for workers is an economic system that helps the jobless *update* their skills to match the needs of prospering firms."[50]

Many writers make the assumption that continuous learning means continuous training, that we will all be trained more frequently than in the past.[51] Certainly I believe that we will all require more training more frequently, but I don't believe that this is the heart of continuous learning. Instead, I think that continuous learning needs to be structured into work processes themselves, so that learning happens as part and parcel of every job.

Since the last part of this book deals with continuous learning in the learning organization, I'll defer more comments on the topic until then. Just don't forget that you can't defer continuous learning until you create a learning organization. It works the other way round: When you get people involved in continuous learning, they create the learning organization.

The Global Competence: Interpersonal and Communication Skills

As the world of work becomes simultaneously more abstract and more complex, the degree of interpersonal and communication competence (the second type of competence) required increases just as rapidly. Perhaps even more rapidly. To an extent, these skills overlap. Individuals on self-managing or quality teams must work together and communicate with each other effectively to a far greater degree than their counterparts in traditional production environments. The same is true for managers on management teams. The number of jobs that can be performed by an individual in isolation or with occasional contact with others shrinks daily. Most job growth is occurring in areas that require sustained contact and cooperation with others.

For instance, have you ever listened to the conversation in a typical fast-food restaurant? Informal chatter occurs, certainly. But many of the transactions have a clearly patterned nature, including the mandatory use of "Please" and "Thanks." Interactions with the customer are just as programmed: "Thank you and have a nice day." The rigidities are necessary to permit individuals who may lack basic interpersonal and communication skills to interact with one another—because even these restaurants require a sustained high level of interaction.

Situations where these interactions can be successfully programmed are few and far between. Consider the line in Saturn's Spring Hill plant, or any other plant based on self-managing teams. A problem develops. In a few minutes, line workers, maintenance personnel, and engineers may be clustered together, all working on the problem. There isn't the luxury to stand on formality, with careful status distinctions, or to talk in functional jargon. The full group may never have worked together as a group before, but they must begin to function effectively at once. Either each member has highly developed interpersonal and communication skills, or the group will sputter and spar instead of solving the problem.

As communication media explode, however, individuals must develop a whole range of communication skills that are only slightly related to interpersonal skills. These skills include the essential ability to communicate clearly, of course. Increasingly, they also involve the ability to select the most effective medium and tailor communications for that medium.

Here's my favorite f'rinstance. During the repression of the student democratic movement in China, President Bush tried (and failed) to communicate with the Chinese leadership via traditional telecommunications. At the same time, pictures of Tiananmen Square were being faxed all over China from machines in the United States. Despite the official news ban, individuals throughout China could see what was happening for themselves.

We used to choose between paying a personal visit, telephoning, or writing. To that, we now add facsimile transmissions, E-mail, teleconferencing, and electronic conferencing via bulletin boards—to recite only the most obvious new choices. The list will probably jump dramatically, now that the courts have cleared the way for regional telephone companies to jump into this market.

Differences between media may be slight, as between ordinary mail and formal E-mail. They may also be dramatic, as in the difference between a telephone conversation and multiway conversations via computer conferencing. As the range of media grows, the variety will probably grow even faster.

To the problems of communication must also be added a final one: cross-cultural communication. This is happening more and more frequently within the United States. As more and more firms become global, however, the problem grows significantly. And it can only increase. On top of high-level interpersonal skills and an understanding of the strengths and limitations of different media, communication thus requires the ability to develop an empathetic understanding of another's culture in a short period of time.

Does all that sound a bit challenging? Welcome to the world of the 1990s and beyond!

Background Competence: The Growing Challenge

The third type of competence is "background" competence—the skills and knowledges we once assumed that any qualified applicant would have. We assumed that typists would be able to alphabetize, accounting clerks would be able to add and subtract accurately, and procurement agents would be able to use the Yellow Pages and their commercial equivalents effectively. We also assumed that all of them would be able to use "common sense"—a very complex and highly developed competence for dealing with the world. That may or may not be the case in today's world, and it will be the case less and less frequently as we go through the 1990s.

For instance, many companies have found to their profound discomfort that many of their workers are functionally illiterate. We've already seen the problems that this caused Motorola and Ingersoll-Rand. But businesses everywhere are finding the same problem. And it's getting worse.

In fact, though, relatively few workers are really functionally illiterate. They are more accurately called "mid-literate." Most of them read; they are not illiterate. What they cannot do is absorb large amounts of information quickly when it's presented via complex texts and manuals and other training methods based on the college model. When training is tailored to their learning level and uses their experience, they can learn rapidly.[52]

Chapter 7 of Rosow and Zager's *Training—the Competitive Edge* contains an excellent discussion of this whole problem of mid-literacy. It also provides six basic principles for training mid-literates:

1. Let students know what they are to learn and why, in such a way that they can understand the purpose of the training or education in their lives.

2. Develop new knowledge on the basis of knowledge that the student already has entry to the program.

3. Develop new lessons on the basis of old lessons, so that the new learning builds on prior knowledge.

4. Integrate instruction in basic skills—such as reading, writing, and arithmetic—into the technical or academic content area courses, to permit students to better negotiate the requirements for these skills in the program at hand and to permit them to transfer such skills to other, related settings.

5. Derive objectives from an analysis of the knowledge and skill demands of the situations for which the course is supposed to be providing human resources.

6. Utilize in the course—to the extent feasible—contexts, tasks, materials, and procedures taken from the setting for which people are being trained and educated.

You'll notice that these principles are remarkably similar to the basic principles of adult learning described in Chapter 4. Regardless of their type of work or reading level or whatever, adults in the world of work are very much alike in what they need if they're to learn effectively.

The central point here, though, is that more and more entry-level workers will need training in background skills. If you're a large firm, your personnel and training departments should already be working on a program to identify the background skills your workers lack and—using these six principles—to provide training in them.

Contextual Competence

When Chapter 2 looked at orientation, it noted how values and practices differ from one organization to another. That chapter concentrated on transmitting these values and practices to new workers so that they would understand what was expected of them in their new organization.

There's another layer of these differences, though—one we haven't touched on yet. Different organizations not only do different things but they do the same thing in very different ways. So do different parts of the same organization. The finance department is a stickler for going by the rules, while manufacturing looks the other way on a variety of rules as long as everyone gets the work out. One design group prides itself in its free, innovative approach, while the second design group takes pride in its ability to move from idea to development quickly.

You may never have thought about it, but knowing how things get done in your organization and knowing how to get them done is a real competence. I would call it "organizational" competence. However, other writers are referring to it as "contextual" competence—so I'll stick with that term.

Contextual competence requires both very global knowledges and very specific ones. Here are a few samples:

- Knowing whom to talk to in quality control to see that a borderline shipment gets out on schedule.

- Knowing who can get you a new hard drive for your PC in a hurry.

- Knowing whose commitments you can depend on in the engineering department, and whose you can't.

- Knowing when the boss is serious about a new program, and when the best course is just to hunker down and wait until it blows over.

- Knowing who has to be at an interdepartmental meeting in order to see that the agreements get carried out.

The list goes on and on and on. Anyone who has moved from one organization to another, even within the same firm, knows how very different companies can be one from another. More important, it takes time to learn how the new organization operates. While you're learning, you're less effective than you might be.

I wish there were a simple way to train contextual competence. If there is, no one has bothered to tell me about it. The beginning of wisdom here is to know that there in fact *is* a problem. No matter how well qualified individuals are formally, it will take time for them to learn how things are done *here*—no matter where "here" is.

We've already discussed one strategy that can help minimize the problem: giving individuals the opportunity to move among various jobs and departments. Individuals who make their careers only in one department learn only one way of doing things, one "culture." They unconsciously assume that this is how things are done everywhere. Moving to a very different kind of organization can be a major shock. Workers and managers may even fail in new assignments for lack of competence in the new organization's way of getting things done. When individuals move among different organizations early on and relatively often, though, they begin to develop a feel for how differently things can be done. A new organization isn't so much of a shock. Learning happens more quickly.

Two final thoughts. The first one was mentioned in Chapter 2: As part of each new worker's acclimation or orientation, try to cover the points that make your organization different from others. If you're a stickler for details, make that clear. If you're proud of your ability to get the job done no matter what, make that equally clear. This will help the individual begin developing the competence necessary to work effectively in your specific context.

Second, and just as important, see that the same thing happens with individuals who come into your organization in senior positions. You may have hired a top-flight industrial engineer or been reassigned a staff executive from another division. See that you and anyone else necessary spend time with them, explaining how things are done in their new organization. This helps them come up to speed quickly; it also may prevent future conflicts.

The Core Competence of the Individual: Self-Management

We've looked at four competencies required in the 1990s: job competence; interpersonal and communication competence; background competence; and contextual (organizational) competence. All of these are at least partly familiar to us. The final, and most important competence hasn't gotten as much publicity—but it's the most important one of all for successful competition. It's simply the ability to manage one's own life, on and off the job.

Let me take you quickly back in history. During the first half of this century, America industrialized rapidly. By the end of World War II, we were the most heavily industrialized country on Earth. We accomplished this primarily by developing ever-more-competent machines operated by less-and-less-skilled workers. We tied this in with the ideas that came from Frederick W. Taylor, the founder of "scientific management." As we've seen, Taylor believed that jobs should be carefully engineered and described, and workers should be carefully trained to perform in exactly the best way.

This approach originated, in part, because Taylor and others believed that the new immigrants were incapable of thinking for and managing themselves. Taylor thought the best way to deal with this condition was to design jobs in detail, and tell workers when and how to work—in equal detail.

Whether Taylor and the others were right, I don't know (though I suspect they were not). What is crystal clear from subsequent history is that what they did *created* a situation in which workers had no motivation to think for themselves or manage their own behavior. Their job was to do as they were told—exactly as they were told. Getting a good education was irrelevant. So was any form of initiative. It became relatively easy for a worker to take the last step and make every aspect of the job the responsibility of management.

As an increasing number of managers realize by now, this kind of worker will not make American firms competitive. A study released in 1990 had this to say about the attitude of business toward the kind of new worker it was getting:

> While businesses everywhere complained about the quality of their applicants, few talked about the kinds of skills acquired in school. The primary concern of more than 80 percent of employers was finding workers with a good work ethic and appropriate social behavior: "reliable," "a good attitude," "a pleasant appearance," "a good personality."[53]

Translated only slightly, American business is saying that its new workers lack self-management skills. They do not know how to identify what they want; set meaningful, practical goals to achieve these wants; make realistic plans to accomplish the goals; manage their daily life so that they follow the plans and achieve the goals, and then evaluate what happens, learn from it, and use what they've learned to develop new and better goals and plans.

Individuals who cannot do this are lost in the kind of effectively competitive firm this book has been describing. Even worse, they cannot be trained successfully in other competencies until they have at least begun to master this one. Finally, they may well believe that there is no purpose in mastering the competence. Take the situation of all too many individuals in urban ghettos; they not only lack this competence but believe it would be useless for them to acquire it. So too with many immigrants, who believe that they should remain obediently in the life station into which they were born.

That's the bad news. The good news is that self-management is a learned competence. Individuals will learn it if—and this is an enormous *if*—they believe they can actually achieve goals they care about.

Firms can show entering workers that there is a future, that there are skills that can be learned and used, *that they can advance both in competence and in income.* When they do this, they lay the groundwork. Then they, probably in cooperation with local community colleges, can offer training in self-management skills that will be absorbed and used.

I know you'd like to see examples of this. Unfortunately, they're few and far between. The whole idea is too new. There are efforts being made to train workers in self-management, but they're piecemeal and scattered. We haven't yet accepted that self-management is a skill and that it can be taught. Until we do, we will suffer far more than necessary from the impact of workers who lack this skill.

What It All Means

These are the five forms of competence required in the work force of the 1990s:

1. *Job competence,* which will increasingly require dealing with abstractions, using day-to-day creativity, and learning constantly.

2. *Interpersonal and communication competencies,* which (because of exploding technology) are becoming more separate competencies than ever before.

3. *Background competence,* including literacy and numeracy, that we are less and less able to count on in our high school graduates.

4. *Contextual (organizational) competence,* which enables workers to get things done in their specific organizations.

5. *Self-management competence,* which is the necessary condition for all of the rest.

Why have we bothered with all this? *Because if we do not see the entire spectrum of competence required we will tend to concentrate on the first two competencies—and become increasingly mystified when our results there are unsuccessful.* Firms that practice smart training will constantly examine their training needs in all five competence areas and shape their training efforts accordingly.

With that, our broad discussion of competence ends. But there's a final and more specific aspect of competence: How do you get it used? The question is more complex than it might seem. The next chapter ends this part with a discussion of that extremely practical question.

How to Use These Ideas

- Are the jobs in your organization changing toward abstraction, creativity, and constant learning? Are you having problems from lack of background competence and self-mastery? Unless someone has asked the question and looked for the answers, you don't really know.

- If you have a training department, they should take the lead in finding out. They may already know part of the answer. If not, it's time for them to start looking. It isn't their job to find isolated problems and provide piecemeal (tactical) training to solve them. You and they need a systematic view of the entire organization and its training needs. Keep pushing them until you get it.

- If you need to use a training consultant, this part may be hard. Many of them are locked into traditional training, or selling some hot new approach. You're not looking for either of these. A local college or university with a strong business department may be your best bet. They should be aware of these changes and able to help evaluate them in your organization.

- This is one of the situations where it's not so bad if you have to do it yourself. Put a team together to evaluate the current situation and the changes that are happening. They can identify the new training needs that these changes are creating. Then you can start planning how to meet them.

9

How Do You Get Competence Used?

The last four chapters took a broad, essentially strategic look at competence. That's where a firm must begin—by understanding how critical competence and mastery are to its success. Unfortunately, broad, strategic programs aren't self-implementing. Until they affect and change the actions of each individual worker, they're just words on paper.

For individuals to get and use competence, certain conditions must be true. Workers must have the *capacity* to perform as desired; an *affinity* both for the work itself and for the work environment; competent *training* in the work; the *opportunity* to perform as desired; at least one *motive* for performing as desired; and adequate *feedback* about how well they're performing.

Start with Square Pegs in Square Holes

The first two factors deal with the match between job requirements and individuals on the job. These are the *capacity* of workers to acquire the skills they must use, and their *affinity* for the kind of tasks they must perform.

Capacity is the point at which the organization's training system is utterly dependent on its hiring system. The first requirement of all new hires is that they have the capacity to learn to do the job. Seeing that individuals hired by a firm are qualified for their jobs is traditionally the task of the personnel or human resources management department. In many firms, this responsibility has now moved to operating organiza-

121

tions. It doesn't really matter who's responsible for it. What matters is that the firm have effective techniques for making sure that the people it hires can perform its jobs.

This hasn't always been easy. An individual with an excellent track record in one kind of work or organization may not be capable of making the transition to a different occupation or organization. On the whole, though, most firms have been able to select individuals capable of learning the skills they need to do their jobs. In over 20 years in the human resources management field, I saw only one situation in which an individual clearly did not have the capacity to perform his assigned tasks.

This picture has been muddied in the last few years, though, and there's every chance that the muddiness will increase in the next few years. More and more, firms must interview and select from individuals who are products of poor school systems, unstable family situations, or deprived environments (such as inner-city ghettos), or who are immigrants, with backgrounds dramatically different from those of traditional employees.

Does this mean that they aren't capable of working effectively in our organizations? Not necessarily. What it means is that *it is becoming progressively harder to determine just how capable many of these individuals are.* Such experience as they possess isn't easy to evaluate. Their education may not mean what it should. They may have cultural characteristics that lead to behavior that—in our eyes—is strange and unexpected.

How do you evaluate these individuals to determine their capabilities? I have no firm answers and few suggestions. The whole field of managing diversity is a new one. In my judgment, it currently has more than its share of wishful thinking and perilously speculative conclusions. In the next few years, if we're lucky, we'll develop solid skills for dealing with diversity.

I just said I didn't have many suggestions, and that's true. But I do have two. The first one concerns hiring, and it's this: The best judgments about the capabilities of individuals from unfamiliar backgrounds can be made by other individuals from these same backgrounds. This is a real strength of diversity in an organization, one that's often overlooked. If you want to make intelligent judgments about candidates that come from a ghetto environment, have someone make these judgments who also grew up in the ghetto. So with any group from a background different from the "standard."

The second suggestion is applicable to the training you give. In Chapter 4, we looked at the design process required for effective training. One phase of good design is what trainers call "learner analysis." Just who will be trained? What is their background? What skills do they already have? What is their motivation apt to be?

These questions are far more difficult to answer with our diverse work force than they have been in the past. Nonetheless, competent trainers—in-house or consultants—have the basic competence to do the analysis. They'll need to sharpen their competence to deal with the more complex current situation, but it's still the same competence. You should be able to expect that their skills are up to date and that they're used.

Then Put Them in Square Holes They Like

There's another aspect to the fit between the individual and the job, one that's far more apt to miscarry. This is the amount of *affinity* workers have for the kind of work they do. When I used *worker* in the preceding section, I meant to include individuals up to and including the executive suite. I also mean to include just that wide a range here. Many a firm has been seriously disrupted because one or more of its top people had no real affinity for their jobs.

Just what is affinity? It's the liking an individual has for the *specific work processes* or tasks which he or she performs, and for the *work environment* in which the processes are performed. Some people have an affinity for jobs requiring high contact with others; some don't. Some people love to work with figures or handle details; others don't. (I'm one of those that deals badly with details; I can do that kind of job, but I cannot do it consistently well.) Some people have an affinity for simple repetitive jobs; most don't. Some people thrive on pressure; some avoid it like the plague. The list goes on and on and on.

This doesn't mean that workers can't do work for which they have no affinity. The capacity is there. An individual who doesn't like sustained contact with others can learn and use sales competencies if necessary. The problem is that they're harder for the person to learn, they require more inner "push" to exercise, and their use is more draining on the person. In the simplest cases, individuals are seldom efficient at work for which they have no affinity. In more serious cases, they perform only marginally well. In the most serious cases, they avoid the unpleasant work—even though it may be essential for the job. When they can, they'll often leave the job.

An individual who worked for me several years ago provides an excellent example of this. She began as a job analyst. At that job, she was mediocre at best. When it became clear she wasn't apt to succeed as an analyst, she moved into a training specialist position. After a short adjustment period, she became an excellent worker. Why? As a job analyst, she had to use analytic skills in an often adversarial situation. She had no affinity for that. As a training specialist, she spent her time fulfilling training requests from managers. It was an almost pure service position, and that was her cup of tea.

Supervisory positions, which we've used as examples before, also make excellent examples here. Virtually every firm has problems because it promotes excellent individual performers to supervisors and then expects them to get work done effectively through others. The supervisory job is completely interpersonal; it requires sustained dealing with people, and sustained dealing with them in specific ways. Many excellent individual performers have no affinity for this. They're more comfortable dealing with the technical processes of the job in which they've developed competence. They may have difficulty learning the interpersonal skills. And they may not *want* to learn them.

As a result, they may avoid situations that are interpersonally challenging and do work themselves that they should delegate to others. Most of us know supervisors who, when confronted with substandard work, take it away from the worker and do it themselves. There are several possible causes for this; one is that they're simply more comfortable doing work than dealing with an individual who's not performing satisfactorily.

Of course, this disconnect isn't limited just to supervisors. The basic reward structure of most organizations centers around promotions— and at several points in the ladder individuals move into positions significantly different from those they leave behind. We've already looked at the major "change points" in individual movement upward: from clerk to specialist, nonsupervisor to supervisor, supervisor to manager, manager to executive. With each change, individuals have the opportunity to move into a kind of work for which they have little affinity.

I've talked with dozens of clerks whose goal is to get a promotion out of the "clerical ghetto." The overwhelming majority of them are only secondarily concerned (if at all) about the line of work into which they want to get promoted. Since organizations seldom worry about affinity, there's no check on whether the individual is really suited for the job— except perhaps the supervisor's judgment in an interview. The same often happens in promotions at each of the other change points; individuals struggle to be promoted whether or not they really have an affinity for the new work.

If you want competence used effectively and confidently, you need to see that people have an affinity for the work they must perform. We've looked at most of the following steps in different contexts, but they're worth quick repetition here.

1. *Provide realistic career counseling and testing for individuals who want to move up.* This is important for clerks, but just as important for man-

agers and would-be managers on the "fast track." The counseling and testing can provide individuals with realistic information on their interests, and how these compare with the requirements of jobs to which they aspire. Then, to make these most effective, combine them with the next step.

2. *Provide as broad a variety of opportunities for movement as possible.* Many firms have positions of expert workers (in everything from crafts to research positions); highly skilled workers without an affinity for supervision or management can move into these positions—in which they're more comfortable and make a greater contribution.

3. *Temporary reassignments can be useful here too—for two different reasons.*

    a. First, they can provide both the individual and the organization with the opportunity to see how he or she likes and performs in a different kind of position. If the present job is a poor fit and the reassignment is a better one, the reassignment can be made permanent. Because mismatch between an individual's preferences and job requirements is so common in organizations, reassignments can many times solve poor or mediocre performance by itself.

    b. Second, they can provide variety and forestall job burnout for individuals who lack the affinity or even capacity for promotion to the next level. Better to have a manager who moves successfully through several positions at the same level than one who gets promoted to an executive position requiring highly abstract strategic skills that the individual lacks and isn't interested in acquiring.

These aren't the only answers, and you may not be willing to deal with lack of affinity to any great extent. In that case, just remember that there is such a problem, and that the greater the mismatch between what individuals enjoy doing and what they are expected to do, the greater the chance of poorly done jobs. Whenever you get consistently poor performance from an individual with an overall satisfactory record, affinity is one of the first factors to examine.

Let me add a quick postscript. As I was finishing this book, I came on an article about Richfoods of Richmond, Virginia. In some of the firm's least skilled jobs, its annual turnover was 100 percent. After numerous failed attempts to deal with the problem, Richfoods analyzed the characteristics of the workers who remained in their jobs. From this, the company constructed a profile of the typical satisfied worker—and started hiring workers that fit this profile. Competence wasn't involved; these were all low-skilled jobs. The whole profile was essentially about affinity. It's use cut annual turnover from 100 percent to about 27 percent—a reduction of almost 75 percent. Yes, affinity really does count.[54]

Who Told You They Were Trained?

You may conclude that it's almost silly—particularly in a book on training—to say that an individual must have the proper training to be competent. Before you reach this conclusion, though, consider what so often happens in the real world.

The vast majority of individuals at every level in the organization receive their basic job training on the job. As we'll see in the next part of the book, few employees, supervisors, managers, or executives give on-the-job training effectively—and almost none are trained to do so. The result? Virtually all workers and managers have holes in their competence for months, years, perhaps even for their entire careers. Even worse, it may take months or years for an individual to realize that the holes are there.

I've emphasized over and over how critical it is that individuals put training to work as soon as they get it. But how often does that really happen? Whenever individuals get trained and then don't put the training to work quickly, they may have a competence that exists only on paper, in their training records. We've already seen that this problem gets compounded when an individual who has only a paper competence gets more training built on the first, deficient competence. (Remember Tom and his spreadsheet training in Chapter 6?) It's not hard for an individual to have impressive amounts of training, yet never develop the competence the training was supposed to deliver.

Finally, an untold number of individuals simply "fall through the cracks" where training is concerned. There isn't time for them to get trained, or it isn't available when it's needed, or there isn't money for it, or _(add your own reason)_ . They manage to absorb enough to get by by watching and asking others; perhaps they even manage to perform satisfactorily. But, like those who get deficient on-the-job training, they end up with holes in their competence.

These three situations are all too common. They may even be typical—not just in organizations in general, but in your organization and mine. And it's crystal clear that, whatever else may be the case, Japanese companies produce high quality products because they train their people better. (Examples: Mazda spent some $11,000 per employee _before_ it opened its Flat Rock, Michigan, plant. Nissan spent almost three times that much before the first car rolled off its Smyrna, Tennessee, assembly line. And highly competitive American companies, such as Motorola, Corning Glass, and GM Saturn, provide as much or more training to their workers.)

What can you do about the situation? This book has already presented a variety of suggestions that may help. However, the real help is in Chapters 10 through 14, which deal in great detail with specific training methods. We'll come to them in just a few pages. But there are three more obstacles to the effective use of competence to consider first.

If You'd Just Give Me a Chance!

Chapter 1 suggested that people decide what to do based in part on what they have the *means* to do. An important part of this factor is the simple *opportunity* to perform. Workers can't use competence on the job unless they're given the opportunity to do so. The lack of this opportunity is a persistent cause of failed training.

We've looked at one form of opportunity several times: The opportunity for individuals to use new skills as soon as training is completed. This is critical for effective training; every day that passes before individuals use their new competence means that they forget more of what they learned.

Let me give you a brief but potent example of this. In the introduction, we saw that Motorola got a 3300 percent ROI on training when managers supported the results of the training and saw that workers used it. The reverse is also true; the single greatest cause of failed training is the failure of managers to support the workers' new competence. As William Wiggenhorn put it, "Workers learned to keep Pareto charts and Ishikawa diagrams—but no one ever asked to see one." [55] Now it may be even clearer why I keep harping on this theme.

Unfortunately, delay isn't the only way that workers lose opportunity to practice what they learn. There are some other, all too familiar, ways in which the opportunity vanishes.

For instance, the current "flavor of the month" may be decreased cycle time. All managers get a one-week course in it. When they return to work, though, the same production demands and production system are still in place. In a week or two, what seemed like a great idea in the training course now seems like an interesting but irrelevant notion. Remember the major corporation we discussed a few chapters ago that spent $7 million to train its first-line workers and supervisors in quality and largely wasted its money? The biggest reason for the waste was simply that the individuals didn't get a chance to use what they'd learned when they returned to their jobs. They had plenty of training, but no opportunity to use it.

Workers miss the opportunity in small ways too. Mary has just returned from a superb course on coaching. She's been having trouble with David, and she plans to use the new skills she has to help him improve. Before she can meet with him, he gets the figures wrong on yet another report. Her boss asks her what she intends to do, and she explains that she plans to coach him. "The hell you are!" he says. "You tell him that if he screws up one more time he's fired!" What's your best guess about when she tried to use these coaching skills again?

We're all tempted to give training in shotgun bursts. If coaching is a good supervisory technique, then let's give it to all supervisors. As inviting as that sounds, it's an almost sure recipe for failed training. Some individuals may be able to apply their new learning back on the job, but others almost certainly won't. Earlier this week I was thinking of a course in effective presentations I arranged for some 100 members of my group. It was competently presented, with clear performance objectives. It was also a dismal failure. Most attendees didn't get a chance to apply the new skills for weeks or months. In addition, at least one subordinate manager saw no use in it. You can imagine how much his workers used what they learned.

I don't know how much your firm could save by ensuring that training was given only to those with the opportunity to use it—but I know that American business as a whole could save billions. The purpose of smart training is improved performance. Training that prepares workers for situations in which there's no realistic opportunity to use it clearly isn't smart.

The solution is simple, though it takes great organizational discipline. We've already looked at it, but here it is again in summary:

1. Do a careful up-front analysis to see if training will give you the performance improvement you're looking for.

2. If it will, or if it's part of the solution, analyze the job(s) carefully and design training that will provide the missing skills.

3. Give the training, then follow up to see whether the improvement you wanted occurred.

4. And see that individuals apply what they learn immediately.

(Since you're probably tired of being bombarded with that particular piece of advice, I have good news for you. The next five chapters, and particularly Chapters 12 and 13, will show you how to develop training that's delivered just as the worker needs it.)

You Can Lead a Horse
to Water . . .

Performance happens only when an individual has one or more motives that the performance will satisfy. Given a motive, people will attempt to find the knowledge, know-how, and means to get what they want. Take away the motive, and all the knowledge, know-how, means, and feedback in the world will accomplish nothing. In short, an action only makes sense to us when we have some motive for taking it. Individuals in organizations—from the shop floor to the executive suite—perform as they do because that's what makes sense to them. Given the existing knowledge, means, know-how, and feedback, *the rewards in your organization are structured to produce exactly the performance that's occurring.*

You may be thinking about your firm's compensation and recognition systems. They're relevant, of course, but don't start there. Start with this:

> *The incentive for the performance any organization gets is the **entire** structure of the organization.*

In other words, how well your workers use competence depends on the pay system, the kind of supervision, the technology, the physical layout, the relations among departments, the feedback provided, the commitment (or lack of commitment) to excellence, etc., etc. All of these together make up your firm's reward system. Here are a few quick examples of how it works.

- You put all of your supervisors through a team-building course, but they don't use what they've learned to work together. Unfortunately, they're all rated and paid on what their individual units produce, not on what they can help others produce.

- You sent your input clerks to training on the new stock-tracking system, but their error rate hardly went down at all. Unfortunately, the system doesn't provide information on errors until the week after they're made—and then the clerks aren't sure what they did to generate the errors.

- All of your fabricators are well trained, and they earn a sizable bonus if they exceed their production quota. They don't; in fact, they barely make the quota. The machines are getting harder and harder to keep in tolerance, so more and more of the fabricators' time is spent devising on-the-spot fixes to keep them running. (You don't know about this because the supervisor in that department is famous for a "can do!" attitude and never tells anyone up the line about problems.)

I think you and I could quickly extend the list for several pages. But the point is already clear: What motivates workers (up to and in the executive suite) is the total organizational situation they confront. Each of us has a good sense of what we want and what to do to get it. As

Chapter 1 stated, we each look at *all* of the four factors, decide what makes sense in this situation, and do it.

The moral is simple: If you want workers, supervisors, managers, and executives to develop and use competence, reward them for doing just that.

1. If you want workers to have and use multiple skills, organize them into teams, train them in each others' skills, give them an opportunity to use these skills, and pay them for using them. "Skills-based pay" is an increasingly popular way of doing this.

2. If you want managers to work together, base at least part of their pay and advancement on how well they work with one another, reassign them to each other's functions (even if only temporarily), task them with significant projects that require them to work as a team, and give out "attaboys" and "attagirls" for team as well as individual achievement.

3. If you want the organization to succeed at any major new program— TQM, JIT inventory, reduced cycle time, self-managing teams— make it clear that you mean it, stick with it, allow for major disruptions, change the standards and if necessary the pay system, provide quick feedback, recognize even the smallest new gain, and— whatever else—get the organization there by praise and support, not by threats and punishment.

Remember, your organization is getting the level of competence and performance that it's structured to get. If you want to "motivate" workers to use increased competence, you have to start by looking at the whole system. Then, when you find out what performance is really being rewarded, you can make the changes necessary to get the new level of performance and competence you want.

I Sure Wish You'd Told Me Sooner

Let's assume that your people are capable and reasonably well matched to their jobs. They're well trained. They have the opportunity to use their competence, and they're rewarded for using it. Now they need one final element. They need to know how well they're doing and what they need to do to perform even better. They need prompt, specific, direct, dependable, useful *feedback*.

Understand that goals, standards, and useful feedback are a matched set. Each works only if the other two are present. Compare the following two statements:

"Charlene, I know you have the makings of a great salesperson. I'm going to put you in the next training class that's available. In the meantime, you go out there and give it your best and when the time comes this fall, I know I'll be giving you a good merit raise."

"Charlene, I know you're going to make a great salesperson. You'll take our basic training starting Monday, then you'll work with Don for two weeks to see how we actually do it on the job. Part of his responsibility is to observe you and discuss how you've applied what you learned in training. As soon as he says OK, you'll be responsible for your own area. Every Monday, we'll give you a report of what you sold the week before and how you did with the items we're currently emphasizing . . . "

Simple common sense says that Charlene will learn faster and apply it better in the second situation (and in this case, research backs common sense 100 percent). Each week, she'll have up-to-date information on how well she did the week before. If she's falling short somewhere, she knows it and can decide how to fix the problem. If she has a consistent problem, her supervisor sees it (he gets copies of the reports) and can help her.

Take away the feedback, though, and all the rest falls apart. Charlene knows how to sell and what items to push. If she never knows how well she does with these items, though, she has a problem. One solution is to get discouraged and just sell what's easiest. (When that happens, her boss concludes that either she doesn't understand or she isn't motivated—so he sends her to training and gives her a pep talk.) The other solution is for her to keep her own records and look them over last thing each Friday. (In that case, her boss congratulates himself on having picked and trained so effective an employee—and wonders why the other workers in the department aren't as good as she is.)

There are a variety of reasons for Japan's success at quality—and one of the reasons is their highly effective use of feedback. In traditional American production, a worker or department produces a large batch of widgets and sends them to the department that uses them. The producers may hear back the next week that the defect rate was double the standard. There's often little they can do with this knowledge except "be more careful"—whatever that means. Their Japanese counterparts, however, produce only a small batch for the next station. If there's a problem, they hear immediately. Because the feedback is quick and specific, it's easy for them to use it to correct the problem. (This, of course, is one of the great benefits of JIT inventory wherever it's used.)

If you want competence used, be clear about the performance you want, train individuals so that they're competent to produce it, and then provide them with feedback that is prompt, specific, direct, reliable, and useful. We looked at this in Chapter 1, but I think it's important enough to repeat quickly here.

- Feedback is *prompt* when it gets to producers in time for them to use it to change their performance. This may be hourly, weekly, whenever—the criterion is that it gets there in time to be used.

- Feedback is *specific* when it contains the exact information producers need to evaluate and, if necessary, change their performance.

- Feedback is *direct* when it comes to the producers themselves. There's nothing wrong with higher levels in the organization getting the same feedback. If you want the people responsible for performance to use the feedback, though, see that they get it directly, not through someone else.

- Feedback is *reliable* when it's consistently accurate and delivered on time, complete, and in the same format each time.

- Finally, feedback is *useful* when it's designed to help producers improve their process, not when it's designed as a "report card" for higher levels. It should be in the format and language that the producers use.

And in Summary . . .

No matter how well you may do at training, people only use their competence well when they are capable of acquiring it; have at least some affinity with the work they do; actually get the training; have the opportunity to use it; are rewarded for doing so; and get prompt, direct, reliable, and useful feedback on how well they're doing. If just one of these factors is missing, the training will be poorly used and perhaps not used at all.

With this sobering thought, we end Part 2 and move on to the specifics of smart training: How do you choose the training method that works best in each situation? That's what Part 3 is about.

How to Use These Ideas

- Most of this chapter has been good, old-fashioned, straight-ahead management. You pick the right people for your jobs, get them trained, let them use the training, and see that they know how they're doing. There's nothing mysterious here. But it has to be done, day after day after day.

PART 3

Smart Training Is Cost-Effective Training

Smart training begins in strategy; it must support the firm's core competence. But, as the last chapter suggested, strategy is always held captive by execution. Part 3 deals with execution—the delivery of the training itself. Its five chapters contain the basics you need to turn the ideas in Parts 1 and 2 into training that's both performance-effective and cost-effective.

Chapter 10 will equip you with overall guidelines for effective training—what works best when.

Since various forms of computer-based and video-based training are so much in the news, Chapter 11 analyzes them and explains when they can be most effective.

As you know so well by now, one of the basic themes of the book is that training must be used immediately after it's given. The best possible training is always just-in-time (JIT) training. Chapters 12 and 13 deal with two methods of providing this JIT training: job aids and structured on-the-job training (OJT).

Chapter 12 is devoted to job aids, including sophisticated computer-based systems that combine training and on-line help. These systems, known as performance support systems, will become more and more commonplace. The lowly printed job aid, though, remains the most economic way to train when the situation permits.

Chapter 13 deals with a second form of JIT training: structured OJT. This method lets individuals learn on the job, where they can make a contribution as they learn, and it also creates a structure so that they learn in a planned and systematic way. Like job aids, structured OJT is extremely cost-effective in the right circumstance.

Chapter 14 describes how to use other forms of training as smart training. It describes a variety of methods and sources that can augment even the most effective in-house program—or become the basic source of training for a smaller organization. Then the chapter ends with a summary of the strengths and weaknesses of each major method of training delivery.

10
The Ground Rules of Economic Training

As IBM, Motorola, Corning, the Coast Guard, and hundreds of other organizations large and small can tell you, smart training doesn't just happen. It has to be carefully planned, then carried out against the plan and evaluated to see how successful it was. Then the cycle starts all over again.

We've looked at many of the ideas these organizations use to produce smart training. Now it's time to gather some of the key ideas, combine them with a few new ones, and recast them systematically as the ground rules of smart training. They're also the ground rules of *economic* training because the goal of smart training is the greatest performance increase for the least expenditure of time, effort, and money.

The Key to Training Success

Traditionally, firms have measured training by the hours provided, the dollars consumed, and similar measures. When a firm uses hours or dollars spent on training, though, it measures the *resources* that the training consumed. It's a lot like measuring light bulbs in watts. You can buy a 25-watt incandescent bulb or a 25-watt fluorescent light. Each consumes the same amount of electricity: 25 watts. But the fluorescent light gives far more light than the incandescent light. The resources used are the same, but the results are very different.

So it is with training. A firm may need to measure training in dollars and hours to get effective training started. Then it needs to turn its attention to making training economical—to seeing that it gets the maximum amount of performance improvement for its expenditures.

The guidelines in this chapter will help you ensure that, no matter how you measure your training, it's as effective as possible. As a way into the topic, look at Fig. 10-1, which shows the relationships between four key training factors: effectiveness, efficiency, cost, and time.

All training involves all four of these factors, and all training is a compromise among them.

- *Effectiveness* means that training improves performance as much as possible. *Efficiency,* on the other hand, means that it is economical to deliver and requires as little of the trainee's time as possible. There is always a trade-off between the two. If development cost and time are held constant, maximizing effectiveness lowers the efficiency of the training, and vice versa.

- The *cost* to develop training is normally the obverse of the *time* that it takes to develop it. Decreasing the time to develop it normally means using more resources (including people), which increases its cost. Alternatively, keeping the cost of development low almost always means taking more time.

- Effectiveness and efficiency together are thus at odds with cost and time. Attempting to keep both time and cost low will decrease the effectiveness or efficiency of the training, or both. Alternatively, training that is both effective and efficient requires a high development cost and time.

All other things being equal, when you raise either of the two output factors (effectiveness and efficiency) you also raise at least one of the two input factors (cost and time). Reduce one or both of the input factors and you reduce effectiveness, efficiency, or both. The goal, of course, is to somehow increase effectiveness and/or efficiency without raising cost or time commensurately. Four factors materially affect your ability to do this—the factors are shown in Fig. 10-2. In other words,

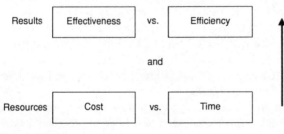

Figure 10-1

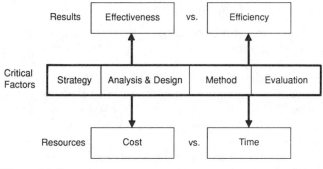

Figure 10-2

If the training strategy is well thought out, the analysis & design well done, the most appropriate delivery method selected, and intelligent evaluation performed, the training will be as effective and efficient as possible while keeping the time and cost required to develop it as low as possible.

The rest of this chapter and the four that follow suggest how you can do this.

Rule 1: Develop Training Strategically

To be smart, training must serve the basic strategy of the firm. It must help the firm develop and maintain its core competence, in every field, at every level. IBM begins with a totally strategic approach, then implements it in a very systematic way. When they're done, this is what they have:

- Key jobs are identified within the organization.
- A curriculum of courses exists for each major job.
- Courses are developed to meet specific business needs.
- Managers and workers are provided with easy-to-understand guidelines for employee training rather than with a thick catalog containing descriptions of several hundred courses, which neither the manager nor the employee can readily comprehend.
- Courses are developed by instructional designers to reduce course length, increase the amount of learning, provide job aids for applying the lessons, and increase the quality of education.

- Cost-effective delivery systems are implemented.

- Measurements of how well students learn, retain, and apply the lessons are incorporated into the course.[56]

This strategy-driven, systematic approach enabled IBM to increase the effectiveness of its training significantly during the 1980s, while at the same time cutting the costs of the training. This was a major endeavor for the company, with a major payoff. In 1988 alone, the firm saved $430 million.[57]

You may have just tuned me out. After all, your company isn't IBM, and it doesn't have IBM's resources. True, but the basic principle here is very simple: If you know just what you want, you dramatically improve the chances that you'll get it. If you know what your business is and what core competence it requires, you can concentrate your training to develop that core competence. To use the groupings we developed in Chapter 7, you will not waste time with massive training for workers in departments that contribute little value to your customers—no matter how very competent these individuals are or think they should be. You will concentrate your training on developing and maintaining the competence of those who do create customer value—whether they wear white, blue, or pink collars.

It all begins, however, by identifying the strategic aims the training will satisfy. When Robert Galvin said that training cost nothing, this was what he meant. Motorola concentrated their attention during the 1980s on becoming world-class quality leaders. Their training supported this strategic goal. It worked.

And it will work for you, whether your organization is in the Fortune 500 or only in your city's Yellow Pages. If you want smart training, start by being very clear about what your competitive advantage is and the value you create for your customers. Then organize *all* your training around that, using the suggestions in this and the next four chapters. It may not be easy, but it is just that simple. Any firm, large or small, can accomplish it.

Rule 2: Focus Training on Improved Performance

Here's where so many firms run into trouble: "Our strategy is to provide world-class service to our customers, and our training goal is to train our people to do this. Let's set up some training to explain what we want done and how to do it." That sounds good, and it's an acceptable global training goal—but it won't provide your training department or a consultant with even 1 percent of the information needed to design the actual training.

This is the step that IBM refers to as designing a detailed curriculum. It's where you take the strategic goals you want to achieve, identify how each major job category will contribute to the goals, and keep working down the ladder until you identify the specific competence that each individual needs to learn and use. *Then* you're ready to start developing the individual courses. True, this takes some time. Remember, taking the time saved IBM $430 million in one year.

Let me explain very briefly how this process works in the organization I'm part of. Several years ago, my group did an exhaustive survey of supervisors, managers, and executives to determine the skills they needed to perform effectively. From their input, we developed an overall curriculum for each category (supervisory, managerial, and executive). Then we took each item in the supervisory category, analyzed the specific competencies it required, and developed a specific training outline for each competency. We're now following the same path for management and executive positions.

Stop and think what this approach means in terms of your everyday job. The managers and supervisors that report to you (and to whom you report) have demanding jobs. What you can do depends on how well they do these jobs. If you have to spend your working day reviewing their work, correcting their errors, and making up for their shortcomings—well, you won't get much of your own work done.

What happens if they get trained in the skills they need? It isn't utopia, but now you can count on them to do their jobs. You can be confident that they know how to perform their everyday duties effectively. This leaves you to help them handle the exceptions—which is just as it should be.

There's another advantage. The training outlines are always available, so you know the training they'll receive. If they won't be trained in a skill you think is important, you can arrange the training on your own. Suppose you're a firm believer in coaching, but the curriculum only gives it a lick and a promise. You know that you'll need to schedule a course for them or perhaps give them on-the-job training yourself.

In brief, this systematic approach makes the organization more effective and life much simpler. Here's how you get from strategic goals to the specific training that workers, supervisors, and managers need:

1. Identify the broad competencies that each job category must have. Whenever possible, get this information from the individuals in the job category itself. If one of the purposes of training is to get individuals in that category to perform differently, get information from

higher levels of management. But, wherever you get the information, make it as specific as possible.

2. Combine these competencies into logical groups (such as "communication skills"). The sum total of these groups is the curriculum for the job category. This is a half-way step between the overall goals and the specific courses.

3. Divide the groups into specific units or courses. For instance, communication skills might be divided into active listening, written business communication, counseling and coaching, and presentation techniques.

4. Identify—again using subject-matter experts—what specific skills are required for each unit. Then create the training to develop these skills.

The result? You've gone from very general strategic goals to very specific, performance-focused objectives in specific training units. Even a small organization can follow the same process; just simplify it and do it as informally as possible.

Rule 3: Analyze, Then Design, *Then* Pick the Delivery Method

If you read and practice just this one rule—and make sure your training department or consultant practices it—the money you spent for this book will be returned hundreds of times over. Don't decide how training will be delivered until *after* the analysis and design have been done. Don't let anyone else decide either.

This sounds oh, so simple, and it's oh, so often violated. Every day, this scene is repeated with training departments and training consultants throughout the world:

> MANAGER: Hi. My people need some training in quality control.
>
> TRAINER: Sure. We can do that. I'd like to talk with you a little about your problem before we get to work.
>
> MANAGER: There's not much to talk about. My people don't know QC [quality control] techniques and they need to. I don't want them to lose a lot of time away from the job, so let's do the course in computer-based training. You do that, don't you?
>
> TRAINER: Sure, we can do CBT. But I really would like to talk with you some more about just what skills . . .

MANAGER: I'm awfully busy, and I know you know your stuff. Why don't we think in terms of a 4-hour CBT module—and when you get it outlined bring it over and we can look at it together. See you![58]

At its best, this approach will result in an inefficient, generally ineffective course that takes too much time and money to develop. At its worst, it will be money thrown down a rat hole. Not only was the analysis step skipped, but the delivery method was chosen without regard for its suitability to the training requirement.

Please don't think I'm exaggerating. I can always tell what delivery method is faddish just from the training requests my group gets. I used computer-based training (CBT) in the preceding example because it's back in fashion as I write this. It could just as easily be performance support systems (based on expert systems), or multimedia, or any of another dozen delivery methods.

I'm not downplaying state-of-the-art delivery vehicles. My group has developed expertise in both video-based and computer-based training. We never try to "sell" any method, though, until we've done an adequate up-front analysis and designed the training. Then we can effectively recommend CBT or another form of self-paced training, traditional classroom training, or another method altogether.

Please take this to heart. You want training that will effectively improve the performance of your people as efficiently as possible. You want it to cost as little as possible to develop and be available as quickly as possible. You'll get the best possible mix of effectiveness, efficiency, cost, and time if you let your training department (or training consultant) do a careful analysis and design *before* deciding on the delivery method. To put the same truth negatively:

Poor training design can never be "rescued" by even the most sophisticated technology. Poorly designed training will be poor in the classroom, poor as basic computer-based training, poor as multimedia, even poor as a job aid.[59]

Now for the other side of the coin. Once the analysis and design are completed, and you know the delivery alternatives available—*you* pick the delivery method. One method might be the most economical, but doesn't fit your overall strategy as well as another one.

Let me give you an example. One of our internal customers wants to move toward a system where both training and help screens are available on-line at his people's terminals. We know that for some of his training needs a paper-based self-paced course is the most efficient delivery method. Because of his overall strategy, though, he chooses to spend the extra development time and money (and put up with a small increase in inefficiency) to deliver the training via computer.

This simply reiterates the first rule: Strategy dictates training, not vice versa. The job of your training department or a training consultant is to perform an effective analysis and design and recommend the proper delivery method. Then you make the decision, based on both the short- and long-term needs of your organization.

Rule 4: Know What the Real Costs Are

One of the great running discussions in the human resources development occupation is the debate over the "real" costs of training. While these discussions are worthwhile, I'm not going to burden you with their finer points. Instead, I'm going to deal with this issue by looking quickly at both the tangible and intangible costs of training, and then making a few suggestions on how you can reduce some of the costs.

Let me begin with a critical point—so critical that I'm going to end this section with it, and then talk about it again in the next section. It's this:

> *Always compute training costs as life-cycle costs, not initial development costs.*

Every training course has a life cycle. Some life cycles are short: a one-shot, one-hour introduction to the firm's new credit card system. Some are longer: how to use the word processing system. And some are virtually endless: the introductory course for new supervisors. How long a course runs and how much it must be changed during that run are critical time and cost issues.

We'll return to life-cycle costs, but now let's look at the various costs of training in general. These fall into three groups. First is the cost of training design and development, covering everything required to create deliverable training. Next is the cost of the delivery itself. Finally, there's the cost of receiving the training, the cost incurred by the trainees. Some of these costs are clear and tangible; others are often hidden and intangible.

Tangible Costs

Most costs of training design and delivery are both tangible and clear-cut. They include the time taken by the individuals who do the work;

prorated costs of equipment such as computers and TV studios; the costs to reproduce the training materials; and the salary and travel expenses of trainers.

If you contract for training or have to do it yourself, these costs are important. If your organization has its own training department, however, the costs may not be that important to you.

[If your direct reports include the training department, by the way, you might want to consider converting the department into an "internal strategic business unit" (ISBU) that sells its services to its internal customers. The group that I head is just such an ISBU. We provide most of our training services via contract with our internal customers—and one of our services is to help them find an external source if they believe we're too expensive. The way it works isn't perfect, and we're constantly trying to improve it, but it does indeed work. You might want to consider it. If you do, and it works, you might want to consider expanding the department's mission to provide training outside the firm. Florida Power and Light clears over $100,000 per year selling other firms training initially developed to train its own workers. Caterpillar provides quality training to its suppliers at cost; both Caterpillar and suppliers profit. With imagination, there are lots of ways to increase the value of your training department.[60]]

The tangible costs of those who receive training are also relatively clear-cut: any loss of production while away from the job, along with any travel costs incurred to get to the training.

This, by the way, is one of my big objections to the "schoolhouse" approach taken by many training departments. It's normally much more expensive to bring students to trainers than to send trainers to students. More on this in Chapter 14.

Intangible Costs

One of the great problems with many human resource issues is that their major costs often fall through the cracks of established cost-accounting systems. These then become "intangible" costs—which automatically makes them suspect to the firm's number crunchers. There are three major training costs that are intangible, and at least one of the three is generally more important than the tangible costs.

1. *The cost of getting it right.* Way back in Chapter 4, we looked at the critical importance of SMEs to effective training. The time these individuals lose from their jobs serving as resources for training designers is a more or less tangible cost. When managers make average performers available as SMEs instead of their top performers, the

intangible cost shoots up. If designers build training around average performance, average performance is all anyone learns.

2. *The cost of disrupted operations.* When training is delivered somewhere other than the work site, the most important delivery cost may be the loss of trainees from their jobs. We've already looked at lost production, which is an obvious tangible cost only in very routine, measured operations (such as data entry). For much of the work force, and especially managers, the cost of being away from the job is more intangible. Not having a senior worker or senior manager around when a crisis erupts can be a major cost. So can the simple delays occasioned by an individual's absence.

3. *The cost of not getting it right.* This is, by a large margin, the most exorbitant training cost of all. Virtually every company that has adopted a systematic, proactive approach to training has made money by doing it. IBM, Corning, and Motorola have learned from experience that the way to make training really expensive is not to give it. Giving it too soon or too late, or inefficiently or ineffectively, is almost as costly.

Reducing the Costs

You can reach your own conclusions about the relative importance of the intangible costs—remembering that the evidence is growing about just how expensive they can be. What's clear, though, is that you can control all of them. Here are a few quick suggestions.

- No matter how disruptive it is, make the best of your SMEs available when they need to be. You have a right to expect whoever's designing the training to schedule around your experts' schedules. If need be, let the trainers travel to meet with the experts. But see that they work with the very best you have. If the training is worth giving at all, it's worth getting the best performance possible from it.

- There are various forms of training that can be delivered on the job site itself; the next four chapters deal with many of them. Whenever they can be used, they cut the costs of disrupting operations—and they often cut them significantly.

- Finally, remember that the basic meaning of quality is "meeting requirements"—not whether the training has heavy flash and glitz. Sometimes trainers are looking for an opportunity to demonstrate how state-of-the-art and up-to-the minute they are. This gives them bragging rights among their peers. If you want the same bragging rights, go ahead and contract for the gold plating. If you want improved performance, contract for the least expensive training that will do the job.

Back to the Life Cycle

I promised I'd be back to this point, and I'm keeping my word. Don't get sucked into planning for training and estimating its cost on the basis of the cost to design and develop it alone. Training that is extremely expensive to develop may be the least costly way of meeting a broad training need. Conversely, if the audience is small and the useful life short, development costs should be held to an absolute minimum.

One of the major life-cycle costs of training is the changes required during the life of the training. These are important enough to deserve their own rule.

Before we turn to that rule, let me make a quick detour. There are many different ways that the costs and benefits of different kinds of training can be calculated. If you'd like a relatively simple way to explore them, you might want to try the *Costs/Benefits Disk* published by Park Row Software of San Diego. Using real data, you could sit down with your trainer and in less than an hour have a good feel for the principle ways to evaluate costs and benefits.

Now, on to the next rule.

Rule 5: Manage Change—Or Else!

A funny thing happens when organizations develop training courses. All too often, both managers and trainers concentrate on the time and cost to develop the initial training. They spend little if any time analyzing and allowing for the changes that will have to be made in the training during its useful life. Some training, such as effective written communication, can be given over and over without change for several years. Other training can literally be obsolete by the time it's developed.

In later chapters, we'll see how the velocity of change affects delivery methods. I'll give you some suggestions there on how to choose the specific method that will let you manage the change as painlessly as possible. Here, we need to look at an overall approach to managing change.

The people who really understand change management are the software companies. Here's an all-too-typical example: You're Ward Prosize, chairperson of WordGlitz, maker of word processors for personal computers. You've just released version 6.0 of WordWhiz, your flagship product. In the three weeks that it's been on the market, this is what you've learned: The "drivers" for three printers don't work as well as they should. The "line delete" command actually deletes an entire paragraph. Your programming staff tell you that a small change they've made to the program will let users generate a table of contents three times as fast. And your marketing department tells you that SuperWord, your main competitor, is about to release a version that will do desktop publishing more effectively than WordWhiz. The department also tells you that your product development people assured them that they can have the same feature available in two months.

Here's the question: When and how do you issue an updated version of WordWhiz? You and I couldn't answer the question. If WordGlitz is successful, though, you can be sure that Ward Prosize knows how to answer it. His firm has a clear, rational system for determining when and how to issue updates. It's called "version control."

Version control is just as important in training that's built around changing technology. For instance, you need training for your data entry personnel on how to use a new order-tracking system. Even as you talk with your training department (or consultant) about the training, you know that there's a new version of the system scheduled for release within 60 days; corporate is discussing a policy change that will require major changes in the information that's input; and the management information system (MIS) department has ordered new terminals that have a very different key configuration from the ones currently in use.

Now you and your trainers face your version of the question Ward Prosize faced: When do you start giving the training? When and how do you update it? Unless the trainers are very adept at answering this question, we have to back up one step. The question now becomes: How do you make this kind of decision?

The basic answer is that you apply life-cycle thinking not only to the costs of training but to its development. Here are some of the basic questions you need to ask to do so.

1. *How long do you expect this training to be given before it is completely revised?* If it's a quick-fix, one-shot course, or one that can be given unchanged for a long time, forget about life cycles. If the subject matter is constantly changing and you intend to use the training for several years, you can't avoid life-cycle analysis.

2. *How frequently will the training have to be updated?* As we've seen, if updates are infrequent you're in one situation. If they're frequent, the situation is quite different.

3. *Can you plan on a regular update cycle?* A critical accompaniment of frequency is *regularity.* If developers know that they'll reissue the training every 6 months, for instance, they can handle the updates efficiently. If updates are hard to predict, though, the time and cost required for them will be much higher—and often much harder to predict.

4. *How will you decide when to do an update?* Even if you update on a regular cycle, you may want to skip a cycle. How do you decide when to do so? Will you plan on minor updates with an occasional major update? If so, how do you tell major from minor?

5. *Can you handle some of the updates through job aids, on-the-job training, or a combination of the two?* Chapters 12 and 13 look at both of these methods in detail—because there are simple and cost-effective ways to provide training just when it's needed. The more you can handle updates by one of these methods, the more easily you can deal with the entire problem.

If it seems that I'm dwelling on this overmuch, I'd like you to consider one point. For many software developers as little as 10 percent of the total time and cost is required to create the software—while up to 90 percent of the total cost and time is required to maintain (i.e., update) it. When training is designed to keep skills current in the midst of fast-changing technology, the same ratio can easily hold.

I haven't brought up the topic to suggest that you're the one who needs to find the answers. Your training department should do that for you, with your help. You do need to see that they ask the questions. If they don't ask these questions, you and they may be up to your armpits in alligators in short order.

Here's an example of what can happen. You ask a training consultant to prepare a short course on the portable computers your salespeople are getting. After analysis, it appears that CBT is the best way to go, especially since the users are scattered over a six-state area. The training is developed and sent to your sales force. Three weeks later a major change in the software (that you knew about but hadn't thought to mention) is released. When you contact the consultant about the change, she says: "I'll be glad to do it for you. Unfortunately, I can't get it done for at least 4 months, and it'll probably be quicker just to rewrite the whole training than to try to update what you've got."

Think early and avoid the pain. Look at all your training in life-cycle terms. Make sure your trainers are planning realistically for the entire cycle. Like so much else, it takes more time up front—but it can prevent truly gigantic frustration downstream.

Rule 6: The Best Training Is JIT Training

Of the several themes that have run through this book, I hope this one is indelibly engraved on your cerebral cortex: Training only really takes when it's put to use immediately after the person has received it. The longer the delay between learning and use, the less effective the training will be.

I'm sure you're familiar with just-in-time (JIT) inventory methods. Your firm may well use them. The theory is that a company wastes space and money when it carries a large inventory. If the company can reduce its inventory to the bare minimum needed for today's (or this hour's) production, it can significantly reduce its costs.

Think for a moment of what's learned in a training course as inventory. It's a stock of ideas and skills that individuals carry around in their heads, waiting for a chance to use them. There's a basic difference between physical inventory and mental inventory, though: The loss rate of mental inventory is phenomenal.

Suppose you had a stock of parts, 30 percent of which went bad on you every day. You'd see that those parts were used quickly because you couldn't afford the loss. That's precisely the situation with training. Individuals don't return from training courses with sets of new skills neatly filed away in their heads and hands, ready for use in a week or a month. They return with new skills that are very perishable. If the skills aren't used quickly, workers begin to lose them. In only a few days, most of them are gone.

We overlook this so many times, in part, because of our educational experience. We learned facts and ideas in school we didn't use for months or years, if at all. We learned skills that we didn't put to use for the same lengths of time. Algebra is extremely useful for some purposes—but several years probably elapsed between the time you took it in high school and the first time you used it for real-world problems. When you did use it, you were probably rusty. You either tried to find an old textbook or you worked your way through the problem slowly and painfully. Because of this, we come to accept that training is effective even if it's not used right away. Wrong!

I have a half dozen phones around the house that can be programmed with the numbers I use most frequently. Most of them have 911 and my wife's business number in their memory, and that's it. I read the instructions when I first bought each phone and entered those two numbers. Now it's months later, and I don't remember how to program most of them. So, they don't get programmed. You perhaps have the same problems with your phones or VCR or all the buttons on your car radio. You read the instructions (i.e., received training) when you first got them, but now you've forgotten most of what the instructions said.

Remember that when it comes to training. If you want your workers to use their training effectively, they need to use it as soon after they get it as possible. That means scheduling the training just before it's to be used, and then seeing that it is used.

But suppose you can't? People are too scattered, or turnover occurs too often, or it's hard to predict when they'll need the training? There are answers for this. Some are new, such as on-line help systems or computer-based performance support systems. Some have been around a very long time: job aids, self-paced study, on-the-job training. Different methods work in different situations. But they enable you to provide training to your people just when they need it.

We'll return to the JIT theme often in the next three chapters, particularly in Chapters 12 and 13. For now, just remember that, whatever the delivery method used, your goal is to get training to your workers just when they need it. Not sooner. Not later. Just when they need it.

Rule 7: Set Specific Objectives and Evaluate against Them

We've looked before at how critical this is. It's also perhaps the hardest of the nine rules to follow. Even in the best circumstances, it can't be done all the time. But it can be done, and it must be done—or you'll never know how smart any training was.

Let me remind you of a point first made back in Chapter 4: If training is developed based on effective analysis and design, it will almost certainly be effective training. As the Total Quality proponents say over and over, if the process is a good one, the result will be good. If your training department (or training consultant) follows a solid analysis, design, and development process, the training will improve performance.

As managers, though, you and I can't afford to settle for that all the time. We have to follow up to see that the training, in fact, was successful. This doesn't mean that we have to spend great amounts of time in the follow-up. Chapter 4 suggested that you set specific performance improvement goals based on the training, and then expect the improvement. Here's how you might do just that:

1. Try to find at least one measure of current performance. For accounts payable clerks, it might be percentage and dollar value of discounts not taken. For supervisors it might be number of formal

grievances or absenteeism rate. For a personnel specialist advising supervisors, it might be the number of grievance decisions overturned at arbitration. If you want to know that training really improves performance, you need to begin with a clear measure of the performance you're getting now.

2. Estimate the performance improvement that should result from the training. This doesn't have to be exact, but it gives both you and the trainer a target to shoot at. If possible, let the individuals to be trained participate in this step and the preceding one.

3. Make it clear, both before and after the training, that you expect the improvement to take place. Measure performance to see if it does. If performance improves as expected, the training was successful. If it doesn't, assess the reasons why and use the assessment to plan future training.

You won't be able to be this specific all the time, so supplement the formal measurement system with an informal one. As part of your MBWA (that's management by wandering around, if you're not a Peters and Waterman fan), ask questions. You might ask:

"Are you using the training you had last week? How? What are you doing differently?"

"Can you do your job better as a result of the training? What do you do better?"

"Did you improve as much as you expected? Why do you think that was? Why didn't you?"

"What really helped about the training? What wasn't as helpful as it might have been?"

None of these are scientific, but they'll give you insights into what's working and what isn't. Then you can use these insights to improve future training.

One last word on evaluation. In the introduction, I mentioned Federal Express's first-year ROI of 24 percent on their two-week basic training course for couriers. That, of course, is superb. Studies like that take time, effort, and money. No company can afford to perform many of them. If you're a manager in a large organization, though, you should see that your training department does a study like that of a basic training course every so often. It helps prevent a lot of arguing.

Rule 8: Evaluate the Alternatives

It's never enough just to evaluate the results of a course in isolation. The first question may be: Was it cost-effective? But there are always other questions: Was it as cost-effective as another method would have been? Would it be more efficient if it used job aids, structured on-the-job training, or other time-saving methods? Evaluation won't have its full impact, though, until it includes the evaluation of one method against another.

Let me return to the example that closed the introduction. I explained how my group had cut the cost of training one of our customers to $10 per student hour. That's a very low cost, but we're trying to cut it even further. The only way we'll be able to do this is to evaluate each part of the training, to see if it can be provided more economically by a method other than the one we're currently using.

It's very difficult for you to do this kind of evaluation, but your training department or consultant should be able to do it. More important, they should actually *do* it for all recurrent training. This kind of evaluation, done consistently, keeps everyone on the lookout for cost reductions without reducing the effectiveness of training.

Comparative evaluation is important for another reason. In the real world, training must often be developed and delivered to meet time constraints that don't permit full analysis and design and that rush development. This gets the training out there, and that's important. If the training is going to be repeated, though, evaluation should begin the day the first training ends. Even the quickest and dirtiest training can be made efficient and effective if a quick and competent evaluation is made and then used to revise the training.

Rule 9: What Counts Is Learning, Not Training

You know by now just how basic a theme this has been in the book. That's the problem with all the ways of measuring training in terms of courses or hours presented, workers trained, even dollars per training hour. They measure training inputs and training efficiency; they *don't* measure training output.

Even more, looking at training rather than learning focuses on the wrong activities. Ninety percent plus of all learning occurs somewhere other than in formal training. The primary job of training is to facilitate overall learning.

We'll return to this in the next few chapters. Then we'll look at it again in Part 4, which deals with the learning organization—the ultimate goal of smart training.

How to Use These Ideas

- The way to use the ideas in this chapter is to *use* them. The nine rules are a convenient summary of the basics of smart training. Whenever you're considering a major training initiative, pull out this chapter and go through the rules. Use them as benchmarks to evaluate the planned training.

- These nine rules are a great conversation starter with your training provider, whether its a training department or training consultant. If they take exception to any of these, both of you need to explore why.

- If you have to provide the training, these rules are your basic guidelines. They'll help you concentrate your efforts where they need to be.

11

How Smart Are Computers and Video?

High-Tech Training: Golden Opportunity or Just Gold Plated?

In the introduction, I mentioned IBM's highly successful use of computer-based self-paced training. IBM used a strategic, systematic approach and saved some $200 million a year in delivery costs.[61]

Now, contrast that with a remark by Dr. David Merrill. Dr. Merrill is a professor at Utah State University and one of the major forces in the use of technology for training. But he's also realistic about the advantages and disadvantages of computer-based training (CBT). At a conference in 1991, he introduced the topic with these words:

> You used to take four or five hours to prepare an hour of stand-up training. Now you can prepare the same hour with CBT in only four or five hundred hours![62]

This contrast illustrates the great promise and equally great peril of technology-based training in general and computer-based training in particular. Such training is extremely expensive and time-consuming to develop, and it requires highly competent developers. When used inap-

153

propriately, it creates extraordinarily expensive, mediocre training. When used properly, it can save big bucks.

Computer-based training and training videos have been hot training topics for many years. Now multimedia and something called "performance support systems" are coming into fashion. Are they revolutionizing training, or just adding more glitz and gold plate? The answer on both counts is "yes." Like basic CBT, these new high-tech training methods have tremendous promise—and pose at least as great a danger of overpriced, ineffective training.

How Organizations Use New Training Technology

How do you use technology-based training so that you realize the promise without falling for the glitz? This chapter will help you answer that question. The heart of the answer is this:

> *Firms use new training technology successfully when they take a strategic rather than tactical perspective and a proactive rather than reactive stance toward it.*

In other words, an organization tends to approach new training technology (and, indeed, any new technology) in one of these four ways:

- It may take a *reactive, tactical* approach and "jump on the bandwagon" for that technology. When this happens, the firm lets the new training technology itself drive what the organization does with it.

- It may take a *reactive but more strategic* approach and "go along for the ride." It lets the technology channel the organization's training development efforts in a particular direction.

- It may take a *proactive but tactical* approach and "use it as a horseless carriage." It successfully uses it to enhance the training the organization is already doing.

- Finally, it may take a *proactive and strategic* approach to the technology and "tame it and ride it." When it can accomplish this, the organization uses the technology to enable it to meet training needs in a way it hadn't been able to before.

You see the first approach, a reactive and tactical one, all too often. A manager calls in a trainer and says, "Hey this _(fill in the latest technology)_ really looks good; I need a training course, and I want you to do it in that for me." Or it can happen the other way; the training department wants to try this sexy new technology, so they try to sell everyone on its benefits—without regard for any training strategy. Either way, the firm *jumps on the bandwagon* with no clear idea of what it will gain from the new technology. We've already seen that this approach, which puts delivery method before analysis and design, is an almost sure recipe for failed training.

The second approach, while at least marginally strategic, is only a slight improvement. A manager or trainer spots a hot training technology that might have some benefit. The firm decides to *go along for the ride* and see what it can learn. In fact, it may learn to use it effectively and get some good from the technology. But it's still just *reacting* to the new technology. For all it knows, another technology might have met its needs far more effectively.

The other two approaches are proactive. The organization doesn't wait for new technology to come to it; it searches for the technology. The search may be tactical, focused on the firm's immediate needs. In that case, trainers will look around, identify what they're doing that the new technology might help them do better, and try it out. This approach very often results in improvement. (For instance, self-paced training can often become more effective when moved from paper and pencil to the computer.)

In fact, it's very hard to use a new technology initially except to *build a horseless carriage*. We tend to see any new technology in terms of our experience; it takes years to see what genuinely new possibilities the new technology holds out. No new technology is really successful, though, until this happens: until the firm is able to *tame it and ride it* where the firm wants to go. When this happens, dramatic improvements in training efficiency and effectiveness generally occur.

A Case in Point: Computer-Based Training

Computer-based training (CBT) has been around for more than three decades in one form or another. It still hasn't achieved its real potential, so it still qualifies as a "new" technology. And the ways that it's been used provide excellent examples of the four approaches just discussed.

Many firms jumped on the CBT bandwagon simply because it was new and high-tech. They've taken existing course designs and translated them unchanged to the computer. The results have often been nothing more than "electronic page turners." The courses have been no more effective than the paper-and-pencil courses they replaced—and often less so. However, they've cost a great deal more in time and dollars to create and maintain. Sad to say, all too much CBT even today falls into this category.

Some smarter training organizations looked at CBT and decided to go along for the ride. They invested in the necessary software, trained one or a few developers to use it, and then waited to see what they came up with. Their success depended on the kind of training they were doing and the creativity of their developers. If the ground was fertile and the developers imaginative, they got good results. The problem is that, because this approach is reactive, they didn't know the quality of the results they'd get until *after* they began getting them.

Most organizations that have early successes with CBT are those that take a tactical but proactive approach and use it to build the training equivalent of horseless carriages. A good example here, and one you'll hear a great deal more about, is *self-paced* training. Workers can take self-paced training at their own speed and as close to their work sites as possible. They can also take it when they need it (JIT training). Self-paced training has been done for years using paper and pencil and perhaps audio cassettes. Many training organizations looked at CBT as a way to make this training more interesting, more comprehensive, and more effective. It didn't produce a dramatic improvement, but it was worth the investment.

Trainers are just beginning to see how they might tame CBT and ride it in new directions. For instance, over the last decade firms that create software for personal computers have developed embedded help systems. Someone using the software can press a key and have an instant explanation of a feature or problem. This is truly JIT training, and trainers are beginning to make increased use of it. It enables developers to put training literally at the worker's fingertips in a way that wasn't possible before.

Don't Throw Away
Your People

For the rest of this chapter, we'll be looking at three major training technologies: videotape, computer-based training, and multimedia. (The latter includes what used to be called interactive video as well as an evolving technology called "virtual reality.") First, though, we need to get one fact solidly in place:

> *Whatever its advantages, all technology-based training is less flexible, less adaptable, and more expensive to develop than instructor-led training.*

This doesn't mean that training using the newer technologies doesn't have advantages over traditional instructor-led training. It definitely does. But these advantages do not include flexibility, adaptability, and on-the-spot creativity. Humans are far ahead in that.

There are two very practical implications of this for training. First, technology-based training must anticipate and allow for a very broad range of student responses. A developer who prepares training for experienced instructors can rely on the instructors to handle any unexpected situations. Not so if the training is computer-based.

This limitation extends to simple points. A few weeks ago, I was talking with a friend who's a real expert at computer-based training. He described a question in a CBT course he'd seen that provided for two answers—one right, one wrong. The problem was that on close analysis a third and horribly incorrect answer was also possible. If the student gave that answer, however, the system would have told him or her it was correct. An experienced teacher or even an alert student would have caught the mistake.

The moral? If the training is technology-based, developers have to catch even the unlikely problems before the training is presented. You can imagine how costly and time consuming this is.

Second, technology-based training is not only costly and time-consuming to develop; it's equally costly to update. A Japanese training manager summed the problem up succinctly:

> The more rapidly technology changes, the more difficult it is to use [CBT] for training. Human beings are always ahead of systems and by the time the new technology areas are systemized and computer software developed, it's too late.[63]

In other words, in fast-changing fields, the cost and development time to produce and maintain effective, efficient technology-based training rise sharply. Without a careful life-cycle approach, a firm can literally spend thousands of hours and dollars on training that is never current enough even to release.

None of this means that technology-based training isn't important or useful. It just doesn't replace human beings. In fact, some of the most useful applications of technology-based training *require* that human trainers or mentors be available. (In my own group, the most successful CBT application we've developed to date is one that's used as part of instructor-led classroom training.)

Now, let's look at the three major electronic technologies used in training today.

Video Worth Watching

The first commercially successful electronic training technology was the videotape. It's still quite successful, though it's generally settled down into its own specific niche. Because of this, it's easy to describe its strengths and weaknesses.

Let me start with the weaknesses. When videotape recorders first became available, there was a great rush to put instructor-led courses on video. (Building horseless carriages again!) Trainers quickly found out something they already knew: Because effective adult training requires interaction, videotape by itself is *never* an adequate medium for an entire course.

Taped video by itself is a one-way medium. All the students can do is sit there and absorb what's pitched at them. Is a point unclear? Too bad. Do students want to test the material against their own experience? Sorry. This has led to a real "jazzing up" of video presentations; one firm even uses John Cleese of Monty Python's Flying Circus. Entertainment is no substitute for training, though. The time that has to be taken keeping the student alert and interested is time taken away from the content of the course.

How then, can videotape be used successfully? There are three circumstances in which it's almost unbeatable:

1. It can create a realistic situation for discussion. This doesn't require video, of course. Two or more individuals can role-play a situation and then the group can discuss it. Many times this is just as effective as video—and much cheaper. But if the situation needs to be just right, and particularly if it's going to be used many, many times, video is the better alternative. Video can also take advantage of professional actors to make the scene realistic. Finally, there are hundreds of commercial videos, at reasonable prices, that provide cases for discussion. No need to reinvent the wheel.

2. It can model effective and ineffective behavior for individuals to evaluate and discuss. Again, a role play can do the same—but often not as effectively. For instance, a training course on customer service might use a video demonstrating poor, good, and excellent responses to customers. After each example, the group can discuss the pros and cons of what they saw and compare it to other examples and their own behavior. Any course intended to teach skilled, *visible* behavior can use video effectively in this way.

(I have to make a parenthetical note here. Remember Chapter 2 and the Montreal Urban Community Transportation Commission's course in cultural diversity. They used bus drivers to teach the course—because no one is so credible to a bus driver as another bus driver. When you want to train individuals in a particular skill and you believe they may resist the training, *don't* use an off-the-shelf video as a first choice. Find someone who is like the students, who has the skill, and who believes in it. Then have him or her model the behavior you want. The individual will be far more credible than even the best professional actor. It's most effective if the individual presents the behavior in person and is available to discuss it. If this can't be done, use the alternative in the next item: Make a video of that person and use it.)

3. Finally, video is effective when real individuals in the firm need to present information but aren't available to do it in person. If the CEO kicks off the new quality program, it may best be done in a video that can be distributed throughout the organization. That's yesterday's news. The next example may not be. Suppose you're acclimating new workers to the company. And you want to make the point that individual workers exercise great initiative and perform challenging work. You could just tell the group that. Or you could use videos of actual workers to tell them. (Do you remember how GM Saturn used actual workers in their commercials to make the point that their work force was committed to their product? This gave an immediacy and genuineness to Saturn's message that no professional actor could have provided.)

A word of caution: If you use videos starring your organization's managers and workers, be sure they're competently produced. Video tends to catch every imperfection. Minor items of dress, inflection, or mannerism that pass unnoticed in live conversation are emphasized on tape. And even the shortest video requires a script. If you want a tape, have pros do it. This isn't the place for amateurs.

Videos can be used effectively to present situations for discussion, model behaviors, and add reality to presentations. Just remember that sitting and watching a video is *never* a substitute for active learning. Videos are most effective when they involve learners—and then give learners the chance to respond. Which brings us to a form of video that does just that.

The Next Step: Interactive Video

Interactive video is almost impossible with videotape. Videodiscs, however, are an entirely different matter. For instance, an interactive video system can show a student part of a sophisticated electronic assembly. Using animation, it can demonstrate how each part of the assembly works. Then it can ask the student to answer critical questions about the part and its function. Depending on the student's answer, it can go to the next part of the assembly or repeat what the student has just studied.

This ability to select one response or another based on a student's input is critical to any technology-based training. Trainers call the ability "branching." The system can branch to any one of two or more alternative paths based on how a student responds. Good interactive training—whether it's based on video or not—uses branching intensively. By constantly requiring a response from students, it keeps them interested and active. As we've seen again and again, that's critical in all training.

Since branching is so significant, the power in interactive video is in the computer that controls it. Interactive video is really a visually intensive form of computer-based training. It extends the power of the computer by giving it more extensive storage—storage that's particularly adapted to images and graphics. In addition, it has undergone a metamorphosis; interactive video is now just a part of "multimedia." We'll look at multimedia in a few paragraphs. First, let's consider the strengths and weaknesses of computer-based training in general.

How Smart Is Computer-Based Training?

Computers are at the heart of almost every electronically based training technology except straight videotape. As a culture, we're infatuated with what the computer can do. (I have a desktop, a laptop, and, as of last week, a palmtop computer.) I've already given you examples of how computer-based training (CBT) often misfires. In this section, I want to suggest how you can use it effectively.

Whenever anyone proposes to provide you training via CBT, ask the person for a sample of CBT he or she has already done. Then sit down and play student. Go through the course. Look at the whole product: professionalism, screen design, clarity, and so on. But pay particular attention to how active you are as a learner. If you mostly sit and watch what's happening on the screen, it's poor training. On the other hand, if you are constantly involved, constantly answering questions and responding to the system, it's probably very effective.

In other words, *on the average, students should never go for more than a minute without having to respond to what they've seen.* That is as close to an absolute as you will find in training.

Good CBT is interactive, but even the most interactive CBT isn't necessarily cost-effective. When, then, should you use CBT? Here are some basic guidelines:

1. With three exceptions I'll describe in a few paragraphs, don't use CBT if paper and pencil and/or instructor-led training will do the

job as cheaply. Just putting training on the computer accomplishes nothing. If it can be done economically on paper or by an instructor, stick with that.

2. CBT usually isn't a good idea when students don't have easy access to the computer on which it runs. In a day when almost everyone has a computer on his or her desk, this isn't the problem it was even a few years ago. However, not everyone who has a computer uses it or is comfortable with it. So take both availability and familiarity into account. Don't go with CBT unless you have both.

3. There's a basic trade-off when you're deciding whether you want CBT or traditional instructor-led training. CBT is more costly to develop, while instructor-led training is most costly to deliver. This means that:

   - Instructor-led training is most cost-effective when there are relatively few students who are all generally in the same geographic region and are all available to attend the training session(s).
   - CBT is most cost-effective when there are a great many students who are scattered widely and aren't available to come to a training site.

4. One of the common uses of CBT is for "self-paced" training. Students can take self-paced training at their convenience and progress at their own speed. Many times, both of these are desirable characteristics. Self-paced training adapts the training to the job demands, not vice versa. Remember, though, that self-paced training can be as simple as a workbook or other paper-based self-study method. CBT isn't an automatic best choice for self-paced training. How do you make the choice?

   - If the self-paced training requires considerable interaction and initiative from the student, CBT will be the best alternative. If it doesn't, paper-based training will almost certainly be better.
   - If the subject matter is complex, CBT will be the best method. This is closely related to interactivity; complex material requires the student to pay close attention and learn each point before moving to the next. Well done CBT excels at this.

I mentioned that there are three situations when you may want to use CBT even though another method might be more cost-effective. Here they are:

- Many individuals spend most of their workday at a computer. They're often more comfortable with training that's computer-based rather than paper-based. This is particularly true if their documentation, instructions, and other reference material are on-line. In this circumstance, CBT may be the best method, even if it's not the cheapest.

- What do you do if you simply don't have individuals available to do training? They're too busy, there are too few of them, or they can't leave their work sites. This may override other considerations and make CBT the most practical way to get training to the workers who need it.

- Finally, some forward-looking firms are beginning to see training as an integral part of their automated systems. They're moving toward a situation like that just discussed in item 1—where individuals can get all the information they need right from the terminal where they work. When training will be integrated into a total system like this, it's often best to develop it as CBT initially. We'll look more closely at this approach when we examine performance support systems in the next chapter.

By the way, you don't have to use CBT (or any training method) just for your own work force. Federal Express uses a self-paced course, featuring Sky King, to train customers to use the firm's automated package shipping system.[64]

There are a number of guides around to help you decide whether CBT is cost- effective. One of the simplest to use is a computer program available from Park Row Software called The CBT Analyst. It lets you estimate the costs and benefits of CBT for any given application and then helps you predict its probable success during implementation. If you want to truly educate yourself on CBT, you might want to look through Gloria Gery's *Making CBT Happen*.

Let me give you a final suggestion before we turn to the more sophisticated forms of training based on computers. When CBT is done poorly, or when it's the wrong method, people won't use it. When it's good CBT, they will. But how do you tell?

Actually, there's a very straightforward and reliable test of how effective CBT is. After a CBT module has been delivered for a few weeks, make a few calls to organizations that should be using it. Ask them what their reaction is. If they have a dozen reasons why they haven't used it yet, it probably wasn't very good CBT or it didn't meet a real need. If they tell you they used it and let it go at that, it was probably so-so at best. If the response is, "How long before we can get the next module?" you know you have a success on your hands. When they get angry that they don't have the next module yet, you can brand it an unconditional success.

That's not very scientific, but it's probably as worthwhile a test of the *usefulness* of CBT as you can find.

The Current Buzzword: *Multimedia*

I'm sure you've heard or read about "multimedia" and its fantastic capabilities. It is impressive, and getting more so all the time. A personal computer with the proper software can present training using text, graphics, full-movement video, and high-fidelity audio. There's no reason in principle why holograms and "virtual reality" couldn't be included. With multimedia, computer training is moving to the point that it can present anything, from any perspective, to any degree of realism. For instance, beginning drivers could learn all the basics—including how it feels to crash when they take a corner too rapidly.

In other words, multimedia offers incredibly rich possibilities for training. These possibilities are also extremely expensive and time-consuming. In addition, multimedia courses require thousands of dollars worth of hardware. This led a national computer magazine to ask, "What costs a lot, takes forever to learn how to use, and makes a simple presentation a complicated thing?" The answer? Multimedia.[65]

This doesn't mean multimedia shouldn't be used. It should—but only when its results justify its high cost.

Careful analysis and design are essential for any training. With the kind of bucks that multimedia involves at stake, the analysis and design must be little short of brilliant. Fortunately, there are more and more guides becoming available. When your training department or consultants evaluate multimedia, they might want to use a book such as Richard Brandt's *Videodisc Training: A Cost Analysis*. This is really a workbook that talks a trainer through the cost analysis. Though it was written before "multimedia" became a buzzword, it's fully useful for multimedia.

The greatest danger in multimedia training is that it can indeed produce flashy, attention-getting displays. Whether these dramatic displays train effectively is another question entirely. No one is better equipped than Lucasfilm to produce dramatic multimedia—but they understand that visual effects aren't the key. According to Steve Arnold of LucasArts' New Media group (which contains Lucasfilm Learning), "We see multimedia as the platform and interactive as the process."[66] Once again, technology-based training must be interactive to work.

Developing multimedia training is extremely expensive and time-consuming. Delivering it properly requires significant hardware investment. Where, then, can you use it effectively? There are three basic situations where it will almost certainly worth the time and expense.

1. *Where basic CBT would be cost-effective but the situation demands the additional capabilities of multimedia.* In part, the next two situations cover

this one—but not always. You may need to show the exact operation of a machine or system, and a CBT simulation isn't adequate for it. You may need to show an individual performing specific tasks in an environment. The common thread is that live action is required to really understand the topic.

2. *When you must give highly technical, complex training and access to expert trainers and equipment is limited.* For instance, you may be ready to use a different and more complex engine in equipment you build. The equipment, and the individuals who service it, are scattered all over the United States. It's expensive to bring people to a central location for training, and you don't have many spare engines for them to work on. In this circumstance, highly interactive training using a variety of computer-controlled media will probably be both most effective and most cost-effective.

3. *When individuals must learn how to handle situations that are too dangerous to create in the real world.* The Department of Defense and the major airlines have been using complex flight simulators for decades. You may remember the DC-10 that crashed on takeoff outside Chicago a number of years ago. Once the airline found the causes of the crash, it programmed a simulation of it into its flight trainers. Now pilots can experience the same situation and correct it—before they actually climb into a plane. Wherever this kind of complex and dangerous simulation is required, multimedia-based simulation is probably the *only* feasible alternative.

Let me close this section with an example of the power of CBT in general and multimedia in particular. Shell Oil has developed numerous applications in interactive video (i.e., multimedia) training operation. The firm has 21,000 workers spread from Maine to Honolulu, in different jobs, working different shifts. Multimedia enables Shell to put the training out in the field, close to these workers. They take it as they're available and/or as they need it. The multimedia capability enables the training to depict situations realistically. How cost-effective is Shell's use of multimedia? One course that would have cost some $3 million to develop and deliver as conventional classroom training was developed and delivered for $100,000 as multimedia. That's a 30-to-1 savings. Not bad.[67]

As firms experiment more with multimedia, and as the cost of developing and delivering it drop even lower, there will be additional practical uses for it. Someday it may become an ordinary way of delivering training. As of late 1991, however, that wasn't yet the case.

Something Called "Virtual Reality"

Virtual reality isn't a training method widely used today; when it's developed, it will most likely be an extension to multimedia training. Since it does offer unique potential, it's worth a brief look. Besides, it must have some promise—because Mattel has licensed the technology to incorporate into video games.

You may have seen news clips or pictures of individuals wearing special goggles and specially wired gloves or suits. The goggles and electronic sensors enable them to operate in a "virtual reality" that is generated and controlled by a computer. Their actions are transmitted by the sensors to a controlling computer; in turn, the computer generates the appropriate response from the virtual world.

For instance, consider an individual learning to be a mechanic. He dons the goggles and two specially wired gloves. From that point on, he can disassemble and reassemble any part of an automobile. He can select appropriate tools from a tool rack. He can start the car, run it—even take it for a test drive. The automobile and its environment exist only as a computer projection—but he can see and manipulate the projection as though it were "really" there. Imagine having the equivalent on an entire auto repair shop on your desk!

Dramatic as this sounds, no one can tell yet what the worth of virtual reality for training will be. It will extend the abilities of multimedia training, particularly in the area of simulation. Virtual reality may make it possible for individuals not only to experience extremely hazardous environments in great detail and with several senses, but to *act* in these environments.

Don't hold your breath until your training department develops practical training using virtual reality. This was the assessment made of it in mid-1991 by the editor of *AI Expert Magazine:*

> The technology is crude and expensive, but improving daily. At some point in the next few years, the tools that allow visual, audible, and tactile feedback will be inexpensive and readily available. Input devices, too, will be improved to make interactive virtual reality easy and affordable. After that, it's a software problem.[68]

The use of virtual reality as an extension to multimedia training does have significant potential. By the mid- to late-1990s, it should be as commonplace as computer-based simulations are today. (If you're interested in a "things to come" demo of virtual reality, Media Magic, Nicasio, California, will sell you a videotape for $30 illustrating it.)

Add a Dash of AI and Get a Performance Support System

The newest and perhaps most exciting technology-based training is something called a performance support system. It incorporates a variety of methods, including artificial intelligence (AI), to deliver training to workers exactly where and when they need it. Though these systems are high tech, they're really a turbocharged form of job aid. The next chapter is about job aids in general, and we'll look at performance support systems then.

It's Not Necessarily Either-Or

Before we turn to that chapter, let me end with a final suggestion about CBT in all its forms. It clearly takes longer and costs more to develop than instructor-led training. Even the best developers will normally take three to ten times as long to develop effective CBT (in any of its forms) as instructor-led training.

Don't think of these two alternatives as mutually exclusive, though. I've already mentioned that my group has produced effective and relatively inexpensive training in some circumstances by combining CBT with instructor-led methods. It works particularly well when individuals are being trained to use a computer system, when the CBT can mimic the system being learned.

This doesn't apply just to CBT. Combining several methods is often more effective than one method alone. Some combinations are obvious. Videotape can be used with instructor-led training or self-paced paper-based training. The next two chapters will suggest how effective a combination job aids and on-the-job training can be. Even very unlike methods can sometimes be used together to produce real successes. In many ways, multimedia does just that. Start with good analysis and design. Then pick the methods, individually and in combination, that will produce maximum learning with minimum training.

How to Use These Ideas

- Don't let yourself get seduced by the glitz and the glamour, but don't be put off because this training is technology-based.

- Here's where a good training department is invaluable. If the department is doing its job, it keeps up with new training technology. It also evaluates it in light of your firm's real training needs. When you ask about the relevance of a particular training technology, you should get a knowledgeable and thoughtful response—one that takes account of your specific needs. If you don't, the department isn't doing its job.

- You should get the same knowledgeable and thoughtful response from a training consultant or a college. This may be a lot harder, because consultants and many colleges specialize in one or two training methods and don't know a lot about others. All you can do is keep looking and keep pushing until you find someone with good answers.

- You have to do your own training? Don't even think about using technology-based training. If you have someone who's just dying to play with it, you have a decision to make. Either turn the individual into a trainer and see that he or she picks up the analysis, design, and development skills good training requires, or decline politely. This isn't a good area for amateurs, no matter how talented they are.

12

Smart Just-in-Time Training: Job Aids

I've pointed out how training is like inventory. Unused training may not cost as much to store as unused inventory, and it doesn't take up space—but it deteriorates much more rapidly than most physical inventory. As with inventory, the most efficient form of training is training that's provided just in time. This chapter and the next will describe two forms of just-in-time (JIT) training: job aids and structured on-the-job training (OJT).

These two forms of training have another advantage: They're both relatively inexpensive. And the ratio of performance improvement to development cost is very, very high. Sometimes you can combine job aids and on-the-job training effectively. At other times, you use one or the other. And many times neither will work. They're powerful enough, though, that you should always consider them before any other form of training.

Job Aids Can Do All This?

First of all, let's define a job aid. That's really quite simple: It's an aid that a worker can use on the job to help do the job. Perhaps the best known of all job aids is the checklist that pilots use to make sure they've checked all their equipment. The instructions that came with your VCR were also a job aid—and probably not a very good one. The sheet of paper in the trunk of your car that tells you how to use the jack is yet another job aid. Most job aids are printed instructions, but this doesn't have to be the case. The slide rule that engineers used to perform math

169

was a job aid. Performance support systems, covered at the end of this chapter, are computer-based, complex job aids. The crucial point is this: A job aid is something individuals can use right on the job, right when they need it.

Let me give you some concrete examples of just what job aids can do. In one firm, installers weren't properly grounding a very large, expensive system that they were installing. About one of every three systems were poorly grounded, resulting in outages, fires, and even loss of the equipment. The company wanted to bring the installers in (from all over North America) and give them a one-week refresher course. A knowledgeable consultant persuaded the firm to use an eight-page job aid, with no training, instead. This cost some $255,000 less than the initial solution, and resulted in the proper grounding of 95 percent of the systems.[69]

The instructions with a product should tell someone how to use it effectively, shouldn't they? That doesn't mean they will. The employees of a commercial spraying company followed the manufacturer's instructions when they mixed insecticides. The result was a 35 percent error rate. The cure? A one-page job aid, written in an hour, that immediately reduced the error rate to 10 percent.[70]

I've mentioned Frederick W. Taylor, the creator of "Scientific Management." He was the originator of time and motion study and the whole occupation we know as industrial engineering. One of the problems that Taylor and his associates investigated was the optimum feed and speed for metal cutting. They identified 12 independent variables that affected feed and speed. They also estimated that it would take a trained mathematician from 2 to 6 hours to solve the problem each time—during which time a machinist would already have completed the job. After literally years of study, the group came up with a slide rule that a machinist could use to set both feed and speed accurately *in less than a minute.*[71]

No organization makes more effective use of job aids than the Caterpillar Corporation of Peoria, Illinois. They've got it down to a science. Most machines have their job aids right there. Each job aid is hand-lettered and hand-drawn—not because they're cheap but because they're easier to read and follow that way. Thousands of hours of training are saved every year by this very practical form of JIT training.

Make Them High Tech, Low Tech, Any Tech

I can't show you an example of a slide-rule job aid, or one etched in metal. I can show you three very different yet very effective paper ones.

The first one, Fig. 12-1, created by the Harless Performance Guild, is as elegant and complete as you could ever want. No one reading this would ever have a doubt about what he or she was to do.

Look how different Fig. 12-2 from the Caterpillar Company is. It's hand-lettered and hand-drawn—to be clear, not to save money. It's not

---

Task: Deal With Charge-denial

1. Locate toll charge on microfiche Long Distance Statement.

2. Ask customer, "Could someone else have made this call *from your phone?*"

IF:	THEN:
YES	a. Thank customer. b. Close contact. c. Stroke as Toll. d. Go to Step 3 below.
NO	Go to Step 5 below.

3. Obtain data about call.

IF Call Is:	THEN Get Name of Party Called From:
Ticketed	Toll Library
NOT ticketed	CNA Bureau

4. Tell customer name and address of party called.

5.

IF Customer:	THEN:
DENIES making call	a. Tell customer to deduct amount of call. b. Prepare AV and forward to Revenue accounting. c. Close contact. d. Post deduction to CAR. e. File AV. f. Stroke as Toll.
ACCEPTS call	a. Close contact. b. Complete CM and file. c. Stroke as Toll.

Figure 12-1. Harless Performance Guild job aid. (*Reproduced with the permission of the Harless Performance Guild.*)

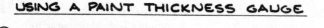

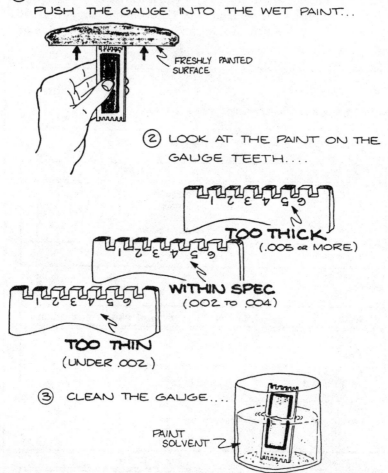

Figure 12-2. Caterpillar job aid. (*Reproduced with the permission of the Caterpillar Corporation.*)

as elegant as the one from Harless Performance Guild, but it's just as easy to follow and just as effective.

What a contrast Fig. 12-3 is. It's hastily drawn, and certainly not elegant or even attractive—but all the necessary information is there. This is what Jeff Nelson calls a "quick and dirty" job aid. It was later revised to be more elegant—but an individual could get just as clear an idea of what to do from this as from the fancier version.

Again, job aids don't have to be words on paper. We've seen that a

STEP 4 – ADD UNLISTED PERSONNEL

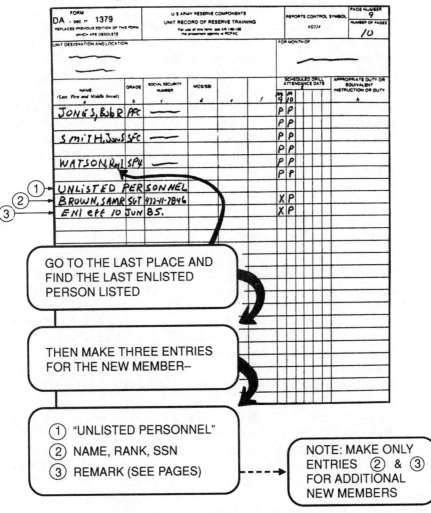

TURN TO NEXT PAGE

Figure 12-3. Jeffrey Nelson job aid. (*Reproduced with the permission of Jeffrey Nelson Associates.*)

slide rule can be one. So can a picture or a diagram. Job aids can be painted on the wall, etched onto products, put on any medium in any way that works. The key point is to create and use job aids—in any way that works. And that brings up the question: When do they work?

When a Simple Job Is
Performed Infrequently

In this situation, you ought *always* to use job aids. If a janitor has to mix a special cleaning solution once a month—fix a job aid for it. If a clerk has to fill out a special requisition two or three times a year—fix a job aid for it. If a supervisor has to prepare an evaluation each time an employee leaves—fix a job aid for it. Whenever the task is simple and performed infrequently, don't ask individuals to remember it. Create a job aid, put it where they can find it when they need it, and go on to more important things. Create a job aid, too, when the task is performed often but spread among different workers so that no one of them performs it frequently.

When a Job Has a Series
of Detailed Steps That *Must*
Be Performed

The pilots' checklist is the classic example of this. Individual pilots go through the list several times each week. The procedure is so detailed, and the consequences of forgetting a step are so serious, that pilots need the job aid each time. You may have the same situation when a technician must use a detailed format for a technical report. Don't expect the individual to remember the format, or dig it out of a manual. Prepare a job aid that's ready to use whenever needed. (Needless to say, the more individuals that can use the job aid, the more cost-efficient it will be to develop it.)

This approach only works, by the way, when there's nothing complex about the checklist. No one has to make any decisions about what to do next. That's important. Suppose individuals have to go through a series of steps that require decisions at several points. If they haven't had training on the process, a job aid won't normally solve the problem. (At least a paper-based job aid won't. A performance support system, which we'll examine at the end of this chapter, may.)

When a Job Is Somewhat
Complex, but the Individual Has
Had Training on It

Job aids are memory joggers—and they can help individuals remember a process they've had training in but may not recall in detail. In most organizations, supervisors must appraise the performance of their subordinates at least once a year. There are always rules for the process, sometimes quite complicated ones. Certain forms have to be used. Certain steps have to be followed. If *x* is the case, then *y* must be done. Supervisors need training in the process, but they don't need to remember it in detail. Provide them with a job aid that walks them through the steps. Then trust them to understand the judgmental parts of the process.

As Part of the Machine, System, or Process It Aids

I looked at a new car yesterday. Every user-serviceable device (dipstick, windshield wiper reservoir, etc.) is clearly visible and painted yellow. This says simply: "If it's yellow, you can take care of it if you want to." Our copying machine has instructions right by every part that might need to be moved to clear a paper jam. WordPerfect has red, green, and blue dots that color code three keys to the cardboard job aid that sits at the top of the keyboard. The possibilities are endless. There's no better way to use job aids than to make them part of the system they aid.

(If you really want to understand how much built-in job aids can accomplish, read Donald Norman's *The Psychology of Everyday Things*, which is listed in the bibliography. You will never look at doors, coffee pots, and the other accoutrements of life in the same way. And you'll learn how much effective design and simple job aids can improve the everyday world—including the world of work—around you.)

What's *Not* a Job Aid?

"What the heck," you may be thinking. "We already have manuals that are just loaded with job aids." I'm sure you have manuals, and I'm equally sure that they're intended to fill the function of job aids. If your firm is like most others, though, the manuals don't fill the function very well. In many organizations, the most common job aids you find are those created by individuals to *replace* the instructions in the manuals. Sometimes they're the same instructions, put more simply and readably. Sometimes, though, they modify the manuals. They describe a less complicated or more effective way to get the same job done.

The fact of the matter is that most manuals are produced by individuals who've never done the specific job. The manual is their best guess about how to do the job effectively. It may or may not work well in the real world. Then, to complicate matters, most of these individuals have had zero training in how to do an effective job aid. This makes the manual even less useful.

How do you prepare effective job aids? The key is for them to be *practical* and *understandable* to the people using them. You watch an individual who knows how to do the job and describe what she does. Then you give the job aid to someone who isn't very familiar with the job and have him or her follow it. If the person does what you expected him or her to do, the job aid worked. If the person doesn't perform as expected—redo the job aid.

Suppose a job aid is for a series of steps no one is performing yet. Perhaps the job aid describes how to back up a personal computer on a tape drive that's about to be installed. Or it describes new safety precautions required by a modification to a milling machine. Have someone familiar with job aids create one and give it to an individual who will be performing the process. If the worker uses the job aid and performs successfully, excellent. If not, revise the job aid until he or she can do the job.

There's another way that's even more effective than these.

The Best Job Aids of All

I mentioned earlier in the chapter that there are job aids all through your organization that you don't know about. These are the ones that individual workers, supervisors, and managers have made for themselves.

For instance, Emily, the receptionist, has a Rolodex of all the individuals in the organization, with their units. On about half the cards, she's written the name of an individual to contact if the person listed on the card isn't there.

Tom got fed up trying to translate the manual's instructions for ordering capital equipment. He got with the organization's expert on capital equipment and they worked out a flowchart that explains each step. Now everybody in Engineering uses the flowchart.

Maureen wants the performance appraisals she does to be a dialogue. To prepare for this, she gives each of her direct reports a list of five performance factors that she believes are most important. The individuals list what they have done under each factor and then discuss them with Maureen at the appraisal meeting.

Whenever Joshua calls on a client, he takes a moment afterward to jot down the highlights of the call. The next time he deals with that client, he reviews his notes—so that he can start the conversation off with a specific reference to the last visit.

Emily, Tom, Maureen, and Joshua are each using homemade job aids. Walk through your organization and you'll see dozens, perhaps hundreds more, of them. Because good job aids haven't been furnished to them, your people make their own. They may be sloppy, dog-eared, even almost illegible—but they work. They fill a gap.

Now let me give you an example of just how powerful these quick and dirty job aids can be when individuals have had even minimum training in how to do the job.

> A firm was installing a new assembly line in a large manufacturing plant. Key operators needed to become familiar with its operation as quickly as possible so that they could train the regular operators on three shifts. Because the operators had been trained in how to do job aids, they wrote "notes" in a quick and dirty (but effective) job aid format and used camcorders to videotape the vendors as they operated the line. They took the notes and videotapes and created more polished and complete job aids. Then they used the job aids and the videos to train the other operators. Result: the line was up in running in two months instead of the six that would normally have been expected.[72]

If worker-created job aids are this powerful, why leave a gap for them to fill? Teach your people how to do job aids and then encourage them to put the knowledge to use.

You can do this in two effective ways. First, you can see that all your first-line supervisors learn how to develop job aids. Then they can train their workgroups and encourage them to prepare their own job aids and share them with one another. But there's another way, ever better in some circumstances. Do you have an active Total Quality program? Your quality teams have learned skills like brainstorming and cause-and-effect diagrams. Now teach them how to do job aids. This gives them another, powerful tool for improving processes.

In each case, nothing has to be elaborate or complicated. Quite the reverse—look back at Fig. 12-3. What counts about job aids is their *usability*. I described briefly how to create a good job aid a few paragraphs back. Here's the process in a bit more detail:

1. Concentrate on the task, not on the background knowledge, the reason the job is being done, or other considerations not directly related to performance. If these other considerations are important, handle them through some form of training. The job aid should contain only the *what* of the job.

2. Create the job aid as the individual is doing the task, if possible. The individual can create it himself or herself or have another person write it down as the job is being done.

3. The job aid should be legible and usable. It doesn't have to be neat or elegant or professional looking.

4. If pictures or diagrams are needed, draw them. Don't put in any more detail than absolutely necessary.

5. When the job aid is done, give it to someone who's not familiar with the task and ask him or her to do the task from the job aid. Revise the aid as necessary until a worker can use it to perform successfully the first time.

6. If several people are going to use the job aid, make copies. If it will be used repeatedly, or under harsh conditions, put it in a plastic sleeve. Then get it out where people can use it.

7. If workers will use the job aid for a long period of time, have an experienced job aid designer redo it. Then test the revised aid and revise it again as necessary.

That's the essence of the process. Yes, it's simple. Yes, it's not very sophisticated. But it *is* very successful.

There are courses available on job aids from a number of vendors. The Harless Performance Guild of Noonan, Georgia, is famous for its use of job aids and offers a 3-day course in them. Jeffrey Nelson Associates of Newport News, Virginia, offers a 2-day course. Both courses show how to combine job aids with on-the-job training—an extra benefit. Either course works for training professionals *and* white-collar workers above the clerical level. A *Handbook of Job Aids* by Rossett and Gautier-Downes (listed in the bibliography) covers the topic in good detail, for the same audience. An individual could use any of these sources to prepare effective training for workers.

Job Aids and Core Competence

Job aids are true smart training; they improve performance with a minimum expenditure of time and money. But they're not for every situation. They work best when they make it easy for individuals to do the inessential part of their jobs—so they can concentrate on the essential or core tasks. Just as firms have a core competence, so do individuals. In fact, the core competence of a firm is simply the combined core competence of each member.

Let me give you an example of what I mean. Earlier I used the example of a job aid to talk supervisors through their annual performance appraisals. The aid might tell them what forms to use, what procedures to follow, and where to send the completed forms. That's appropriate. After all, you don't need your supervisors to memorize these details. They're simply not essential to a supervisor's job.

Suppose, though, that someone suggests a job aid to help supervisors arrive at the appraisal itself. If the aid is simply a checklist of items to be considered—dependability, initiative, work quality and quantity—it will be helpful. If it's intended to substitute for the supervisor's judgment, though, it won't be helpful. This can happen, for instance, if the aid reduces the appraisal to a simple formula, such as "an employee who is late five times during the year will be rated average."

Neither job aids nor any other form of training should ever reduce workers' competence in any core functions of their jobs. Conversely, whenever a firm can reduce the time and attention that workers have to pay to their inessential duties it should make every effort to do so. That's the area where job aids pay off quickly in improved performance *and* worker satisfaction.

Souped-Up Job Aids: A Closer Look at Performance Support Systems

Traditional job aids don't support complex tasks well. They also lose their effectiveness when they pile up to the point that the individual has trouble keeping track of them. A new form of computer support for training, performance support systems, (also called electronic performance support systems), may remedy this lack. These systems are still in their infancy, but they do show promise.

What are they? They have three essential features: They're computer-based, they normally use some form of artificial intelligence, and they provide advice, assistance, and support to workers—at the job site, in the midst of their work, just when they need it. They are, in short, intelligent job aids. Many of them use databases and graphics. They can employ the full tools of multimedia, often in a form called "hypermedia" that permits easy browsing and searching. In short, they can use any tool or method available that is required by the work situation.

To see how performance support systems might work, consider the so-called help desks that many firms use to support a variety of products. Customers call these help desks for answers to specific problems. The individuals at the desks apply their expertise, generally supported by manuals or automated technical manuals, problem summaries, and a variety of other background materials. When you call customer support in a firm like WordPerfect, for instance, you'll often hear, "Just a minute—I'm checking our problem database to see if we have anything on that."

The problem with traditional help desks, even when they use automated databases, is that as the reference material gets bigger and bigger it's harder and harder to find what you need. On top of that, new workers have trouble finding solutions for all but the simplest problems. The result is delay in answering questions and the potential for a high number of wrong answers.

To correct this situation, organizations are increasingly turning to performance support systems. By asking questions, these systems can help identify the probable cause of problems and suggest where to look for answers. This particularly helps less-experienced workers. For more-experienced workers, the system might offer a highly efficient system for browsing rapidly through the material.

Many of these systems already exist, and more are being created all the time. They show enough promise that firms such as Intel, Amdahl, AT&T, and American Express have begun to use them. Don't think that they necessarily replace paper-based job aids, by the way. Caterpillar uses performance support systems in addition to its paper-based job aids.

Actually, you may already have used a basic performance support system. If you use any of the top software packages for personal computers, you've been exposed to on-line help systems. These systems are immensely more sophisticated and useful today than they were even 3 or 4 years ago. Most of them are "context sensitive"; instead of providing help in general, they provide it for the specific function you're using. Even a neophyte using the help system can run the software passably the first time out.

These on-line help systems pioneered an important idea: incorporate the training and the help in the software package itself. We've already seen that this approach partially solves the problem with CBT: that it's so hard to update. The more common this approach becomes, the more practical it will be to bundle both training and performance support with the total system.

One of the characteristics of performance support systems is their use of artificial intelligence (AI). The most popular form of AI used in them at present is expert systems. If you're not familiar with expert systems, they're a way of making a computer behave "intelligently" by providing it with a number of decision rules. For instance, a rule in a help desk expert system might be "IF printer is functioning AND print quality is poor THEN replace the ribbon." By combining a number of rules, an expert system can guide a human being to the likely solutions for a variety of problems.

Expert systems are already widely used. Digital Equipment Corporation uses a system with thousands of rules to configure their computers. The Du Pont Corporation uses hundreds of systems. Each of their systems, however, has only a few dozen or few hundred rules. Small or large, such systems make the expertise of experienced workers available to less-experienced ones. You can see how short the jump is from these systems to full-fledged performance support systems.

To end this section, there are four major points I'd like to make about performance support systems:

1. Because they're fashionable, there will be pressure to use them everywhere. The problem is that, like any other form of training, they're effective in some situations and ineffective in others. We're back to rule 3 from the last chapter: Analyze, then design, *then* pick the training method. A performance support system is one method among many. It may be just the ticket—or it may be an immensely more expensive substitute for a series of simple job aids.

2. Because performance support systems can use expert systems to make decisions formerly made by humans, there's a real temptation to use them to *replace* the skills of workers. As you might expect, this has advantages and disadvantages. The best guideline to use is that between essential and inessential job duties. If you attempt to substitute expert system–based performance support systems for essential employee skills, you'll reduce workers' core competence—and thus the overall core competence of your firm. On the other hand, if you use these same systems to take over the often irritating inessential tasks, you'll preserve core competence. You'll also make your workers happier. This is exactly the same point made in the section on job aids and core competence. It's a useful reminder that, for all their electronics and electronic glitz, performance support systems are simply fancy job aids. And that's the way you should use them.

3. Performance support systems will come into their own when they're built into the systems they're designed to aid. We've seen that many software packages contain on-line help systems. These are limited but very real performance support systems, and they're integrated into the software itself. There's no reason why these help systems can't be expanded by adding computer-based training, on-line manuals, access to distant databases—whatever's needed for individuals to perform effectively regardless of their level of skill.

4. This suggests the last and, I think, most important point. Performance support systems will realize their true potential when they incorporate *embedded training* for the systems in which they're embedded. Let me sketch you a quick picture of how that might happen.

Your firm has just released a major revision to its integrated receipt processing–inventory–accounts payable system. Your training department provides a day of training to the individuals who use the system. This training describes the differences between the old system and the new, then covers the basic skills that all users must have.

When workers go back to their desks, the system is in place, complete with its resident performance support system. Whenever individuals access screens that are new with the revised system, the performance support system takes over and talks them through the screens. Workers who don't understand what to do can ask for more information. As the users become more proficient, the performance support system slides further into the background. At that point, individuals using the system simply do their jobs, perhaps forgetting that the performance support system is even there. If an unusually difficult situation arises, the performance support system may insert itself again—furnishing the information needed to deal with the situation.

This description is somewhat fanciful; virtually no performance support system can perform at this level yet. But we're getting closer. As the technology matures, and firms begin to incorporate it routinely into their systems, it will become both easier and less expensive to use. The time may come, and in not too many years, when this is simply the way that training is done on new and revised systems.

In the meantime, you have an organization to manage. You still want to get maximum performance improvement for minimum training investment. See that your training department or consultant becomes familiar with performance support systems, their capabilities and limitations. Then, when the analysis and design point toward such a system as a training solution, everyone is prepared for it. A good place to start learning is Gloria Gery's book, *Electronic Performance Support Systems.*

My final advice is this: start small. The best way to get a big performance support system is to develop several successful small ones and start combining them. This is another point at which the Total Quality approach of constant small performance improvements is right on target.

How to Use These Ideas

- Job aids are always the first training solution to evaluate. Unless something prevents it, get at least some of your work force trained to develop them. Then develop them.

- Use your training department or consultant to turn your home-grown job aids into professional ones and/or supplement them with other training if necessary. *Don't let your training provider sell you on anything else until you or they have tried to solve the problem with job aids first.*

- If you have to give training yourself, this is the chapter you've been waiting for. Use job aids. If you and your workgroup can create job aids to handle the whole training need, great. If not, create job aids to handle as much of it as possible. Then try to take care of the rest of it with on-the-job training. (The next chapter will show you how to do that.) Consider classroom training *only* if one or both of these methods won't solve the complete need.

13

Smart Just-in-Time Training: Structured OJT

What's the most common form of training in American business and industry? By a wide margin, it's on-the-job training (OJT). But it's not systematic, planned, *structured* OJT. Typical OJT is hit-or-miss, catch-as-catch-can training delivered by a less than highly motivated supervisor to a generally confused worker. That's a shame. Carefully designed and presented OJT is effective. When used in the right situations, it's not only as effective as any other method of training, it's also much less expensive.

Few companies, though, think out how training should be presented on the job. Fewer still train supervisors and senior workers to be effective trainers. As a result, OJT is inefficient and often an irritant for the trainer and trainee alike. It doesn't have to be that way. For a relatively small investment in planning and training, structured OJT produces significant performance improvements. And that's the definition of smart training.

Just what do we mean by "structured" OJT? Like most other effective training concepts, this one is basically simple. OJT is structured when it's planned and then delivered in accordance with that plan.

Let me give you three very different but effective examples of structured OJT. The first occurs in my own organization. All individuals hired into a major career field (such as contract administration, management information systems, or quality assurance) serve a 2- or 3-year "internship." Their training is based on a careful analysis of the competencies that workers in each field must have. Some of the training is formal classroom training. Most of it, though, is structured OJT. Supervisors are provided with a detailed outline of the topics to cover and the sequence in which they should be covered. Interns receive their "diploma" when a manager certifies not only that they have taken the formal training but that they have also completed the structured OJT.

At the other extreme is the 10- to 30-minute OJT a firm can use to familiarize workers with job aids. Some job aids can just be given to workers to use; the task they aid is simple enough that individuals can read the aid when they need it and perform the task. A job aid explaining how to request vacation time is normally this kind of aid. Other job aids are more complex; they work effectively, but they have to be explained to the individuals who will use them. For instance, a supervisor would want to spend time explaining the job aid for emergency situations to a worker—to ensure that the worker understands the critical procedures.

Most work situations fall between these two extremes. Workers receive some formal training, perhaps pursue some self-paced training, and pick up the remaining basics of the job on the job. Machinists, for instance, typically complete very formal apprenticeship programs (which rely heavily on structured OJT). When the new machinists arrive on the job, they'll get some additional formal training, but most of their instruction in the specifics of the job will come through OJT. That's also how they'll learn the shortcuts and tricks of the trade that are so important to any job.

In short, OJT exists in many forms. Whatever its form, it's essential to the learning process in any organization. It will always be done. A basic goal of smart training is to see that it's done well.

How Not to Do OJT

Before we look at how OJT is done effectively, we need to look at how it's done *ineffectively*. Few organizations have any form of systematic OJT. As a result, this is what usually happens.

First, there's seldom any plan or sequence for the training. Because of this, OJT is almost never scheduled. New workers get OJT only when they walk up to a supervisor or senior worker and ask for help. (Willie is revising a spreadsheet to make cost projections for the section when he runs into a formula he can't understand. He puzzles over it for a few minutes, then gets up and goes in search of someone to help him with it. "Oh, that!" Rosalind tells him. "We use that kind of formula all the time!") Right there, two people—the new worker and the worker who's been asked to help—have had their work sequence interrupted.

(For simplicity, I'm going to write as though the new worker asks another worker for help. That's usually what happens—but the worker may ask anyone in the workgroup, including the supervisor. I'll save a lot of "ors" and "ands" and thus make everything considerably more readable, though, if I just refer to the person on the spot as a worker. Just remember that it could as easily be a supervisor. The new worker will probably make the decision of whom to ask by seeing who's close, or friendly, or just available.)

So what happens when a new worker asks for help? The other worker often reacts to it as an interruption, because that person has his or her own work to do. And there's no guarantee that the interruption comes at a slack time. Quite the reverse; Murphy's Law virtually guarantees that the other worker will be right in the middle of a demanding and/or timebound task. (When Willie asked Rosalind about the spreadsheet formula, she was right in the middle of debugging a spreadsheet of her own. Since she can't find anyone else to help him, she'll deal with his problem—and then go back to her work complaining to herself about the 15 minutes she "lost.") To cap it all off, there's a good chance that the other worker isn't responsible for any OJT or that it's an added duty that takes the individual away from "real" work.

Most workers are conscientious and willing to help, so they either give the new worker the necessary training or try to find someone else who will. This raises its own problems, because these "trainers" get little if any training in how to train others. Supervisors are simply expected to see that new workers learn their jobs. No one really asks how this happens, or whether anyone is proficient at it, or how much time it takes. For all these reasons, the "training" is all but guaranteed to be brief and rushed.

(This part of the exchange between Willie and Rosalind is worth a paragraph. Rosalind had her own problem with this kind of spreadsheet formula when she was a new worker. The only person available for her to ask was Doug, who always liked to learn one way to do his work and stick with it. There were three or four different ways of developing the formula, and each way worked best in certain circumstances. Doug only learned one way, and that was what he taught Rosalind. Consequently, she often spends more time on a formula than she'd have to if she knew the alternatives. And that's the level of competence Willie learns.)

Since supervisors don't understand good training methods, there's virtually no follow-up to see whether the new worker has learned correctly. The supervisor assumes that if an individual isn't causing visible problems the training must have been effective.

It's not surprising that the new worker learns this way. After all, this is how the supervisor and the other workers learned to do their jobs. It just seems like the natural order of things. Experienced workers may well believe that new workers ought to show initiative and take responsibility for their own learning.

Even if somehow the new worker gets past all this and does learn how to do the job, there's yet another problem. No one, including the supervisor, knows whether any new worker has learned the *best* way to do the job. The supervisor isn't necessarily the most competent worker. If someone else provided the training, it may be because that individual was available—not because he or she was particularly good at the job. The new worker may have learned a relatively inefficient way to do the job. Since it gets done, no one notices, but the individual's competence gets pegged well below what it could be.

Smart training requires analysis, design, development, testing, delivery, and evaluation. The OJT I just described—typical OJT—has none of these. Since the average supervisor never passed Miracles 101, typical OJT doesn't work very well.

Many organizations respond to this situation by minimizing OJT and providing formal training in place of it. To a point, that's an effective strategy. After this point, it's not. The question, of course, is where that point is. Let's tackle that question now.

Why OJT Is Smart

When OJT is carefully done, it has several significant advantages. First of all, it's *inexpensive to deliver.* Both trainer and trainee are already on the payroll. The trainer is already expert at the job.

Furthermore, it's *convenient.* Neither the trainee nor the trainer has to leave the workplace. Because they don't have to go anywhere for the training, the lost time is minimal. Just as important, the interruption in the work is minimal too.

It's also *productive.* Trainees often perform their actual jobs while receiving training. This may not amount to much. On the other hand, over several weeks or months of OJT, it may amount to hundreds of hours. You can even add more hours—the hours that would have been taken up traveling to somewhere else for the training.

For all these reasons, OJT is *effective.* It's given right when the worker needs it, and it can be put to use immediately. In part, this is because the training can be planned to correspond to the work cycle. However, OJT by its very nature is flexible. Even though it's structured, supervisors can vary their schedule. They can give OJT sooner or later than planned so that trainees can use the new skills immediately.

The final advantage isn't a training advantage, but it's a very real gain for the organization. Done well, OJT *reinforces effective work relationships.* When supervisors willingly take time to present effective training, they communicate to new workers that the organization is concerned about them. They also reinforce helping rather than judgmental relationships between themselves and workers. If your firm got nothing more than that from the OJT, it would be way ahead of the game.

Let me pause right here to emphasize a critical point. You won't get any of these benefits—OJT won't work—*unless supervisors understand that OJT is an intrinsic part of their job.* That isn't the case in many organizations now. Supervisors and senior workers are responsible for getting out the work. If something goes wrong, the supervisor is expected to straighten out both the situation and the workers. Training, like counseling and coaching, is a luxury—to be indulged in when there's some spare time.

Never mind that untrained and undertrained workers produce neither the quality nor quantity of work that they should. That's not a problem *right now,* when today's production needs to be gotten out the door. Because workers lack proper training, they make more mistakes than they should. These mistakes take time to identify and correct. This builds more time pressure, which shortchanges training even further. And so it goes.

Unless you change this pattern, OJT won't work. Period. Firms use so much formal training because it gets the trainees away from their work. Once in the classroom, they can devote uninterrupted attention to the topic they need to learn. It works. It's also unnecessarily expensive and disruptive whenever OJT is a realistic alternative.

OJT has the potential to make your training far more effective, but only when supervisors understand that training is one of their core responsibilities. This isn't easy to accomplish. The time pressures described two paragraphs ago are very real. Supervisors are often called on the carpet for missed production, but seldom for missed training. You have to help them change a basic pattern. It can be done, and later in this chapter I'll give you some suggestions on how to do it.

When OJT Is Smart

On-the-job training works well in some circumstances and less well in others. Here are some basic guidelines for when it can work well:

1. *When the OJT is directly related to the work of the unit.* Put yourself in the shoes of the supervisor or senior worker who's supposed to be doing the training. You're taking time away from your own work, work that you're under constant pressure to produce. What are you getting in return? If the OJT you're providing will help the workgroup function more effectively, there's a clear payback from it.

Suppose that the OJT is partly or mostly developmental (as with the "intern" program previously described). Even worse, suppose the work unit only has the individual for training, and knows that he or she will move on when the training is done. In other words, a lot of training is expected for very little return. What do you do if you can't avoid this circumstance? The best answer is to pick trainers carefully. Some supervisors and senior workers get a real kick out of developing new workers, even when they won't stay in their units. This is especially true if the trainers have "plateaued" in their current jobs; they can get genuine satisfaction from acting as a mentor to a beginning worker.

What if you can't identify enough supervisors for whom training is satisfying in itself? Then at least make the supervisor's performance rating and promotion opportunities depend on how effectively he or she does the training. This means, of course, that someone will have to follow up so that you *know* how effective the training is.

I can give you a strong, definite suggestion on what *not* to expect an OJT trainer to do: spend time explaining administrative procedures that have little to do with the work of the unit. Unfortunately, this is one of the chores that often gets dumped on supervisors. They're expected to explain leave and holiday provisions, which are definitely related to the job. But they're often expected to explain how to apply for promotions, how to sign up for the bond program, what the benefits program is, and a host of other matters that they're neither expert in nor much concerned about. *Don't* assign them the task of explaining these matters. Cover it in a formal orientation for new workers or in self-paced courses and job aids.

2. *When the trainer is completely familiar with the OJT topics.* Now this may sound somewhat silly, but it isn't. For instance, you might ask the supervisor to do OJT in travel voucher processing. The supervisor's unit, though, may perform only the preliminary verification, or may deal only with a certain type of voucher. If that's the case, arrange for some of the OJT to be given by someone from another unit who knows the specific subject matter to be trained. OJT takes the trainer's time away from production; if he or she has to research the topic before giving it, more production is lost. Because of this conflict, the trainer will be sorely tempted to skimp on the research. Try to avoid putting the individual in that situation. Arrange for any OJT to be given by individuals who are clearly expert in the topic.

3. *When the OJT can be given in short modules.* If you want OJT to be smart training, trainers need to be trained in how to give OJT; we'll cover that a few paragraphs from now. Even after supervisors or senior workers have training in OJT, though, they don't become expert trainers. It's not realistic to expect a typical OJT trainer to hold a trainee's

attention for more than an hour. Trainees will also learn best if they have to absorb only a limited amount of training before using it on the job.

4. *When the trainee can* see *what he or she is supposed to learn.* This isn't absolute. Even so complex a topic as creativity could be presented through OJT—though not easily. In general, the more concrete the training is the more adapted it is to OJT. It's easier to use OJT to teach balancing the books than to teach the theory of double-entry bookkeeping, to teach setting a jig on a boring machine than to teach the properties of different types of steel.

There's an additional advantage of teaching visible skills in OJT. Expert performers tend to operate on automatic pilot; often they literally don't know what they're doing. When they explain what they do, they can easily leave out steps. When they *demonstrate* the skill, though, the steps are visible. The trainee can ask, "Wait a minute—why did you do that?" This makes the training both easier and more reliable.

5. *When OJT is given by genuine experts.* The individuals presenting the OJT should really know their stuff. I've already said that, but I mean it just slightly differently here. Not everyone who's done a job for 20 years does it the best way; there are significant differences in competence even among long-term workers. To the greatest extent possible, assign OJT trainers that both know and use the best procedures. You don't want your new workers learning how to be mediocre workers.

By the way, this suggests one of the times that you don't want to use OJT: If you're implementing major changes that are being resisted by your existing work force. Perhaps you're trying to achieve a higher level of productivity or quality, or quicker response to customer requirements. If your current work force is dragging their heels on these changes, *don't* let them train your new workers.

(One organization I know followed this advice with dramatic results. It brought in a group of college students to help with a peak work load. Instead of integrating the new workers into the existing work force, though, the organization formed them into separate units and trained them separately. The result was a continuing level of production almost 50 percent higher than that of the existing work force. It wasn't just that the college students were brighter or harder working, though they may have been both. They simply didn't learn the informal restrictions on production that the rest of the work force practiced.)

How to Do Smart OJT

How do you turn a charging rhinoceros? A little bit at a time. How do you implement structured OJT? The same little bit at a time. You begin by selecting a pilot group of supervisors (and senior workers, if appropriate) and introducing them to effective OJT. Here are the seven basic steps:

1. Identify a small group of supervisors and senior workers. You want individuals who'll not only give OJT but who'll give it frequently and take it seriously. You want individuals to give frequent OJT so that they'll use the OJT skills they learn. You want individuals to take it seriously so they'll take the time necessary to present the training. One effective way to get these individuals is to ask for volunteers and select the best of those who volunteer.

2. Make it clear up front that effective OJT is a priority for you, and that you intend it to be an *opportunity* for those in the pilot project. Some of the trainers will have difficulty learning OJT skills. *All* the trainers will make mistakes along the way. And you may find one or two who elect to drop out. All of that is overhead necessary to get the program off the ground.

3. Get your training department or a training consultant to work out a general "curriculum" for OJT in each supervisor's unit. A curriculum is simply a grouping of the different skills a new worker in the unit must learn. For instance, a new claims examiner might have to learn the claims process, logging in claims, identifying whether a claim is complete, entering claims into the system, etc., etc. Nothing fancy, and it doesn't have to be a time-consuming process. At the end, though, the supervisors and senior workers should possess a clear idea of (a) the skills a new worker needs to learn and (b) the best grouping and sequence in which to learn these skills.

4. Train the supervisors and senior workers to present effective OJT. The basic steps used to present it are simple, and I'll summarize them in a few paragraphs. The training should be built around an OJT manual that every trainer receives. The manual should be simple and straightforward, and trainers should be able to use it easily to help them deliver the training. In short, it should be an effective job aid.

5. Have someone available to work with and support each trainer. Be careful—you don't want this person peering over the trainer's shoulder to make sure everything is done just right. The ideal person for this job is another supervisor, one who's good at OJT. Clearly, when you're first starting the program you won't have a lot of these individuals available. Use someone supportive from your training office or elsewhere in the organization.

6. Don't simply delegate the program to your training department or some other specialist and forget it. Show that effective OJT is an impor-

tant item to you. Check with the individuals doing it every so often—and plan formal conferences with them to review results. If you're several organizational layers above them, still make it a point to meet with a trainer every so often. Managers tell their organizations what's important by how they spend their time.

7. This final point applies only if your organization is large and structured OJT is broadly used within it. In this circumstance, you'll probably want a permanent oversight committee to evaluate the program periodically and recommend changes. You may well have an established steering committee for training. If so, simply make them responsible for OJT. If not, create a small committee that has a few managers and have a representative from your training department be executive secretary. Once the program is on solid footing, the committee doesn't need to meet more than once or twice a year. Simple interim reports can keep everyone on the committee informed between meetings.

That's the essence of what you need to do to begin an effective structured OJT program. It isn't difficult or particularly time-consuming. If you approach it carefully, the individuals you want to be trainers will support it—particularly after they've used good OJT methods and seen the results in their organizations. Like any other new program, though, it requires continuing attention at first. Unlike many other programs, its benefits begin to show up fairly rapidly. You'll know the program is in place and working when the first supervisor stands up in front of a new OJT training class and tells them that structured OJT is the only way to go.

The Secret of Effective OJT

I don't pretend that in a few paragraphs I can teach you or anyone else to be an effective on-the-job trainer. For one thing, you learn from doing something, not from reading about it. For another, OJT is a significant task, one that can't be learned in a half-dozen easy steps. The core of effective OJT, however, can be summarized in a few, relatively simple points.

First, remember that the goal isn't for the worker to know something but to *be able to do something*. Like all smart training, the goal of OJT is improved performance. When you or I or anyone else presents OJT, we're tempted to share what we *know* with the trainee—perhaps at great length. For instance, as a new worker you may need to compute economic order quantities for supplies that are used regularly. That's something you *do*, and you do it by following certain very specific rules. If I get sidetracked into what I know about economic order quantities, I may tell you about the theory, or how the approach to them has changed in the company, or even other ways of computing them that we don't use but could. If I'm concentrating on performance, though, I'll focus on showing you what the rules are and when to apply them. I might also tell you a horror story or two about when they were set carelessly, to help you understand the importance of them. But I won't get into the theory or history of them if you don't need it to *do* them.

Don't forget job aids. If at all possible, prepare a job aid for the process and use the OJT to *explain how to use the job aid.* Because this is so effective a way to do OJT, always explore it first. If it can't be used, fine; present the OJT some other way. If the task can be summarized even partially in a job aid, though, use a job aid. It may even be that a series of job aids will work. Just don't overlook this opportunity.

Take the example of economic order quantities again. Suppose, because it's a relatively infrequent task, you do it manually. You certainly can develop a job aid that shows how to perform each step in the process. Perhaps you can use a simple worksheet that guides the new worker through the procedure. In the last chapter, we looked at how a job aid might be used to help supervisors do annual performance appraisals. The same job aid can be used as part of a new supervisor's OJT.

Remember that no one learns very much from listening to someone else describe how to do something. We learn best by *watching* it done and then *doing it ourselves.* The standard pattern for OJT that came out of "vestibule training" in World War II was Tell-Show-Do. *Tell* workers what to do, *show* them how to do it, have them *do* it. You can tell individuals what to do and then show them—but it's even more effective to tell them *while* you show them. Most effective of all, if they can see what you're doing, do it and ask them to describe what they see.[73]

Let's return to computing economic order quantities one more time. OJT might begin this way:

> TRAINER: This top block is where we begin. What do you put in that block?
>
> TRAINEE: It says I should put in the average amount used per month for the past 6 months.
>
> TRAINER: That's right. You get that information from this report. Why don't you look on it and find the average usage for the last 6 months for ballpoint pens.
>
> TRAINEE: Oh, yes, here it is. We average 216 a month.
>
> TRAINER: Good. Now what are you going to do with that figure? . . .

You get the idea. Involve trainees from the beginning. If they can see what you're doing, have them describe it as you do it. Then get them doing it as quickly as possible. (In the economic order quantity example, there's probably nothing to be gained from showing the trainee how to fill out the worksheet. You can simply let him or her fill it out, helping as necessary.)

Provide immediate feedback to trainees both when they're doing it right and when they're not. In general, it's better to do this when an error is made, rather than waiting until the complete task is done. Stop and ask the person to tell you what he or she just did. If you can help identify the problem by asking a question, do that. ("Do you remember when you review the individual's last merit increase?") If you can't use a question, point out *gently* what should have happened. Then have the person repeat the step. At this point, you can decide whether to have the worker continue from that point or go back to the beginning and go through the complete process.

There are two key points in the preceding paragraph. First, stop and have the individual do the step right immediately. Second, do this in a completely noncritical way.

Those are the essentials of effective OJT. Practiced regularly, they'll increase the effectiveness of any OJT trainer. Don't even think of stopping with just this much, though. If you implement the structured OJT plan I've given, including an effective job aid for the trainers, you'll reap far greater benefits.

How great are these benefits? Recently, a major American corporation did an analysis of its training costs. The conclusion: 17 percent of the costs was for formal training—while *83 percent* was for informal, unstructured, and often ineffective OJT. To see what this means, take your organization's total identified training costs and multiply them by 4.9. That's what you spend for largely ineffective OJT.

Compared to other programs, establishing job aids and structured OJT throughout your firm is relatively easy. It's very difficult to measure the return on that effort directly. However, it will affect supervisory and worker morale, productivity, quality, and the time it takes a new worker to begin performing effectively. And, done properly, it will permit you to reduce your formal training costs or provide additional formal training for the same amount.

What are you waiting for?

How to Use These Ideas

- You already know what I need to say here. Use structured OJT wherever you can. If you have supervisors working for you, see that they're trained in OJT. Then let them use the training.

- Your training department can be a material help. They can help you plan the OJT and then train your supervisors in how to do it. They can also help evaluate the effectiveness of the OJT program.

- An external training source can be almost as much help to you, if that's all you have. They may or may not be able to help you plan the OJT—but they can provide OJT training for your supervisors. Several firms specialize in just this kind of training.

- If you have to give training yourself, this is the other half of your solution. Learn how to do OJT, then do it—by itself or (preferably) using job aids. Concentrate your training energies here and go for other training only if these clearly won't satisfy your needs.

14

Other Smart Ways to Train

The last three chapters have spanned quite a range of training. We began in Chapter 11 with the most popular technology-based methods: videotape, computer-based training, and multimedia. From those high-tech heights, we dropped to the low-tech but high-efficiency world of job aids (Chapter 12) and structured on-the-job training (Chapter 13).

As useful as those methods are, they only scratch the surface of what's usable for smart training. Nor will this chapter cover all the other alternatives. Instead, it will touch on a half-dozen of the major options for training that any firm, large or small, should consider. Quite possibly you use one or several of them already. It's unlikely that you'd use them all at any one time, but you should never write off any of them.

The greatest virtue of most of the methods described in this chapter is their *flexibility*. You can use them for primary training, to complement your in-house efforts, or to deal with the peaks and valleys of training demand. A firm that's effective at training uses a wide variety of methods, not just one or two, because the training situations it faces are varied. This chapter can help you achieve that variety.

A final word before we dig in. Nowhere in this chapter or any other do I describe instructor-led classroom training as a separate topic. That's not because it isn't important. It is, and it's an essential component of many effective training programs. However, you're already familiar with it. When you get canned training or a course put on by a consultant, you probably assume that it will be a classroom course. You've had enough classroom training yourself to have your own judgments of its good and bad points; I don't need to repeat the obvious to you.

So much for prologue. Now to the meat of the chapter.

Let's "Train the Trainer"

Suppose you want to familiarize everyone in your organization with some new program—say a new customer-focused initiative. You could mail a videotape to each location or develop a CBT course to get the idea across. Either of these might work, but they both take considerable time to develop. Instead, you might develop a short instructor-led course and train one or a few individuals from every location to present the course. Without adding extra staff or paying outside sources, the training gets presented promptly and effectively throughout the organization.

Welcome to a training technique often called "train the trainer." Typically, the training department (or consultant) gives training to those for whom it was developed. In this approach, though, the training department trains workers as trainers—and they, in turn, give the training. Instead of training workers, then, the training department trains trainers. Hence the name.

Firms can use the technique in a variety of ways. The trainers may be trained to deliver one specific instance of training, as in the example just mentioned. Or they may present one or a few courses several times. But the trainers remain in their primary jobs, providing training as an additional duty. As you might guess, the train the trainer technique can be extremely efficient and effective.

Before we look at the situations where this technique works, though, we need to look at its major limitations. First, because these individuals aren't full-time trainers, they don't reach the level of proficiency of professional instructors. In addition, because they don't use their training skills continually, these skills can become rusty. For these two reasons, the courses they deliver can't use sophisticated training methods; they must stick to basics.

Few organizations have the quality control of training they need. With occasional instructors, the problem is even worse. Because they teach infrequently and often in dispersed locations, observing them is difficult. It's very hard to know just how competent these instructors are or where they might be improved. For most of them (though certainly not all), the competence they possess at the end of their own training is the maximum they reach.

Also, you don't always get individuals with the motivation and expertise necessary to perform effectively as trainers. When you're hiring professional trainers, you can be selective. When you're taking individuals from their jobs, though, you can't always be as choosy. You often have to settle for trainers who will do an adequate job, but no better. This compounds both of the problems in the two preceding paragraphs.

Having said that, there are situations in which the train the trainer approach produces excellent results. We've already looked at one—when instructor-led training must be presented rapidly and broadly. Here are a few other situations in which the approach normally works well.

1. Many firms must provide highly technical training to a relatively small number of workers. The training may also be sporadic: once this year, three times next year, not at all the following year. Training one or two subject-matter experts to present the training when and where it's needed is often the best possible solution. You lose some instructor proficiency, but this is balanced by instruction given by trainers who are completely up to date.

2. Experienced specialists and technicians can provide a reservoir of instructors for times of peak demand. If your organization is large, you have individuals scattered through it who have some teaching/training experience or would like to have some. A central training department can ensure that they develop and maintain the basic training skills. Then they can be used to lead courses when demand is too great for the permanent instructor cadre. This is far less expensive than hiring and training new instructors, and it lets you get new training fielded much more quickly.

3. Certain individuals are clear experts at certain parts of their jobs. Manuel is a supervisor who's superb in his role as a coach and counselor. Eleanor really understands how inventory is managed throughout the system. John can create expert systems more rapidly than anyone else in the programming branch. With a minimum of training in how to train, the individuals can take over portions of larger courses. Manuel might take one day of a two-week-long supervisory course, John takes one day of a week-long course in expert systems, and Eleanor takes one week of the two-week inventory management course.

Besides the efficiency and effectiveness I've mentioned, there are two other advantages to this approach. First, it gives individuals the opportunity to do something different, challenging, and worthwhile. Particularly for those who've "seen and done everything" in their jobs, training others can be a welcome break. They can bring a freshness and motivation to their training that professional instructors may lose.

They can bring freshness in another way. Many fields are both highly technical and constantly changing. Picture the job, for instance, of a personal computer repairperson in a retail computer store. Two or three major new styles of computer are introduced each year—not to mention the new and improved printers, disk drives, and other elements of computer systems. Even the best full-time instructor will have problems keeping up with these changes. If the training is given or supplemented by a working technician, though, it will be completely up to date.

From Worker to Trainer to Worker

Trainers who are workers are more up to date. They also have much greater credibility with those they train. After all, they've been there and they know how it really is. This brings up a point that's broader than the train the trainer approach.

A permanent training group has one of two choices when recruiting new trainers. It can hire experienced trainers and train them in the subject they're going to teach. Or it can hire experienced individuals from that career field (true "subject matter experts") and teach them to become trainers. Most groups, my own included, choose the latter. We select individuals with solid experience in their subject, train them to be trainers, and send them to deliver training throughout the country. We expect that most of them will remain with us 2 to 4 years, then return to their career field. In those 2 to 4 years, we get effective instructors and they get career-enhancing experience.

This principle is practiced by many firms in technical fields. If you have a permanent cadre of individuals training supply clerks, machinists, inventory managers, or computer programmers, you probably draw them from your technical work force. But what about your supervisory and managerial training? I think that being a supervisor or manager demands complex, high-level skills. Yet where do most firms get their instructors for these courses? Normally, from anywhere but the ranks of supervisors and managers.

Let me tell you a quick and painfully true story. Over a decade ago, I attended a course in management by objectives. Almost everyone in the course was a manager, and many of us were senior managers. The two instructors between them had zero experience in managing. Before an hour of the course was over, they had completely lost credibility. The course continued for another 4 hours and 7 days. Everyone attended, and several individuals entertained themselves and the class by challenging the instructors. But no meaningful learning occurred. The class knew beyond a shadow of a doubt that neither instructor knew how it really was as a manager. So, they ignored the instructors and what they had to say.

How many times do you think this situation repeats itself every day in American business and industry? Instructors with no experience in the field try to tell experienced supervisors and managers what they should do. I'm willing to bet it's happened to you at least once. I hope no more than that.

Take a lesson from this. The best possible alternative is to recruit your management instructors from your managers. If you don't want to make them permanent instructors, use the train the trainer approach. But see that the guts of your supervisory and managerial courses are taught, at least in part, by individuals who've been in the trenches and know how it really is. The trainees will listen to them.

"But," you say, "we don't want to train our supervisors and managers just to do it the way it's being done. We want to train them in new methods and new ideas." I understand. If you try to do this by using staff specialists who've never been managers, you'll hold the courses—but you won't really train anyone. Instead, find one or two managers who do what you want done. It may not be practical for them to teach the full course (though it may), but at least let them serve as models for the skills you want to train.

(What if *none* of your managers have the skills you want to train? Select one or two who will be most receptive and send them to the best possible training you can find. Then use them as subject-matter specialists when you design training for other managers.)

The Virtues (and Vices) of Canned Courses

I'm sure you've noticed: There are dozens of companies out there who want to sell you prepackaged, standardized training. In an average week, I will get flyers for training in subjects as diverse as key management skills, personal computer repair, executive skills for secretaries, team building (currently very hot), and how to prepare a budget. For a price ranging from $75 per day up, there's a company somewhere that will teach all attendees almost any subject you can imagine.

What about these courses? Should your firm use them? If so, how? My first caution is this: Be very skeptical of what the courses promise. I received a flyer just before I began this chapter, one that touted a basic course for supervisors. The flyer promised that supervisors who completed this *one-day course* would be better equipped to bridge age gaps and differing backgrounds/lifestyles; deal with different personality types and understand individual needs; redirect problem employees; keep high achievers performing at peak levels; promote employee loyalty and commitment; and accomplish a number of other worthwhile goals. And all for $95!

Do you think it achieved its objectives? Of course it did, because all it promised was that each attendee would be "better equipped" to handle each of these situations. How could you ever prove someone wasn't "better equipped"—whatever that means?

I mention this to introduce an important point about canned training. Because they must appeal to a wide audience, many canned courses promise far, far more than they can deliver. While some of the courses that promise the moon may be good, I'd avoid them like the plague. Watch for the courses that state clear, limited objectives—objectives related to improving performance in *your* organization. Forget the other courses, no matter how sexy and interesting and fashionable they sound.

Let me make a distinction, by the way, between what I'm calling "canned" courses and the prepackaged courses offered by experts in the field. Many, many consulting firms offer training in their specialty: EPA regulations, structured programming techniques, team development, and so on. They may offer only a set course or two, or they may be willing to customize training somewhat for your firm. This is part of the training we'll cover in the next section. By canned training, I mean training offered by firms whose mission in life is to offer training itself. Normally they offer general, administrative, and supervisory training—though they're often willing to move into any field that is currently popular. Their instructors are usually employees or subcontractors and may lack any real expertise in the field(s) they teach. That doesn't make the courses poor courses. It is a limitation—one you need to keep clearly in mind.

When you find courses that appear to have realistic, relevant objectives, send someone to the course. Not a whole group, just one individual. Find out from that person how well the course met its objectives. If it delivered what it promised, you can send other employees with a clear conscience.

Now that we've narrowed down the courses to consider, when do you use them? Let me begin by emphasizing when you *don't* use them.

Never depend on a canned course as the sole source of skills in any area where it's important that your performance is better than that of your competitors.

Let me give you a quick example. One staple of canned courses is the range of courses on dealing with customers, from telephone courtesy to improving service-call effectiveness. Every one of these courses is available to any firm that wants it. If you depend on customer service for competitive advantage, its suicidal to rely solely on canned courses for training. That guarantees that every competitor of yours who sends workers to the course will know *at least* as much about customer service as you do.

The same is true for any area in which you need to excel. Canned courses are a way of making knowledge available quickly to a broad range of companies. You can profit from that; I'll suggest several ways to do so beginning in the next paragraph. But you don't dare depend on canned courses to provide your firm with important competitive skills.

When do you use the courses? Here are my suggestions:

1. Use canned training for basic, generic skills—as long as the training can be given when it's needed. For instance, almost any city of any size has at least one vendor offering training on personal computers and different software packages. If you're large enough, you may want to develop your own training in-house. Otherwise, use the vendor to provide most personal computer and software training. This same principle holds for a wide variety of basic training, from telephone courtesy to customer service to the role of a supervisor. (Yes, I did include customer service. There's nothing wrong with using a canned course to provide the *basics* in this or any other field. The key is to provide additional training of your own.)

2. Use canned training as a stopgap while you're developing in-house training on the topic. Many vendors have very efficient systems for developing courses; they can put together and field a canned course much more rapidly than the average training department or training consultant will. The course will likely be lower quality than you'd want any training you developed to be, but that's the trade-off for speed. For instance, while you're getting together a course in self-managing teams for managers, you might well send a group of them to a commercial course on the topic. They'll have covered the basics—which means that you can concentrate on the parts of the topic that are most important to your firm.

3. Use canned training to fill out your in-house training. Let's take team building again as an example. You need to train your managers and workers in your firm's approach to teams, how and when they'll be used and what you expect from them. But you don't need to develop a course in basic team skills. That's generic. Somewhere out

there are vendors who can provide you with this course just when your people need it. Use them.

You can probably think of more uses; just make sure to keep your hot air detector on high when you evaluate the claims that vendors make. When you do find a useful course, and enough employees need the training to fill the course, have the vendor bring it on-site. You'll get a lower rate, and sometimes a vendor will tailor the course at least slightly for you. (If you don't have enough employees of your own, you can sometimes go in with another firm to fill a class.)

Now to my final suggestion in this section. I'm sure you've heard that the way to maximize training such as canned training is to send an individual and then have that person train others. It's a good idea, and it works occasionally—but I have never seen it work regularly. I'd recommend a different tack. Wherever possible, select courses that provide effective job aids to attendees. Then the attendee can use the job aids to train others in a minimum amount of time. One word of caution, though. You'll find that most of these job aids are copyrighted. If they're effective, get permission to copy them *before* you do so—even if you have to pay. Remember that no form of training is more efficient or effective than job aids and OJT.

I'd go one step further. If you contract for training, from either a commercial vendor or a training consultant, insist that they furnish the most effective job aids possible to the attendees. You'll be doing them, yourself, and your people a favor.

How to Use Consultants and Customized Training

If your people need classroom training, you can develop it yourself or use canned training. But there's another alternative. There are thousands of consultants in the world, and many of them are very competent at designing and delivering training. Some of them focus on relatively canned courses. Others prefer to develop and give more customized training. But almost any of them will be willing to tailor training to your own requirements.

There are at least five situations when it makes sense to contract with a consultant to provide training for you:

1. When you're a *small organization* with no training department of your own. It costs money to develop and maintain an effective training department. When the department does effective up-front analysis and then designs and delivers smart training, it earns its keep many

times over. (That's one of the core messages of this book.) But if you're small you can't afford a large training department, no matter how effective it is. Even if you're part of a larger organization, the corporate training department may not be able to support some of your training needs. In either situation, working with a consultant to provide you with the training you need is smart. If you're too small to support the training by yourself, you may want to join with another firm or two to create a base large enough to make the training economical.

2. To provide your firm with *specialized training*. Many consultants specialize in specific areas: OSHA regulations, materials handling, computer connectivity. If you need specialized training for which canned courses aren't a solution, look to customized training from a qualified consultant. When the training need is broad enough you can even combine in-house, customized, and canned training effectively. Develop the material that's specific to you in-house, get the truly generic material from canned courses, and use a consultant to provide the rest. For instance, a firm moving toward Total Quality could effectively develop basic training on its philosophy and overall approach, supplement it with canned courses for workers in team and problem-solving skills, and use a consultant to deliver the technical quality control skills.

3. To help meet *peak demands*. We've dealt with this issue before; the train the trainer approach is one way of dealing with short-term heavy work loads. A good consultant is another way. If you build up a continuing relationship with one or more of these individuals, they can often step in and help deliver training.

4. To handle training in *other geographic areas*. This one is iffy, and won't always work—but it can be a money saver. If you have operations in other areas that need training, hiring a consultant in that area may be less expensive than sending your own trainers to present the training.

5. The final situation is a broad one: Use a consultant whenever it *makes more sense than developing training in that topic in house*. In the last chapter, we discussed how efficient and effective structured on-the-job training is. Your training department can train supervisors in how to do OJT. On the other hand, you can hire a consultant who's been doing just that for several years. Either alternative will work. Which one you choose depends on your overall training strategy.

When I mention how a training consultant can provide training, do you automatically think of a training *course*? You shouldn't. A training consultant worth using has a full range of training methods available. He or she may not be able to do CBT or create a performance support system; many consultants don't have the expertise required for this. But any consultant should be able to provide formal training, paper-based self-paced training, job aids, and training in OJT. Before you make any long-term commitments to a consultant, make sure that this is the case. If he or she does only one or two forms of training, those are the kinds of training you'll get—whether they're smart or not.

That brings me to my final point about training consultants. Many of them are ex-trainers, with little experience in up-front analysis or design. Individuals like this are fine to develop a course after your training department has done a proper analysis and design. If you don't have a training department, or it's weak at analysis and design, a consultant without these skills will be of little help to you. Find one who is strong in analysis and design. At the risk of terrible repetition, good analysis and design are the two most critical elements in smart training.

Use Your Local Colleges and Universities

No matter how small the town in which your firm is located, there's probably a junior college no more than half an hour away. If you're in a city, there are probably one or more junior colleges and at least one university. These can be a tremendous resource for you.

You know by now that I often put a word of caution near the beginning of a discussion, and this time is no exception. The fact that a course is offered by a junior college or university guarantees neither that it's good nor that it's relevant. Many colleges (of both kinds) have yet to discover that the purpose of training is improved *performance*. And some of them slant their courses toward what's fashionable whether their staff is properly equipped to teach it or not.

So don't think of college training as a panacea. You need to focus just as intently on performance when you deal with a junior college or university as with anyone else. If you keep this performance focus and insist that the institution respect it, however, you can reap significant dividends. Here are the most likely ways in which they can help.

- A junior college is often the best source you can find for *technical training*. Many junior colleges began as technical institutes, and almost all of them offer 1- and 2-year technical courses. If your workers must be trained or updated in electronics, accounting practices, computer operation, or a similar topic, a junior college may be just the ticket.

- Junior colleges (and some universities) are also excellent sources for training in *literacy and numeracy*. Because of the impact of mid-literacy on colleges in general and on junior colleges in particular, they've had to start finding ways to deal with it. In many instance (as we've seen) combining basic training in literacy and numeracy with skills training is a highly synergistic and effective approach. The Institute for the Study of Adult Literacy at Pennsylvania State University, for instance, has developed a number of programs for developing both literacy and technical skills.[74]

- Many junior colleges and universities offer *supervisory and managerial development* sequences. These won't equip your managers with many of the specific skills they need in your firm. However, they can provide them with important general skills, like delegation, coaching, and work scheduling. No matter how impressive the sequence sounds, though, see that it focuses on getting and using *skills*, not just on pumping knowledge into the students.

- You can also use the staff of a junior college or university as *consultants*. You may select a single individual or use most of a department. Many institutions can and will develop and deliver training that's tailored to the needs of specific firms—if there's sufficient demand.

There are more ways that you can use junior colleges and universities, but these ideas may help you get started.

How Well Does Teletraining Train?

Teletraining is an idea whose time may or may not have come. Transmitting instruction by TV is a useful idea. Many educational TV stations carry televised courses. A number of private firms and federal agencies use televised courses transmitted by satellite in this country. Abroad, such organizations as the Japan University of the Air and the Japan Management Association sponsor teletraining.

Teletraining can be developed in-house or by a local junior college or university. It's capable of reaching individuals or small groups in isolated locations. Televised training can also spread new training quickly through the company—for instance, to provide sales personnel basic information on a new product line. It can let executives and senior managers speak directly to learners. And while a "downlink" for satellite training is expensive, the cost can be amortized over a number of years.

Stop and think for a moment, though. Without some specific provision for interactivity, there's no difference between a televised course and a course delivered via videotape. Actually, there is a difference: An individual can take a videotape-based course when it's convenient rather than when it's broadcast. And this is the critical point. Unless specific steps are taken to make the teletraining *interactive*, it's just a more expensive way to do what videotapes do.

Interactive training is always more expensive than "sit and listen" training. Instructor-led classroom training takes less time and money to develop than any other method precisely because the interactivity is handled by a human being on the spot. Just as soon as you add interactivity to any technology-based training, though, development time and costs rise. And the more interactivity you add, the greater the costs.

Teletraining can be done interactively—but not easily. The simplest way is probably a phone link connecting the trainer with each training site. Other, more sophisticated ways can also be used; needless to say, they also cost more.

This may give you the idea that I don't value teletraining highly. That's basically correct. I believe that most of the time there are alternative ways of delivering training that are just as effective but less expensive. How true this is, though, depends in part on whether the hardware needed to produce and propagate teletraining is in place. If your firm already has a video studio and access to downlinks, the actual cost of specific training is relatively low. If it lacks either, the initial investment is quite high. And while it's easy to concentrate on the hardware, the time and cost required to develop competent video production is probably the more significant factor.

I'll leave this one up to you. Just remember that teletraining only differs from training on videotape when it allows trainees to take an active part in the training. Unless the teletraining provides this interaction, videotape will accomplish the same purpose much more cheaply.

Don't Build a Schoolhouse

This last section isn't about a training method. Instead, it's about a training *orientation*—one I think you should avoid.

This is particularly relevant for large or growing firms, especially those that operate in several locations. When a firm's training operation gets to a certain size, the urge strikes to build a central training facility and conduct the firm's training there. The idea sounds attractive and it fits the model we have from school and college. It may be worthwhile—but I'd suggest you think seriously about it before you commit yourself to it.

Recently a friend was telling me of a particular organization's prowess at teletraining. You already know my reservations about teletraining, but this did sound a cut above the ordinary. I wasn't as impressed with it as he was, though, for a simple reason. This organization operates a large centralized training facility. Its students come to it, not vice versa. For this firm, teletraining is a way to bring training to its students without having to leave the schoolhouse.

There are several reasons to question this strategy. First, training concentrated in a central location tends strongly to be classroom training. Teletraining is an extension of this. As we've seen, classroom training often isn't the best training method. Once an organization commits itself to a centralized facility, however, it almost invariably begins to think of training as something led by an instructor in a classroom. After all, if you've got a bright, shiny training facility, you want to keep it full. That's a great full-employment program for instructors, but a questionable strategy for improving corporate performance.

This leads to the second, closely related point. A large facility concentrates attention on the *training* itself, not on performance improvement. It becomes all too easy to focus on "number of hours given," "number of students trained," and the like. As we've seen, these are all cost figures; they don't tell you a word about whether performance improved. To a certain extent, you can't escape this approach—but you don't have to emphasize it. Having all those dollars sunk in a training facility tends to create just this emphasis.

Finally, it becomes equally easy to think of the head of your training (or human resources development) department as the "dean" of the school. This leads the organization to identify training with what it produces in-house. The firm should be looking at training as a way of improving performance that can be procured from a variety of sources. Instead, it begins to see it as what the instructors in the schoolhouse produce. After all, you want to keep the dean and the instructors busy.

What's the alternative? I've tried to avoid holding my group up as an example, but at this point I'm willing to. We have over 50 instructors, but only about 6 classrooms. The training we present in those classrooms, augmented by CBT, self-paced study, and job aids, is all for one organization located in the immediate area. Only 15 instructors work there. The others present their training across the country—*where their students are*. This is immensely cost-effective. We conservatively estimate that if someone were to provide the same training to our students in a central location, with no cost but the travel expenses of the students, it would cost more than *$2 million* more per year than the total cost to hire and train our instructors and keep them on the road.

While we don't completely escape the classroom-oriented mentality, we at least have a minimum commitment to keeping a building filled. We even conduct most of our management development in classrooms leased from a local university and staffed by instructors drawn in part from there. This makes it easier to concentrate on improving performance—our real job.

There are various reasons why you may want a central facility. Perhaps you should have one. I'd strongly suggest, though, that you do the following. List each reason why you believe the facility would be helpful. Then list the alternatives available for meeting that need. Build the facility *only* if the economic and other benefits clearly outweigh the organizational costs of maintaining and institutionalizing a classroom facility.

By the way, avoiding the schoolhouse approach doesn't mean you can't organize corporate training on the university model. Most states use some form of a university model to systematize and streamline higher education and avoid unnecessary duplication. IBM and Motorola both systematized and streamlined their training. Though IBM didn't call it that, they both used the university model.

Remember, at the same time that IBM was systematizing its training it was creating more and more self-paced training to replace classroom training. It combined centralized administration with decentralized delivery. A university is a *philosophy*, not a building. A firm makes smarter training decisions when it keeps this distinction clear.

How to Use These Ideas

- This is short and to the point—and it applies no matter how you get your training. First, always look at the full spectrum of delivery methods. Second, pick the delivery method that best fits both the specific training need *and* your overall strategy. The Quick Guide to Media and Methods, which follows Chapter 16, summarizes the material in the last four chapters. The guide will help you focus quickly on the methods and media most likely to work for each specific training situation.

PART 4

How Smart Training Fits into a Learning Organization

We're nearing the end of our search for truly smart training. We've examined broad strategic considerations like core competence. Then we looked at the nitty-gritty of selecting a delivery system. What could be left? Not a lot, in terms of length—but a great deal in terms of importance.

The last two chapters examine the learning organization and its relationship to smart training. Chapter 15 considers how learning organizations learn, and the kind of training that these organizations require. It also talks about the "acceptable learning risk" that learning organizations must take in order to learn.

Chapter 16 explores three themes. First, it explains why firms must use smart training to become learning organizations. Then it describes the difference between tactical and strategic learning. Finally, it ends the exploration with a look at the dilemmas that core competence and mastery create for learning organization. That's not really the end, because the last words of the chapter are three suggestions on practical steps you can take immediately to move toward a learning organization.

15

How a Learning Organization Learns

The Missions of a Training Department

In many organizations the training (or human resources development) department sees that operating managers get the training they request, develops courses, and generally oversees the training delivery effort. This is true whether the operation is one trainer or a nationwide department headed by a vice president. Let me suggest right up front that if it's what your training department and its leader are doing, you won't be able to become a learning organization, because the department is concentrating on the mission that's *least* important to your firm. If you want to become a learning organization, it has to change.

What should your training department, large or small, be doing? An effective department performs five very different functions:

1. It helps the firm develop and keep updated an appropriate training strategy.

2. It identifies the specific training that will be required to meet this strategy.

3. It identifies the specific performance needs that can be met by tactical training.

4. It ensures that the training developed will meet both the strategic and the tactical needs.

5. It sees that the necessary training is delivered.

While these are separate functions, they can be grouped into three basic missions: (1) strategy support, (2) analysis and design, and (3) development and delivery. It's critical that the first mission be performed by every training department. It isn't as critical that the second be performed in-house, but it's normally preferable. The third mission is by far the least important to perform in-house—though many firms prefer to do so. Let's look more closely at what all this means.

The Strategic Mission

Training is smart only when it's strategic—when it helps create and maintain the core competence of the firm. It cannot be separated from the overall goals and strategy of the firm.

The first job of the manager responsible for training is to see that the entire training operation is aligned with the firm's overall strategy. This means looking anywhere from 2 to 10 or 20 years downstream, anticipating the performance needs that will be created, and identifying the training resources that will be required to meet these needs.

In *America's Choice: High Skills or Low Wages!*, the National Center on Education and the Economy presents an interesting dilemma. On one hand, most companies believe they will be able to hire the individuals with the skills they need. On the other hand, fewer and fewer individuals are available with the skills needed to staff and run operations with highly empowered workers. No firm considering a strong move toward such methods as self-managed teams can wait until the schools find an answer to the dilemma. Instead, it must begin planning *now* the training and development sequences its workers must have to succeed in the last decade of the twentieth century.

Firms that develop, update, and use a training strategy reap a number of benefits. They concentrate their training efforts; as a result, they get the greatest bang for their total training buck. They don't get caught by surprise when the types of workers they've been hiring come into short supply. And they increase the odds that the training actually delivered will be the training needed.

There's one more advantage, one that was mentioned in Chapter 11 but bears repeating here. Training, like management in general, is subject to fashions and fads. And, like management fashions and fads, the ones in training are often disruptive and wasteful. For instance, many firms have decided to produce or contract for computer-based training and CBT/multimedia because these methods are highly publicized. In the overwhelming majority of cases, what they get for their efforts is a computer-based self-paced course considerably more expensive but no more effective than a paper-based course would have been. They've jumped on the bandwagon—with no clear idea of why they should be in that particular parade.

A firm that has a clear strategy can avoid far more easily this kind of mistake. It has a standard against which to evaluate any and all training technologies. Not only does it avoid wasting money on unnecessary technology, but it can identify potentially useful technology much more rapidly than can a firm without a strategy.

The first mission of a training department is to help develop *and regularly update* this strategy and to see that the training operation functions consistently within the strategy.

The Analysis and Design Mission

The bridge between the overall strategic mission and the delivery of smart training is competence in analysis and design. The training operation should be able to both identify how to implement the firm's training strategy *and* help managers find ways to improve their day-to-day operations with effective training. These involve the same basic skills (analysis and design), but apply them in very different ways.

Think back to the Petaluma Coast Guard Station. Before it began to stress analysis and design, it had concentrated on course development and delivery. After the Coast Guard Station adopted a systematic approach to training that emphasized both analysis and design, training hours went down, staff costs went down—but the impact on performance went up. IBM pursued the same strategy on a far broader scale during the 1980s to increase the effectiveness of its training at the same time that it reduced total training costs.

Traditional training organizations concentrate on development and delivery, but this is precisely the wrong place to put the emphasis. The needs analysis and training design mission are where their effort must be focused. That shouldn't be surprising, since we're finding that the same thing is true for most other endeavors—from building cars to writing computer software.

The Development and Delivery Mission

Many training organizations concentrate on the development and delivery mission—yet of the three missions we're looking at it's by far the one that can most easily be contracted out. I'm not recommending that you contract your training. I am strongly recommending that you not give development and delivery priority over analysis and design.

When I first took over the group I now head, it had just over 90 individuals in it. Because I believe what I've said in the last few paragraphs, I wanted to reduce the size of the group. Twenty-five seemed like a good number to me. Three years later, with this goal in mind, the group had *grown to 135*. This year, we will top 150. In one way, that's good; people like our work enough that they want us to do the development and delivery. (This may be a little more remarkable than it sounds; remember that we charge even our internal customers for our services.) The growth has posed the traditional problems, though: Under the day-to-day pressures of development and delivery, we've tended to slight analysis and design. We're currently reorganizing specifically to restore the balance we need.

There's another, even more compelling reason for a training department to concentrate on analysis and design. If it concentrates on development and delivery, its staff thinks of that as their job. They automatically assume that training means what they develop in-house. So, one job of the training organization becomes that of protecting its staffing and its turf.

Putting the people who do the analysis and design in the same immediate organization with those who develop and deliver the training encourages this inward-looking approach. If the two groups are organizationally separate, designers have more freedom to recommend a broad range of training sources. This will be far more economical and effective in the long run than simply assuming that training will be done in-house.

If your training organization expects to find outside sources for some of its regular training needs, your firm gets an additional benefit. When times get tight, training is one of the first functions cut. It shouldn't be that way, but all too often it is. If you have a large training operation that does all the training, the cutting gets bloody fast. If you use "train the trainer" techniques, contract some of the training out, and even use canned training, it's far easier to cut. You simply don't purchase training from external sources for a while. You keep your internal staff and you keep it busy—but your overall costs drop.

If your training department understands and prioritizes its basic missions, it can help you create a learning organization. Now we need to take our first look at what a learning organization really is and the part that smart training plays in it.

What an Organization Needs to Learn

Two of the strongest emphases in management thought in the early 1990s are the learning organization and shortened cycle time. This is no coincidence; the two go together. The shorter a firm's product (or service) cycle and the greater the experimentation it tolerates, the more individual workers and the firm as a whole can learn in a given period of time. Since the goal of smart training is the greatest performance gain in the shortest time for the smallest outlay of resources, nothing accomplishes the goals of smart training better than an effective learning organization.

Such a learning organization is, above all else, one that learns effectively as part of everyday work. This is how economist Michael Rothschild put it in a recent book:

> Only after the reality of the learning curve is accepted do the two paramount principles of economic competition become obvious. First, gaining an efficiency advantage by accumulating experience faster than competitors is the key to any organization's long-term growth and survival. Therefore, if a firm can somehow accelerate its own experience growth and/or slow down its competitors' experience accumulation, its competitive position will improve. Also, when a firm is very far behind in experience accumulation, it can catch up only by obtaining the proprietary technology of a leading company.[75]

Gary Hamel and C. K. Prahalad are major proponents of the importance of core competence to a firm. They also understand how important it is for firms (like individuals) to learn by doing. Writing in the *Harvard Business Review*, they put it this way:

> Staking out uncharted territory is a process of successive approximations. Think about an archer shooting arrows into the mist. The arrow flies at a distant and indistinct target, and a shout comes back, "right of the target" or "a bit to the left." More arrows are loosed and more advice comes back until the cry is "bull's-eye!" What counts most is not being right the first time but the pace at which the arrows fly. How fast can a company gather insights into the particular configurations of features, price, and performance that will unlock the market, and how quickly can it recalibrate its product offering? Little is learned in the laboratory or in product-development committee meetings. True learning begins only when a product—imperfect as it may be—is launched.[76]

Hamel and Prahalad cite a number of firms that are particularly good at getting products out, learning from them, revising them, getting them out, learning from them, and so on. Unfortunately, most of the firms they cite are Japanese.

Finally, Rosabeth Moss Kanter, currently the editor of the *Harvard Business Review*, had this to say about organizational change and experimentation:

Encourage incremental experimentation that departs from tradition without totally destroying it. Many companies begin Major Change Programs with training when they should really begin with doing. Experimentation produces options, opportunities, and learning—and training can be provided to the innovating teams. A proliferation of modest experiments provides the organization's own experience with elements of many different business models.

... A rapid succession of experiments from an existing platform resolves an important dilemma surrounding the very idea of corporate transformation. A company cannot neglect existing businesses while leaping into new ones.[77]

Rothschild looks at learning from a broad competitive perspective. Hamel and Prahalad approach it from the viewpoint of product development. Kanter concentrates on organizational change. Their points are directed at the same target: The best way for a firm to learn is to learn from experience—to learn by doing. But we can take this one step further. The only way that firms or individuals learn *is* from experience. Those who learn best are those *who set out on purpose to learn and who know best how to do it.*

The question, of course, is: How do you do it?

Learning to Act; Acting to Learn

What has to happen for a firm to introduce a product or a quality team to come up with a more economical manufacturing method? Essentially, each goes through this three-stage process:

Recognize → Decide → Execute

First, someone has to *recognize* that something needs to be done. The firm identifies an opportunity for the product, while the quality team may begin with a problem. Either way, nothing happens until someone recognizes that there is an opportunity or problem.

The next step, of course, is for the organization or individual to *decide* what to do about the opportunity or problem.

Then someone must *execute* the decision. The best planning in the world is useless unless it's implemented by skillful execution.

That's the traditional sequence. A firm recognizes a new market opportunity, decides how to approach it, then executes its plan. A quality team recognizes a problem with the milling machine, decides how to fix it, then accomplishes what it decided to do. A supervisor recognizes a performance problem, decides how to approach the individual, then carries out that decision by holding a counseling session.

That's the traditional sequence—but it's not enough. We've all too often assumed that what we've recognized, decided, and done would be right. The purpose of training was simple: Train the individual to do it right. We train the supervisor to do counseling and coaching. The person goes back and does it the way he or she was trained. Eureka—problem solved!

It may be that once upon a time it was this simple (though I'm personally dubious). With the rate of change in today's world, however, this kind of "closed-loop" training and learning is completely inadequate. Instead, we need to carry the action process two steps further and convert it into an open loop. For an organization to continuously improve its performance, it must not only *recognize* what to do, *decide* to do it, and *execute* its decision. It must also *assess* the results of the action and then *assimilate* the learning from the action into its planning for the next action.

This may sound to you like what's generally called "feedback." It is, in a way. But it's more than that. When we use a term like *feedback*, it's all too easy to think of it as something automatic. We act, get feedback, and we're ready to go again. The process just isn't that simple. Instead of a single feedback step we have the double steps of assessment and assimilation.

Individuals and organizations cannot wait for the results of their actions to come to them. They must actively *assess* the outcomes of what they do. This may mean building formal reporting systems covering units produced, scrap, and rework. It may mean what Tom Peters calls "management by walking around"—getting out with the organization and seeing what's happening. Most of all, it means being able to identify the results of our actions that we didn't expect. Very few of us do this well.

Just assessing what happened isn't enough. That adds to what a firm or individual knows about the world, but it doesn't change anything. To convert assessment into know-how that can be used, firms and individuals must *assimilate* it. Then they can improve their performance the next time around.

This is the kind of process that Rothschild, Hamel and Prahalad, and Kanter are describing. When assessment and assimilation are built in from the beginning, every process has two outcomes. The first is the product or service it was designed to produce. The second is the learning it makes possible.

Where products are concerned, no one has mastered this better than Sony. No other electronics firm I know of has launched so many ultimately unsuccessful products. Think of Beta-format videotapes. Or the Elcassette—a larger version of the audiocassette that was on the market so short a time that few people even remember its name. Is Sony a failure? Hardly. It gets products out, assesses and assimilates the impact, and uses that information for the next round.

If Sony does it with products, Toyota does it with processes. Toyota is the pioneer in process improvement within the auto industry worldwide. For instance, die changes that used to take several shifts are now done in less than an hour. And Toyota is still trying to reduce the time.

Happily, it isn't just the Japanese who're learning these lessons. Giant General Electric has a clear strategy to get products to market rapidly and with minimum risk. This is how *Fortune* magazine described GE's strategy:

> GE learned to make a multigenerational plan—aiming to introduce a first version that uses only tried-and-true technologies, then gradually introducing new ones as they are perfected. That gets the product to market faster and eliminated costly mishaps when an unproven technology turns out to be full of bugs.[78]

Motorola has clearly gotten religion in its internal processes. One of their products used to take 44 days from the day the order was placed until it was received. In early 1991, after constant process improvement, the same order was being shipped in less than 2 *hours* from the time that the factory received it. Chaparral Steel has also mastered the art. The people who produce Chaparral steel—the people on the floor—are responsible for improving the process. In the words of founder Gordon Forward, "[T]he lab is in the plant."[79]

In other words, the firms that prosper most in today's world are institutionalizing a *five-step* action-learning cycle. Figure 15-1 shows how I would diagram this cycle.[80] The cycle is actually *two* interlocking cycles. The first cycle, the action cycle, runs from recognition through decision to execution. The second cycle, the learning cycle, begins with execution and then runs through assessment to assimilation. Note that both

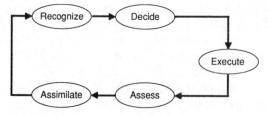

Figure 15-1

cycles include the execution step. The message is simple: Learning begins with action.

More and more, competitive advantage will accrue to firms that can institutionalize this full five-step cycle of acting that leads to learning that leads to better action that leads to more learning, that leads to even better action . . . In the learning organization, learning is intrinsic to action at all levels.

This is how organizations learn most effectively. Now we need to examine how training—especially smart training—can support this process.

How to Train Learning Organizations

Firms don't become learning organizations simply because they're trained more and more. On the other hand, they can't become learning organizations without training. Part of the strategic mission of your training department is for it to furnish the training required to help your firm become a learning organization. Just what kind of training is this? We know that the focus of smart training is always on performance. We can restate the question this way: What are the crucial skills that individuals must learn if they're to perform effectively in a learning organization? There are several answers to this question. Here are the major ones.

The Skills to Get the Work Done

That doesn't change just because an organization becomes a learning organization. Machinists must know how to machine, word processing operators must know how to process words, and supervisors must know how to counsel and facilitate. In one way or another, the basic skills must be taught and learned.

In fact, training basic skills will probably be an even bigger job in a learning organization—because it requires a higher level of basic skills than a traditional organization. Remember the long list of competencies in Chapter 9 that firms must have and use in the 1990s. One of these competencies is particularly important. It is . . .

The Skills to Learn How to Learn

It seems strangely logical that in a learning organization individuals must first learn how to learn. In the late 1980s,

   . . . the American Society for Training and Development [ASTD] conducted a study of 6000 small companies, 438 large corporations, and 500 post-secondary institutions for the U.S. Department of Labor. The goal was to identify the skills industry and education believe to be essential for a strong and competitive workforce to sustain America in the 90s and beyond.

The result: The ASTD's study identified one skill as fundamental to all others: the ability of workers to have "learned how to learn."[81]

Just what is this skill of learning how to learn? According to the ASTD, individuals become effective learners by using these four component skills:

1. Asking the right questions and knowing when they have asked enough of them.

2. Identifying the essential components within complex ideas and tasks.

3. Finding informal ways to measure their understanding of pertinent material.

4. Applying these skills toward the goals of specific training material and job tasks.[82]

It's hard to argue with any of these. Any firm that intends to be a real learning organization would be hard pressed to succeed if these skills weren't spread throughout the organization.

The Skills to Create and Maintain a Learning Environment

It sounds inviting when a firm thinks of becoming a learning organization. Like apple pie and motherhood, who could be against that? The reality of operating as a learning organization, though, is more difficult than it seems. Companies that intend to follow the Act → Learn → Act cycle must organize themselves to operate that way at every level—from the shop floor to the executive suite. They must create an environment in which learning flourishes.

How do they do this?[83] There are several steps they can take. First, they become proficient at all forms of training, but particularly at job aids and structured on-the-job training. They see that the skills to support job aids and OJT are widely distributed and widely used. Supervisors and their workgroups become effective trainers so that effective learning occurs every day, right on the floor. Individual workers are also comfortable using various self-paced training, including computer-based training and multimedia when they're relevant.

Then they continually reinforce the idea that learning is an essential part of every job. This sounds natural and right—but it's only now becoming accepted in most American firms. Companies that have embraced Total Quality have been the first to realize this. Any organization that truly wants to be a learning organization has to follow their lead. It must create an environment in which constant learning is the norm.

They also know how to create and maintain an environment in which both managers and workers can identify and take the intelligent risks necessary for effective learning. This is the key to the entire enterprise. In traditional organizations, workers and managers alike are rewarded for avoiding mistakes—even though this means avoiding opportunities. If learning does occur when individuals and firms take action and then learn from the action, they cannot help but make mistakes. This is only possible when there's a shared understanding of what it means to take intelligent risks, and how to do it.

I think you can see the immense amount of training it will take to inculcate the skills needed to create and maintain this environment. Before we look at this training in a bit more detail, let me elaborate briefly on the last point—the learning environment.

Finding an "Acceptable Learning Risk"

The change from a traditional organization to a learning organization isn't a simple one—and the concept of an acceptable learning risk is the fulcrum. Traditional organizations have an elaborate system of controls designed to prevent failures. Just removing these controls and "leaving everyone free to fail" is hardly an improvement. Instead, an organization must find the appropriate level of risk it can bear while it learns. This takes time, a great deal of thought, and more than a little experiential learning.

Many firms, through Total Quality, are passing ownership of basic processes down to the workers responsible for these processes. Do these workers, on day one of their new responsibilities, dramatically improve the processes? Of course not. They learn gradually what will work and what won't. They may try several, perhaps even dozens of ways to solve a specific problem. Each attempt is a risk, but the risk is small enough to be worth taking. In the end, the time lost from all the risks is typically far less than the gain from solving the problem.

Rax Restaurants is a fast-food chain headquartered in Columbus, Ohio. No other chain maintains so ambitious a schedule of new-product introductions. While McDonald's and Burger King are carefully researching a new addition to their product line, Rax will have tried out three or four new additions to theirs. Most of these won't last. But they provide a constant stream of tests for Rax, from which the company can select the few that are clear successes. The profit from these few more than justifies the cost of the greater number of failures. (Just to illustrate the success of their approach, the firm boasts in public ever so often of its innovations that its competitors have copied.)

Quality teams in Total Quality and Rax's approach to new products are two examples of organizations learning by taking limited, intelligent risks. Now let me give you two *non*-examples, both from the computer market. In the mid-1980s, Mattel came out with the Adam personal computer. It strove to bring the price of home computers down dramatically while increasing the capabilities of these computers. Virtually every component established a new price-performance category for the market. What happened? In less than 2 years, the Adam had vanished from the market. Too many of the innovations performed poorly. The overall quality was wretched. The company tried too many simultaneous experiments. The level of risk was so high that the system as a whole didn't work, and Mattel pulled completely out of the market.

The second, a bet-the-company risk, is still up for grabs as I write this. When Steve Jobs was forced from Apple Computing, he founded NeXT Computers. The first computer produced by the company was a dramatic step forward—fast, with enhanced capabilities at virtually every point. It fell far short, though, of the market acceptance NeXT anticipated. The company has changed its strategy, begun to make changes in its machine, and prepared for round two. NeXT is learning—but it's not yet clear whether the firm will learn quickly and effectively enough to stay in business as a viable competitor.

Both Mattel and NeXT illustrate, by the way, the problems of trying control risk when you're not a market leader. Sony has such a market presence that even the failure of a major project such as Beta-format videotape is an acceptable risk. Rax is an established competitor in its market. NeXT, on the other hand, is betting the company on its product. Mattel didn't bet the company; it survived the Adam debacle, but got thoroughly bloodied in the process. NeXT had to differentiate itself from its competition from the beginning; it didn't have the luxury of taking small steps. Mattel, on the other hand, would have profited immensely had it thought of GE's product introduction strategy (start with off-the-shelf technology, then improve it) a half-decade before GE did.

New and small firms frequently develop bet-the-company products as their way into a market. Often that's unavoidable. Large firms don't

have this excuse. They should be introducing a stream of product innovations and learning from them. All too many of them don't, so they
don't learn as they go along. As I write this, Philips, the giant Dutch
electronics company, is making major changes in every aspect of its operation. In the words of *Business Week*, "[I]t shapes up as a radical re-
structuring that will either restore Philips to its role as a global
powerhouse or relegate it to a has-been."[84] This is businesspeak for
"Philips is betting the company." They simply stopped learning.

The moral? It's much easier to become a learning organization when
you're already successful—but being successful won't make you a learning organization. If you combine the two, you have a true powerhouse.
Chaparral Steel, the home of the "lab in the plant," provides a final
example of this. Chaparral has among the lowest production costs *in the
world.* It thus has the ability to take more learning risks than its competitors with higher costs. This ability, on the other hand, results from
its skills at constant learning. It takes both to be a true learning
organization.

How Do You Train a
Learning Environment?

This is going to be a short section, and for a simple reason. This is an
area in which we need to learn a great deal. At present, there are few
true learning environments in American firms. The Chaparral Steels
are very much an exception to normal practice. Even schools, supposed
to be the learning environment *par excellence,* have generally opted for
the safe course of regurgitated rather than creative responses from students. And because so much "creativity" training is divorced from the
real world of organizations, it, too, is of minimal help.

We can't wait for someone to create a detailed road map before we
start. In the words of José Maria Arizmendiarrieta, a founder of Spain's
Mondragon cooperative, "We build the road as we travel."[85] We must
use the Act → Learn → Act cycle to create the road.

We can make some highly educated guesses, though, about what will
be involved. A firm can begin with the competencies required for effective competition in the 1990s that were described in Chapter 9. Here is
a very brief recap of the competencies.

- Individuals must be highly competent at *dealing with abstractions.* Understanding and responding quickly to information in displays and
  automated reports will be a requisite for effective performance.

- They will also need to be *creative in everyday work*. Strange as the two words may sound together, we will all need to be routinely creative.

- They will need to *learn rapidly and continuously*. The skills for learning how to learn, discussed earlier in this chapter, are part of this. They are not all of it.

- Individuals will need to use advanced *interpersonal skills* and *communication skills* that span a variety of situations and media. Individuals separated by thousands of miles and cultural barriers will nonetheless need to deal and communicate effectively with one another. So will those separated by the equally real barriers of function and occupation.

Before individuals can acquire these competencies, they must possess two others. Since a declining percentage of those entering the work force appear to possess them, these competencies will become a major training challenge. First, they will need what I've called *background competencies,* including competence at reading, writing, and 'rithmetic (literacy and numeracy). Then they must have a high degree of *self-management competence.* Every aspect of a learning environment requires expert self-management skills from each participant.

Competency-Based Testing and Training

Not everyone will need to have all of these competencies, and different individuals will need them at different times. Because of this variability, you may train workers in skills they don't need and fail to train others in skills they require. This is where a competency-based testing and training program might pay off for you. Very briefly, this is how competency-based testing and training work:

1. You analyze a group of jobs to determine what competencies they require.

2. Now that you know the competencies, you develop a test—preferably a *performance* test—to find out whether individual workers have the competencies they need.

3. When you find individuals who lack one or more of the competencies they need, you train them in these competencies. Then you re-test them to make sure they've mastered them.

You can see how similar this is to the training matrix for managers we looked at in Chapter 6, and to IBM's systematic approach to curriculum development and delivery. The basic difference here is the *specificity* of this approach. It virtually guarantees that individuals will receive the training they need, and only that training. It requires a heavy up-front investment, but it is immensely economical once it's up and running. The U.S. Navy has had real success with the approach, and my own organization is implementing it throughout our distribution centers.

There's no single way to move toward a learning organization. Different firms will move in very different ways. But world-class firms have already begun to move.

16

What a Learning Organization Learns

We've followed the path of smart training through a variety of scenarios—from the very detailed to the very strategic and back. In the previous chapter, the path ended at the learning organization, with a look at how smart training might help create it. In this last chapter, we're going to look at the relationship between smart training and the learning organization from a different perspective. We'll follow that with a recap of two themes as they affect the learning organization: core competence and mastery. Then the chapter will end with a few suggestions of what you might start doing this coming Monday morning to move your part of the world toward a learning organization.

Want a Learning Organization? You've Got to Have Smart Training

There's a critical relationship between smart training and the learning organization we haven't explored yet. It's really quite simple, and it's this:

> *Only firms that practice truly smart training will be able to afford to become learning organizations.*

We've already seen a glimpse of the training burden that firms must bear in the competitive 1990s if they intend to become learning organizations. They won't be able to bear this burden unless their training is very, very smart. Only this level of training competence will leave a firm with enough training resources to tackle the tremendous training challenge that is the learning organization.

How can you and your firm achieve this level? We've been looking at the answer all through the book; here's a recap of the high points.

1. You concentrate on performance improvement instead of training. You seek maximum performance improvement for a minimum training investment. That step alone would be revolutionary for many firms today. This means that, as a manager, you can identify the opportunities for improvement in your organization. And you'll be able to set reasonable improvement goals that the training will accomplish.

2. Then you take a strategic approach to training. You spend fewer of your resources jumping on bandwagons and more on developing competencies that count. You concentrate most of all on your organization's core competencies, which will make or break it as a competitor. This isn't an abstraction. It means knowing what the organization does well now and what it will need to know how to do well 5 and 10 years from now.

3. You focus not just on competencies but on mastery as well. Your firm's workers and managers are competent and *know* that they're competent. As a result, they stretch themselves further to apply the expertise they have and develop more. You encourage this by giving them challenging assignments and coaching them as they learn new skills.

4. You see that all training is approached systematically, moving from analysis to design to development to delivery. Then you evaluate the effects of the training *and* see that your training providers do more formal and complete evaluations. The goal isn't to keep score but to learn how to do it better the next time around. As part of this, you see that individuals put their training to work as soon as possible, and you follow up to see how helpful it was.

5. You expect your trainers to choose delivery methods carefully, fitting the methods to the needs of the training. If you have a training department, you expect it to make use of the full range of training sources—both internal and external. You don't pick the methods before the training need is identified, but you make sure the methods chosen fit with your overall training strategy.

6. As part of this, you avoid technology-based training for its own sake. Instead, you pursue techniques such as CBT, CBT-based multimedia, and performance support systems as ways of delivering just-in-time

(JIT) training in situations where the strength of technology can be utilized. You go for the gold, not the gold plate.

7. Whenever possible you use "train the trainer" techniques, job aids, and structured on-the-job training (OJT) to provide JIT training *and* to spread training skills as broadly as possible through the organization. You see that your workgroups know how to create and use job aids and do OJT as a normal part of their work.

Any one of these seven points, implemented conscientiously, increases the efficiency and effectiveness of a firm's training. Each additional one makes the training that much better. Just imagine this, for instance. You get your people trained to create job aids. Then you and they embark on a systematic attempt to put all the inessential knowledge they use into job aids, available when it's needed. Then you see that all the supervisors know how to give effective OJT so that your workers learn their essential skills from pros, just when they need them. How much would these two relatively simple, relatively inexpensive steps increase your organization's performance?

But there's one more step to take.

Making Training Smarter and Smarter

In this day and age, it's not enough for any organization just to do well; it must constantly improve how well it does. Nowhere else is this more true than in training.

As a way into this topic, let me address a question that may have been troubling you. If smart training doesn't concentrate on training, if training won't produce the learning organization by itself, then why are globally competitive companies like Motorola and Corning establishing specific training goals?

Corning, for instance, set a companywide goal that 5 percent of each worker's time will be spent in job-related training each year. It seems to be paying off. The company is booming and earned an editorial in *Business Week* that held it up as a shining example of American competitiveness.[86] Motorola's results are perhaps even more impressive. If training isn't the proper focus of the learning organization, why are these extremely effective companies doing it?

The first answer to that question is basically a simple one. The average American company so undertrains its workers that something has to be done to shake it out of its lethargy. Robert Galvin at Motorola and James Houghton at Corning did just that. They made training a front-burner issue—instead of the nice-to-have-but-let's-not-spend-too-much-on-it back-burner concern that it is in 90 percent-plus of American firms. A company that sets a specific training bogey will certainly waste some money on training. But it will at least begin to make intelligent discussion of training an internal priority. And smart training can't happen until that happens.

There's a second answer, and it's even more important: *At both Motorola and Corning, training is part of a strategy that is clear, public, and driven from the top of the company.* Both Galvin and Houghton decided that Total Quality was a competitive necessity—and their emphasis on training was part and parcel of their strategic vision. This meant that an absolute minimum of the training was wasted. It had a focus and a direction because it was so closely linked to the firm's strategic goals. And these goals included very specific increases in the quality of each firm's products. In other words, the emphasis on training was part of a strategy that had performance improvement at its core.

That's a great beginning. Many firms (perhaps even yours) would do well to begin there. But it's only the first step. The second step is actually seven steps—the seven steps we looked at in the last section. But there's a third step, and few organizations will have the resources to become a true learning organization unless they take it.

This final step is to ensure that *the firm's training takes decreasing time and cost to develop and is increasingly effective and efficient.* That's how smart training becomes even smarter. In a learning organization, most learning occurs in the process of work itself, but it takes a tremendous amount of training to kick-start and maintain this learning process. The firm can afford this training only if it gets better and better at delivering *all* kinds of training.

In other words, your training providers should work consciously and constantly to reduce the life-cycle cost of all the training they deliver. Over time, they should be able to deliver the same training at a constantly decreasing total cost. This means that they can constantly expand the amount and scope of the training they provide without blasting the training budget through the ceiling.

(I need to put on my training manager's hat for a moment here. If you came to me with the proposal that I just outlined, I'd agree to it in a flash. But I'd put a condition on it. I'd ask you how we were going to divide the money I saved the firm by making training more efficient. From my point of view, I need income for research and development in training, for staff development, and for other long-term activities. These are just as important to the firm as the short-term savings I know I can deliver. How we negotiated the division of the spoils would determine the overall quality of the training effort in the long run.)

Most training providers aren't typically good at constantly improving efficiency and effectiveness. This shouldn't be a surprise. Few firms know how to constantly improve the efficiency and effectiveness of any of their "knowledge workers." This is true even for those that have signed up for Total Quality and continuous process improvement. Many of them don't apply these principles to their accountants, engineers, sales personnel, human resource managers, trainers, and other knowledge workers. When they do use Total Quality methodology with knowledge work, it's often in only the most routine operations in these departments. And relatively few firms are attempting to use high-performance work systems—such as self-managing teams—with knowledge workers.

This needs to stop. One place to stop it is with your training providers. Because training is so crucial to the development of a learning organization, your providers must know how to constantly increase its results while reducing the resources it consumes. They may already know well what your training's life-cycle costs are. In fact, they may have a much better hold on the real costs of training than your accounting department does. But they need to turn this knowledge into clear improvement goals. If continuous performance improvement is a proper goal of a learning organization, what better place to start than with your training department or training consultants?

I believe you should be able to expect the following from whoever provides your training:

1. They can tell you, with reasonable accuracy, the life-cycle cost of any training they deliver in significant amounts. If they can't, this is where they should start. Chapter 9 included several references that will help them do this.

2. They should use a systematic analysis, design, and development process (as described in Chapters 3 and 4). If they don't, just converting to one will increase both the efficiency and effectiveness of their training significantly.

3. If they know life-cycle costs and use a systematic process, they should be able to set reasonable goals to improve their training performance consistently. Perhaps a standard course they deliver is a one-week introduction to the basic processes in a specific occupation. It's not unreasonable to expect that, over a year or two, the course can be reduced to four or even three days—not by cutting out material and shorting the students, but by making intelligent use of job aids, self-paced training outside the classroom, OJT, and other efficient methods.

Delivering all this won't be easy for even the best training department or consultant—mainly because they've operated for so long in an organization that never asked it or rewarded them for it. Don't expect them to produce it overnight. Do insist that they start without delay.

This is the way that training becomes smarter and smarter—and how you get the resources you need to become a learning organization. In the last chapter, we looked at some of the characteristics of learning organizations. Now we need to be even clearer about what a learning organization is.

Tactical Learning and Strategic Learning

In the last chapter, I quoted a section from Michael Rothschild on experience and learning. In part, he said, "gaining an efficiency advantage by accumulating experience faster than competitors is the key to any organization's long-term growth and survival."[87] We saw that firms can do this by taking constant, controlled learning risks. They act, then assess and assimilate the results of their actions, and feed this into the next action cycle. A firm that does this effectively becomes, in the words of Bill O'Brien of Hanover Insurance, "a system intending to learn from its environment more rapidly than its competitors."[88]

Chapter 15 went on to deal with some of the practicalities of accumulating experience rapidly and then learning from it as rapidly as possible. It might seem that this is the core definition of a learning organization. It is, and it isn't. Specifically, it captures the *tactical* dimension of a learning organization, but doesn't deal with the *strategic* dimension. The distinction is critical.

Let me put the difference this way. When an organization learns tactically, it learns how to achieve its strategic objectives more completely and cuts its costs more rapidly (à la Rothschild). When it learns strategically, it learns to identify the best available strategic objectives.

Peter Senge summarized this strategic dimension superbly in *The Fifth Discipline*. He described a learning organization as "*an organization that is continually expanding its capacity to create its future.*"[89] An organization that masters the skill of tactical learning becomes, in Senge's words, effective at "adaptive learning." When an organization goes beyond this and builds learning into its very core, it engages in "generative learning." That kind of learning enables it to create its future.[90] That's *strategic* learning.

The kind of learning that enables an organization to create its future is hard indeed to come by. Most organizations appear to get locked into their current view of themselves, their products or services, and their markets. They thus prepare only for a future that is a repetition of the past. Perhaps a bit better, perhaps a bit worse, but a repetition of the past nonetheless.

How does an organization accomplish the strategic learning it needs to create its future? I'm not sure we yet have enough answers to this question. But I believe we have some answers—and they all center around the kind of strategic planning that a firm does. Three general guidelines seem to suggest themselves.

Maintain a Long-Range Perspective

By "long-range" here, I really do mean *long-range.* Japanese firms, currently the world leaders in long-range planning, use a planning horizon of decades, even a century or more. What does this accomplish? It enables a perspective on short-term events quite different from that taken by an organization whose sights are set one to 5 years ahead.

A superb example of this was provided by Sony's takeover of Columbia, followed by Matsushita's acquisition of MCA. We looked at Sony and Matsushita through short-range goggles and saw them as makers of consumer electronics. From their long-range perspective, they were envisioning themselves in a very different business. They saw themselves as total providers of entertainment. The lessons they learned from the last decade have been dramatically different from that of their erstwhile American competitors.

It's well known that most American firms, for good reasons and poor, have short planning horizons. This makes strategic, *generative* learning difficult because the firms spend all their time making tactical, *adaptive* decisions. The best they can hope for is effective adaptive learning. And even that's harder with a short-term focus. When a firm must encase its decisions in a 2-to-5-year horizon, it simply never sees the variety of options that a firm with a longer perspective can envision.

Understand That Strategic Plans Are Made to Be Revised

Many firms latched onto strategic planning when it became fashionable a few years back. The general view seemed to be that a firm made strategic plans, normally covering 5 to 10 years, and then followed them. Oh, sure, a little tweaking was required here and there. But the plans were made to be followed; that was their strength.

What most firms found was that reality is consistently unkind to long-range planners. Before a firm could get deep into the plan, something unexpected happened and part of the plan wasn't relevant any more. And it's not only firms. The United States' plans for the Gulf War worked remarkably well. We sometimes forget, however, that the U.S. military had planned for a Mideast war because it expected to be facing the Soviets. Saddam Hussein was simply obliging enough to launch the kind of threat that the planners—anticipating a different foe—had counted on.

Long-range plans are helpful because they make a company's vision concrete. If the vision can't be translated into a plan, it's an empty promise. But nowhere is it written that the plan must work. Nowhere is there a guarantee that the world will cooperate with the vision *as it was initially understood.* Furthermore, such a guarantee might be counterproductive. In Tom Peters' words,

> . . . planning and thoughtful resource allocation surely make sense, but innovation is an inherently messy and unpredictable business, growing more so every day. *And the unpredictability cannot be removed, or perhaps even substantially reduced, by excessive planning.*[91]

What use, then, is planning? It does express a direction, and the longer the planning horizon, the greater the flexibility available to move in that direction. But there are other virtues as well. When plans are carefully made and then frequently updated, the surprises themselves become a source of learning. When a plan assumes one series of events and another occurs instead, one is prompted to ask: "Why didn't we expect this?" Just asking and answering that question can help refocus the attention of the organization.

There are other ways of accomplishing the same goal. One firm uses this highly innovative process:

> One executive described how the planning process in his organization is energized by producing "competitor plans." Regular task forces are established with the mandate of adopting the perspective of a primary competitor and of producing a plan that gives that competitor an advantage. This view from the outside, free from the constraints of how the organization presently conducts business and free from the internal politics of decision making that lead people to favor a particular strategy, provides the basis for a critical evaluation of the organization's position and what it should do to take account of the strengths and weaknesses revealed by the competitor plan. This approach allows the organization to see and challenge itself openly and constructively through a process bounded only by the imagination and ingenuity of the task force producing the competitor plan.[92]

The common ingredient in the last few paragraphs has been *surprise.* There's another way to deal with surprise, and that's to build it in up front. That's the particular strength of the third and final method.

Convert Plans into Scenarios

Scenarios are both like and unlike plans. They're like them to the extent that they're attempts to deal with the future. They're unlike traditional plans, though, because they attempt to plan for *alternative* futures. Shell Oil was one of the first firms to use scenarios systematically. The company was immensely successful in the 1980s because, by mastering the technique of scenario building, it was able to anticipate the dramatic drop in oil prices in 1986. When these events occurred, Shell—unlike most of its competitors—was prepared to take advantage of the changed conditions.[93]

When a firm builds scenarios, it deliberately sets out to create several alternative versions of the future. One version may be the expected future, while a second is a more pessimistic view, and a third a more optimistic one. This enables the firm to anticipate and prepare for a variety of events.

The real value of scenario building is much deeper. When a firm forces itself to consider unexpected futures, it must confront its unconscious blinders and biases. Instead of waiting for events to turn out in unexpected ways, scenario builders can project these unexpected events—and then ask *why* they're unexpected. Because so much of Shell's management had grown up in exploration, they had an innate, unrecognized bias that exploration would continue to be profitable into an indefinite future. When presented with a scenario in which oil prices tumbled, these managers had to surface and deal with this previously unrecognized bias.

By forcing itself to envision alternative futures, a firm stretches its mental muscles and loosens its mental blinders. It can then take in a greater range of current reality and deal with a broader range of possible futures. The firm's potential for strategic learning increases exponentially when this happens.

These are a few suggestions. You may have other, better ways of opening your organization up to strategic learning. The exact means aren't critical. That strategic learning occurs is.

Now we need to shift our attention. Earlier in the book, we looked at two factors critical to smart learning: core competence and the cycle of mastery. These factors are even more critical to the learning organization. But each factor presents the learning organization with a major dilemma. The next two sections of this chapter deal with those dilemmas.

The Strategic Dilemma: Finding Core Competence

Chapter 7 reflected the view of many economists that the key competitive factor in the 1990s and early 2000s will be the knowledge embodied in their human resources that firms can tap and use. This is often called "intellectual capital," but I think the term is misleading. To revert to the structure introduced in Chapter 1, it's not what a firm *knows* intellectually, but what it *knows how* to do that enables it to compete.

This is why I've emphasized the idea of a firm's *core competence*, what it knows how to do so well that it constitutes its competitive advantage. We can now see that a true learning organization has a dual core competence. It is expert at identifying its markets and creating the products and/or services its markets want. It's also expert at learning how to do this better and better. Remember Robert Galvin's statement that Motorola's current goal is to *anticipate* its customers' requirements.

Chapter 15 looked at ways smart training can contribute to your organization's ability not only to do but to learn. And it can; there are actions you could take tomorrow that would begin to increase your firm's learning ability significantly. It would take time to do this; you and your training providers would not lack for work in this area for years.

You'd make significant progress. But then a moment of truth would come. You'd sit down together and say to each other: "Well, we've done it. We've really developed our core competence both to produce effectively and to learn from what we do." And then a hesitant voice would ask, "How do we know we've done it? And how do we know how well we've done it?"

In today's world, those questions would generate a perplexed silence. The fact of the matter is that we've no way to measure core competence at doing, much less at learning.

Let me give you a quick example. A traditional assembly plant employs workers who use minimal competence to complete their individual portions of the assembly operation. These workers show up on the books as a pure cost. In tough times, they're treated that way; they're simply "let go" to reduce cost. GM Saturn employs assembly workers in Spring Hill, Tennessee, as does Corning, Inc. in Blacksburg, Virginia. These workers are also carried on the books as costs. Because they function in partly or fully self-directed work teams, the competence these individuals bring to their jobs is a full order of magnitude greater than that of the traditional assembly worker. They know how to do a wide variety of jobs, and they know how to learn on their jobs. They would be far more expensive to replace. But how is their competence accounted for? That's right—it's on the books as a cost. Why? No one knows how to carry it as the asset it clearly is.

If core competence is to be anything other than an abstraction, we must find meaningful ways to measure and record it. Not necessarily precise ways; it's probably not possible ever to say "Our core competence is up 3.7 percent this quarter!" But we must find ways to define and capture it—and then to give it a meaningful value. We can assign a definite value to our physical plant, our machinery, even the carpets on the floors and the pictures on the walls. But we can't assign a value to our human resources. We have only the sketchiest ideas of how to identify, much less measure, our core competence. (There's one exception, of course; core competence may show up under "goodwill" when a company is sold. That's a little late to value it.)

Many companies try unsuccessfully to use secondary measures. They keep careful track of the percentage of college graduates in their work forces, with no idea of the quality of results these graduates are producing. They count workers in different occupations, with only the vaguest idea of the level of competence they represent. Or they measure the grievance rate, as though satisfied workers were automatically competent, or vice versa.

Some companies use other secondary measures that are at least a step in the right direction. Both 3M and Rubbermaid, for instance, have specific goals for the percentage of sales revenue that must be generated by new products. Some firms in businesses that require effective research to prosper track the number of patents earned by their research staff. Universities attempt to measure the value of professors by their "A pubs" (publications in first-tier scholarly journals). None of these measures competence directly, but they do measure some of its more-or-less direct results.

If core competence really does mean something, the situation must change. I don't have any quick answers. I doubt that there are any. There are bits and pieces already out there, and we need to begin with them. Unfortunately, they don't measure gains and losses in core competence well, and they don't measure learning competence at all. We have a very long way to go.

The Tactical Dilemma:
Revisioning Mastery

Chapter 5 suggested that firms successful in the 1990s and beyond will have competence broadly spread through their ranks, vertically as well as horizontally. Chapter 6 broadened this view to encompass mastery—the possession not only of competence but of the self-confidence to use it. Just as core competence is a key strategic ingredient of the learning organization, mastery is a key tactical component.

Here is one description of an organization in which mastery—including mastery at learning—is widespread:

> Difficult as it may be for Americans to believe, at some large work sites—factories as well as offices—rank-and-file employees look forward to coming to work and feel genuinely excited about their jobs. When asked why they like the job so much, one of the most frequent replies is "We learn something new every day." In such workplaces, opportunities are continually presented for learning new skills. Employees are motivated to take advantage of these opportunities by the chance for self-development and professional growth as well as for the sheer enjoyment of learning.[94]

This would be a boon for any organization, of any kind. For a learning organization, however, this kind of work and this kind of worker are essential. And that brings us to our second dilemma: Mastery simply isn't a word or concept used much in organizations these days.

Of course, it's not just organizations that pay little attention to mastery. George Leonard is certainly convinced that the topic is not only ignored but positively avoided. The third chapter of his latest book (entitled, appropriately enough, *Mastery*) is entitled "America's War against Mastery." It ends with these words: "In the long run, the war against mastery, the path of patient, dedicated effort without attachment to immediate results, is a war that can't be won."[95]

Chapter 6 emphasized the *results* of mastery—the self-conscious use of greater and greater competence. Leonard emphasizes the *path* to mastery, which is long and demanding. The two are intimately connected, and the dilemma of mastery is closely related to that connection. Mastery demands time and patient effort. With this thought in mind, how many jobs in your organization permit, much less require, mastery? If your firm is typical, the answer is "few indeed."

Because we place such a low value on mastery, few jobs are engineered to require it. Because so few jobs require it, we place a low value on it. It's a classic chicken-and-egg situation. Even worse, both the chicken and the egg are getting smaller with each generation.

The automotive industry provides perhaps the best illustration of this. Early in the century, Henry Ford created the assembly line as we know it today. Each job required minimal knowledge and skill, and that's what the individual in the job was able to use. Two generations of American autoworkers have grown up performing jobs that could be "mastered" in one or two weeks. This tradition of overengineered jobs never caught on fully in Europe, which still has a strong craft tradition in which mastery is meaningful. The Japanese approach is even more interesting. They took the American assembly line, completely routinized, and then expected their workers to become problem solvers and troubleshooters. This is a form of mastery far different from that of European workers, but mastery it is.[96]

Not only American businesses but American workers as well pay dearly for this lack of mastery. As thousands of laid-off autoworkers have found, their few skills command little more than minimum wage outside the assembly plant. As painful as this sounds, the reality is even worse. Because they have performed the same narrow range of duties for years, perhaps even decades, these workers identify with the work they do. They *are* painters or welders or fitters. Attempts to teach them new skills strike them as attacks on their very identity. They thus are firmly stuck in their lack of mastery.

This is the dilemma of mastery that any learning organization must face. First, it must transform itself so that its jobs require mastery—both of doing and learning. The basics of how to do this are becoming well known. *Empowerment* and *self-managed teams* are catch phrases that describe real changes in some American companies. Making these changes is another matter entirely. Empowering workers, whether individually or in teams, is no simple process. It requires dramatic changes in how the firm sees itself and in its basic structures. (If you doubt how far-reaching these changes are, read "GE Keeps Those Ideas Coming" in the August 12, 1991, issue of *Fortune*. Jack Welch, a dynamic and determined executive if there is one in the country, expects these changes to take more than a decade at GE. That should be no surprise; Motorola was one of the leaders in employee empowerment, and after a decade it's still learning, changing, and growing. So is American Transtech.)

So it's no snap to create jobs that require mastery. And at the same time that the jobs are being created, firms must find workers who are willing and able to master them. The firms that have moved first and furthest—Gaines Dog Food, Procter and Gamble, GM Saturn, Corning, IBM—have been able to tap the thin upper strata of the job market. Saturn, for instance, filled its slots in Spring Hill with workers drawn from the entire country. The firms that try to follow them will find the pickings slimmer. I don't mean by that the workers are incapable of seeking and exercising mastery. In many cases, however, they lack the skills to begin. In perhaps even more cases, they don't believe that there will be any real payoff for their efforts.

The dilemma is how we create from these raw materials a culture based on respect for mastery. How we do it as a nation is important, of course. For the moment, though, the question is how you do it where you are.

Throughout this book, I've described ways that smart training can help a firm deal with this dilemma. I've also suggested management actions that you and others can take to create organizations that support competence, mastery, and learning. And this brings us back to the theme with which Chapter 16 began.

Smart training will not get you all the way to the learning organization. But you almost certainly will not get there without smart training. The first part of this chapter dealt with the efficiencies that smart training creates. Let me end with a different aspect of smart training. Smart training is efficient, and that's good. But smart training is also *effective*— and that's great.

Smart training, with its emphasis on clear strategy, up-front analysis, and careful design, is the most effective way to get from here to there. Remember,

> *Smart training isn't about training at all. It's about learning—learning that produces the greatest performance improvement for the smallest training investment.*

Hold that thought!

How to Get There from Here: Three Goals for Monday Morning

1. If you don't do long-range planning, you need to begin. If you do it, you need to begin converting your plans into scenarios. Traditional organizations live in the present; learning organizations are always on the edge between present and future. Scenarios are the best techniques we have for living there. Find out about them and begin using them. If you don't have the time, put a team on it.

2. Strategic planning goes hand in glove with your core competence. If you intend to thrive in the 1990s, you must know what your core competence is. What is the value you provide, or intend to provide, your customers that your competitors can't? What are the steps you'll need to take in order to extend this value and to counter your competitors? *In detail,* what are all the skills you must have to do this? You can't answer all three questions completely in a short time. If you start asking them, though, you and your organization may begin to look at yourselves in a different light.

3. Finally, start the wheels turning to make learning a part of work. Your first step is to see that honest mistakes are never punished. That may take quite a while. Next, open the organization up to new ideas that may or may not work but carry a low risk (no tragedy occurs if they fail). Then start training everyone—*everyone*—that learning (assessment and assimilation) is as much a part of their job as the work product itself.

Your training providers are valuable consultants in this process. But only you and I, the managers, can create a learning organization.
See you at the top!

Quick Guide to Media and Methods

This guide quickly summarizes the advantages and disadvantages of the different methods and media used to deliver training. With the guide, you can identify the few ways to deliver specific training that possess the greatest potential for success. The guide identifies the pages in the book that describe the method or medium in greater detail, so you can explore it further there. Then you can discuss these choices with your training staff and arrive at the best solution.

Why not just pick from the guide? Let me give you a quick idea of the answer. In Chapter 12, I mentioned that AT&T uses performance support systems. One of these systems helps managers decide which training delivery system will be most effective in a specific situation. That sounds neat and simple, but the system evaluates variables with *more than 1000 different values* in order to come up with its recommendations. Even then, the recommendations are starting points for intelligent discussion rather than final decisions.

I doubt that you're in the mood to look at some 1000 different rules for selecting training methods, even if I wanted to provide them here. What I can do, and what will help you even more, is to arm you with basic guidelines. As long as you take them with a sizable grain of salt, they will help you avoid serious mistakes and raise the probability that your training will succeed.

As you read the summaries, please keep these points in mind:

1. To repeat: The guide is a stimulus to discussion. It will enable you to talk intelligently with your training department or any other training

provider. It will *not* provide you or anyone with the final answer for any specific training.

2. When evaluating different media and methods, don't forget that you can effectively combine several different training methods. Don't let the guide mislead you into picking only one method or medium when a combination may be more effective.

3. Time and cost figure into method and media selection in two different ways: the time and cost to develop and the time and cost to deliver. In general, the greater the impact of delivery, the smarter it becomes to spend the time and cost at the design and development phase. The reverse is also true: If the training is routine training for a small number of workers, don't take a lot of time and money to develop it just right.

4. Above all, remember that smart training requires a training strategy, followed by effective analysis and design, before selection of the delivery methods and media. If you choose methods and media first, you will almost certainly end up with training that is inefficient, ineffective, or both.

The following list covers the media and methods for delivering training that are most generally available today, listed roughly in order of the time each takes to develop. Performance support systems hold great promise, but they haven't been widely implemented yet. Virtual reality is years from practicality for everyday training. The other media and methods are in more or less common use.

Advantages and Disadvantages of Different Training Methods

Delivery Method	Major Advantages	Major Disadvantages
Job Aids (pages 169–179)	Very quick and inexpensive to develop. Can be used at the job site while performing a job; can deliver true JIT training. Can be revised and updated quickly and easily. Can be used as a supplement to virtually any other form of training (particularly structured OJT).	Not effective by themselves for complex training or interpersonal or skills-intensive training. Unless carefully prepared, can become overly complex and/or confusing. If used in the wrong situations, workers can become dependent on job aids instead of learning necessary skills.
Structured On-the-Job Training (pages 185–196)	Relatively quick and inexpensive to prepare, because individuals giving OJT are familiar with the material. Can be used at the job site, close to or at the time the job is being performed. Assuming that the individual providing the OJT remains competent, the training is updated automatically. Can be combined effectively with job aids and self-paced training.	Requires training and initial oversight of OJT instructors. Competes for supervisory time and attention with pressures of daily production. Quality control is very difficult. Can only use basic training techniques.

(*Continued*)

Delivery Method	Major Advantages	Major Disadvantages
Instructor-led Classroom Training (no single reference—see index)	Comparatively quick and inexpensive to develop. Most flexible (humans adapt much more easily than do machines or paper). Handles change well (you can update a human much faster than a computer). Does not require high-tech support, but can effectively use technology-based training as an adjunct. Can use a wide variety of training methods, from very directive to very interactive.	May be difficult to hold class when and where it's needed by participants. Takes participants away from their work areas. May create significant travel and lodging expenses. Competent instructors take significant time to train. During this time, the instructor is almost a pure expense. Classroom effectiveness depends on both the skill and personality of the instructor. All instructors are not equally effective or interesting.
Teletraining (pages 207–208)	Takes somewhat longer to develop than in-person instructor-led training, but is still relatively quick and inexpensive to develop. Can deliver training to isolated locations. Has many of the same advantages as instructor-led classroom instruction.	Requires significant hardware support for videotaping and for downlinks. Also requires studio and trained staff to present the training effectively. Difficult to make interactive. (If not interactive, it has no real superiority to videotape.) Subject to the same basic scheduling problems as in-person training. May also take students away from the work site—though travel is minimized. Has even higher demands on the instructor to maintain interest—especially since available training techniques are limited.

(*Continued*)

Delivery Method	Major Advantages	Major Disadvantages
Videotaped Training (pages 157–159)	Has many of the same advantages as teletraining. Can be combined effectively with other training methods (classroom, self-paced, etc.). Does not require extensive hardware to deliver. Excellent for "slice of life" presentations such as case studies. Also enables actual workers and managers to speak, giving authenticity to the training.	Very ineffective as a stand-alone training method because it lacks interactivity. Requires a somewhat higher level of studio production, since the material is not live.
Canned Classroom Training (pages 201–204)	When canned training will meet the training need, it is less expensive for limited numbers of students than developing training in-house. Possesses the basic advantages of instructor-led classroom instruction. In-house instructors do not need to learn the subject matter and can concentrate on more essential subjects.	May not be available when needed. Teaches only generic skills, which may or may not fit the specific needs of the organization. Dependent on the skills and personality of the instructor. Vendors of canned courses often depend on completely scripted courses in place of well-trained instructors. This limits flexibility sharply. Instructors may or may not be familiar with the subject matter. They may not be able to deal with student questions in depth. Takes participants away from the work site and may require travel and lodging.

(Continued)

Delivery Method	Major Advantages	Major Disadvantages
Semicustomized Training (pages 204–206)	When done competently, has all the advantages of in-house training.	Is normally more expensive than in-house training would be if presented often.
	Does not have to be limited to classroom training. Can include any form of training.	The competence of the trainer is difficult to assess in advance.
	Especially effective for highly technical training (such as workers' compensation regulations) in areas where the firm does not need in-house expertise.	Many training consultants are not strong in analysis, design, and selection of delivery methods.
		Training may not be able to be prepared and/or delivered when needed.
Training Furnished by Junior College and University (pages 206–207)	Can provide the combined benefits of canned and semicustomized training.	Schools are particularly oriented toward classroom training, which may not be the most effective for the training needs.
	Generally high-quality control of training content, though not necessarily of delivery.	The college or university may not have competence in areas important to you.
	Colleges and universities are often anxious to work with local organizations.	Training in universities in particular may be oriented toward theory at the expense of practice.
	Can be an excellent source of basic literacy and numeracy training in conjunction with skills training.	Unless you are a major consumer of training, the school may not have time to do a large amount of training for you.

(*Continued*)

Delivery Method	Major Advantages	Major Disadvantages
"Train the Trainer" (pages 198–201)	Permits a firm to expand its training at minimal cost.	Hard to maintain quality control.
	When the training is in their field, actual performers are more up to date than instructors.	Because trainers are not experienced, only a limited number of training techniques can be used.
	By having trainers in different locations, diminishes travel and lodging costs.	Training of the trainers is normally limited; trainers have little flexibility and cannot be used for other subjects.
	Permits training to be developed and fielded very rapidly.	Like OJT, requires constant attention to remain effective.
Paper-Based Self-Paced Training (no single reference—see index)	Once developed, can be fielded rapidly.	Requires much longer to develop than instructor-led training.
	Can be used in *any* location, including very isolated ones.	Not effective for skills training, complex training, and other training that requires high interaction in order to be effective.
	Permits trainees to go through the course at their own pace.	
	An effective way to get training to a large number of scattered individuals.	

(*Continued*)

Delivery Method	Major Advantages	Major Disadvantages
"Basic" CBT (pages 155–157 and 160–162)	Has all the advantages of paper-based self-paced training. Unlike paper-based training, however, is very good for material that requires student interaction. Because of interaction, can present complex material far more effectively than paper-based self-paced training. Can be combined effectively with instructor-led training.	Takes longer to develop than paper-based self-paced training. Can easily require 10 to 20 times the development time of instructor-led training. Requires that all trainees have access to appropriate computers. CBT works best if delivered through computers that trainees use regularly. Requires a high degree of development skill. Unless interactivity is used well, the course becomes an expensive "electronic page turner." There are no current CBT authoring systems that significantly reduce development time or permit much development flexibility. One CBT course is very much like another. Unless propagated on a single mainframe, both updating the CBT and controlling the version used by trainees can be extremely difficult, time-consuming, and expensive. *This is true of all computer-based training.*

(*Continued*)

Delivery Method	Major Advantages	Major Disadvantages
CBT with Multimedia (pages 159–160 and 163–164)	Has all the advantages of basic CBT, with added capabilities. Because of these capabilities, can train in a broader range of skills than basic CBT. Very effective if a machine or process must be shown in detail and simulated. Extremely effective at many kinds of simulation. Currently the best means available to simulate dangerous conditions or those where a mistake in the real world would have unacceptably serious consequences.	Extremely expensive when done well. Very easy to add glitz and glitter to training without increasing effectiveness. Requires highly skilled developers supported by a full studio of equipment. Requires that trainees have access not only to computers but to videodiscs, videotapes, and so on. (This is becoming less of a factor as small disks similar to compact disks are adapted for training uses.)
CBT with Virtual Reality (page 165)	Will extend the abilities of multimedia to permit touch and kinesthetic experience as well as sight and sound. Once perfected, will be the method of choice for training when mistakes are expensive and for hazardous environments. As an extremely new technology, probably has significant potentials that cannot be anticipated at this stage.	Still in research stage (in 1992). Extremely expensive and requires very sophisticated developers and equipment. Probably not practical for most applications until middle to late 1990s. (But keep a weather eye on its development.)

(*Continued*)

Delivery Method	Major Advantages	Major Disadvantages
Computer-Based Performance Support Systems (pages 179–182)	Combines the advantages of traditional job aids with those of CBT. Provides training precisely at the point when and where it's needed, with virtually no disruption. The performance support system is incorporated into the tools the individual uses to do a job. Unlike non-computer-based job aids, can use forms of artificial intelligence to provide advice and suggestions in the middle of tasks (high-level on-line help). If well designed, can enable knowledge workers to locate and use information far more rapidly than any other method. Can range from simple computer-delivered assistance to more elaborate multimedia resources.	Barely out of the experimental stage. Applications so far are quite limited and do not test the limits of performance support systems. Extremely costly, in terms both of time and money. Also requires a very high level of developer skill. Many workers do not yet use computers and software with the power to incorporate a performance support system of any size. This, of course, is changing. In short, a technology to become familiar with and watch carefully—and perhaps even to experiment with.

Notes

Introduction

1. This was the 1991 Hunter Conference of the Madison (Wisconsin) Area Quality Improvement Network. Robert W. Galvin was the keynote speaker at this conference.

2. John V. Hickey, "Corning Glass Works: Total Quality as a Strategic Response," in Jill Casner-Lotto and Associates, *Successful Training Strategies,* p. 69.

3. This is the first of several precisely documented cases furnished by J. H. Harless, president of the Harless Guild and a leader in performance-based training.

4. Referenced in Jack Gordon, "Measuring the 'Goodness' of Training," *Training,* August 1991, pp. 22–23.

5. Jack E. Bowsher, *Educating America: Lessons Learned in the Nation's Corporations,* p. 69.

6. William Wiggenhorn, "Motorola U: When Training Becomes an Education," *Harvard Business Review,* July-August 1990, p. 75.

7. Paquet, Kasl, Weinstein, and Waite, "The Bottom Line," *Training and Development Journal,* May 1987, p. 30.

8. Peter M. Senge, *The Fifth Discipline,* p. 4. The emphasis is his.

9. Senge, p. 14.

Chapter 1

10. In Levering, Moskowitz, and Katz, *The 100 Best Companies to Work for in America.* The first edition was in 1984, the updated edition in 1987. The information on Preston Trucking is taken from Gloria Pearlstein, "Preston Trucking Shifts to Performance Management," *Performance & Instruction,* August 1989, pp. 1–5. Robert Levering also devotes Chapter 10 of *A Great Place to Work* to Preston Trucking and its transformation.

Chapter 2

11. Harold D. Stolovitch and Mike Lane, "Multicultural Training: Designing for Affective Results," *Performance & Instruction,* July 1989, pp. 10–15.

12. Linda Honold, "The Power of Learning at Johnsonville Foods," *Training,* April 1991, p. 56.

13. Gareth Morgan, *Images of Organization,* p. 104.

14. Hickey, pp. 66–67. The Corning program was adapted, with permission, from the program used by Texas Instruments.

15. Wiggenhorn, p. 75.

16. See F. K. Plous, Jr., "The Motorola Training and Education Center: Keeping the Company Competitive," in Jill Casner-Lotto and Associates, p. 56.

17. See Jerome M. Rosow and Robert Zager, *Training—The Competitive Edge,* p. 146. The same idea is also stressed in H. James Harrington's book, *Business Process Improvement* (New York: McGraw-Hill, 1991).

Chapter 3

18. Roger D. Chevalier, "Improving Efficiency and Effectiveness of Training," *Performance & Instruction,* May/June 1990, p. 21.

19. This account is taken from Mark Graham Brown and Kathleen Chartier, "Improving Financial Service Quality," *Performance & Instruction,* October 1989, pp. 17–22.

20. The idea of the PIP was first introduced, to my knowledge, in Tom Gilbert's landmark book *Human Competence.* The book is tough sledding, but many of the ideas are dynamite—even though it was written 15 years ago.

21. From a presentation by the Fixit Four of the GE Superabrasives plant, Worthington, Ohio.

Chapter 4

22. This material is adapted slightly from the findings of Malcolm S. Knowles, one of the pioneers in adult learning. His findings are presented in detail in his book *The Adult Learner: A Neglected Species.* They are also presented, in much more condensed form, in "Adult Learning," *Training and Development Handbook,* 3rd edition, pp. 168-179. Both are in the bibliography.

23. Quoted in Gordon, "Measuring the 'Goodness' of Training," *Training,* August 1991, p. 24. This short article is a superb overview of the issues involved in evaluating training.

Chapter 5

24. John Hoerr, "Sharpening Minds for a Competitive Edge," *Business Week,* December 17, 1990, pp. 72–78.

25. In the eyes of Womack, Jones, and Roos, the increased competence of Toyota's work force is part of the firm's development of a totally new approach to production. For a detailed description of Toyota's "lean production" system, see their book *The Machine That Changed the World.*

26. For more detail concerning many of the firms referenced in this section, see my book *Teampower.*

27. Robert B. Reich, *The Work of Nations.*

28. National Center on Education and the Economy, *America's Choice: High Skills or Low Wages!,* 1990.

29. Bruce G. Posner, "My Favorite Company," *Inc.,* April 1989, p. 99.

30. William J. Hampton, "GM Bets an Arm and a Leg on a People-Free Plant," *Business Week,* September 12, 1988, pp. 72–73.

31. James L. Sheedy, "Retooling Your Workers along with Your Machines," in David Asman (ed.), *The Wall Street Journal on Managing,* pp. 76–79. In its attempt to organize broadly around self-managing teams, Corning is also finding that it must train a large portion of its work force in basic skills. (See John Hoerr, "Sharpening Minds for a Competitive Edge," *Business Week,* December 17, 1990, pp. 72–78.)

32. Richard E. Walton and Gerald I. Susman, "People Policies for the New Machines," *Harvard Business Review,* March-April 1987, pp. 98–106.

33. Michael A. Pollock, "Business Is Dragging Its Feet on Retraining," *Business Week,* September 29, 1986, p. 72.

Chapter 6

34. Dr. Albert Bandura, who has written extensively on mastery, calls it "self-efficacy." I chose *mastery* because it's far less academic. Both terms mean the same thing: confidence in one's competence at a task or job. If you want to do some heavy-duty reading about the importance of self-efficacy, see Chapter 9 of Bandura's book, *Social Foundations of Thought and Action.*

35. Tom Peters, *Thriving on Chaos,* pp. 167ff.

Chapter 7

36. Reich, "Who Is Us?," *Harvard Business Review,* January-February 1990, p. 54.

37. Thomas A. Stewart, "Brainpower," *Fortune,* June 3, 1991, p. 44.

38. In Prahalad and Hamel, "The Core Competence of the Corporation," *Harvard Business Review,* May-June 1990, p. 81.

39. Prahalad and Hamel, p. 81.

40. Stewart, p. 46.

41. Prahalad and Hamel, p. 90.

42. See S. C. Gwynne, "The Right Stuff," *Time,* October 29, 1990, pp. 74–84.

Chapter 8

43. You can find more information on these types of positions in Barbara Garson, *The Electronic Sweatshop*, and Shoshana Zuboff, *In the Age of the Smart Machine*.

44. Lund and Hansen, *Keeping America at Work: Strategies for Employing the New Technologies*, pp. 93–94. This process is also described, in much greater detail, in Zuboff.

45. Zuboff deals with this phenomenon. Feigenbaum, McCorduck, and Nii draw a picture of how expert systems may not only de-skill work but make it more abstract in *The Rise of the Expert Company*.

46. On the day I wrote this paragraph, the Timken Company ran an ad beginning: "Who would have imagined that one day there would be bearings so advanced they could actually think?" Who indeed! (The ad appeared in *Business Week*, July 1, 1991, p. 20ff.)

47. For an example of this, see John Seely Brown, "Research That Reinvents the Corporation," *Harvard Business Review*, January-February 1991, p. 108.

48. GM ran widespread advertisements in the summer of 1991 making this claim.

49. Russo and Schoemaker, *Decision Traps*, p. 187. The authors devote two of the ten chapters in this excellent book to learning from experience.

50. In Rothschild, *Bionomics*, p. 103. (Emphasis added.)

51. For instance, Rosow and Zager make this assumption in *Training—The Competitive Edge*.

52. This and the following list are taken from Rosow and Zager, pp. 181–182.

53. National Center on Education and the Economy, *America's Choice: High Skills or Low Wages!*, p. 3.

Chapter 9

54. Described in George Korzeniowski, "To Clone the Contented," *Human Resource Executive*, June 1991, pp. 62–63.

55. Wiggenhorn, p. 75.

Chapter 10

56. Bowsher, p. 38.

57. Quoted in Ursula F. Fairbairn, "Lessons in Education at IBM," *Personnel*, April 1989, pp. 12–16.

58. If you're interested in an extended discussion of this problem and its implications, you might want to look at my article "Total Quality Training" in the November 1990 issue of *Training*.

59. I'm indebted to Valorie Beer of Apple Computer for suggesting that I put it this way.

60. The two examples are taken from Marc Hequet, "Selling In-House Training Outside," *Training,* September 1991, pp. 51–56.

Chapter 11

61. Bowsher, p. 69.
62. Remarks delivered at the third annual Utah State University Institute on Technology Enabled Training, Logan, Utah, July 24–27 1991.
63. Sam Stern, "The Use of Technology for Training in Japan," *Performance & Instruction,* July 1990, page 1.
64. Walter L. Sanders, "Cost-Effective CBT at Federal Express," *Instruction Delivery Systems,* July/August 1991, p. 19.
65. Nico Krohn, "Users Aren't Embracing Multimedia," *Infoworld,* August 26, 1991, p. 13.
66. Eric J. Adams, "Lucasfilm Learning: In Search of the Elements of Design," *Instruction Delivery Systems,* July/August 1991, p. 6.
67. Ron Zemke, "Shell Scores with Interactive Video," *Training,* September 1991, pp. 34–38.
68. Alan L Zeichick, "Virtual Editorial," *AI Expert,* August 1991, p. 5. Note that Zeichick doesn't attempt to predict *when* interactive virtual reality will be "easy and affordable."

Chapter 12

69. Another example furnished by J. H. Harless of the Harless Performance Guilds. Harless is well known for developing effective and innovative job aids.
70. One more example from the files of the Harless Performance Guild.
71. Frederick W. Taylor, *Scientific Management,* pp. 104–111.
72. This example was kindly furnished by Jeff Nelson of Jeffrey Nelson Associates.

Chapter 13

73. Again, I'm indebted to Jeff Nelson of Jeffrey Nelson Associates for this suggestion.

Chapter 14

74. Referenced in U.S. Department of Labor Center for Advanced Learning Systems, "CALS Notes," March 29, 1991, pp. 12–13. The Center is located in the College of Education, Pennsylvania State University, University Park, Pennsylvania.

Chapter 15

75. Rothschild, p. 192.

76. Hamel and Prahalad, "Corporate Imagination and Expeditionary Marketing," *Harvard Business Review,* July-August 1991, p. 87.

77. Rosabeth Moss Kanter, "Change: Where to Begin," *Harvard Business Review,* July-August 1991, p. 9. (Emphasis added.)

78. Thomas A. Stewart, "GE Keeps Those Ideas Coming," *Fortune,* August 12, 1991, p. 44.

79. The information on Motorola is from an address by Robert Galvin to the 1991 Hunter Conference on quality improvement in Madison, Wisconsin. For the account of Chaparral, see Tom Peters' book, *Thriving on Chaos,* pp. 167-168.

80. You may notice the similarity between this cycle and the Shewhart or PDCA cycle used by Total Quality teams. The two are very similar. I developed the version used in this book both because I believe it's more complete and because I wanted to make the point that the cycle isn't limited to quality control.

81. Quoted from "Learning to Learn on the Job," a publication of Learning Resources, Inc., Stamford, Connecticut, p. 1.

82. Paraphrased slightly from Marcia Heiman and Joshua Slomianko, *Learning to Learn on the Job* (Alexandria, Va.: American Society for Training and Development, 1989), p. 2. See also n. 81.

83. The material in this section is summarized from my book *Teampower.* For a more detailed discussion of a learning environment and its relevance to effective teams, see Chapter 8 in that book.

84. Jonathan B. Levine, "Philips' Big Gamble," *Business Week,* August 5, 1991, p. 34.

85. Quoted in Roy Morrison, *We Build the Road as We Travel.*

Chapter 16

86. "Corning's Object Lesson on Competitiveness," *Business Week,* May 13, 1991, p. 122.

87. Rothschild, p. 192.

88. A. P. deGeus, "Planning as Learning," *Harvard Business Review,* March-April 1988. Quoted in Charles Hampden-Turner, *Charting the Corporate Mind,* p. 59.

89. Senge, p. 14. (Emphasis added.)

90. Senge, p. 14.

91. Peters, p. 196. (Emphasis added.)

92. Gareth Morgan, *Riding the Waves of Change,* p. 40.

93. Senge refers to Shell's use of scenarios at some length in *the Fifth Discipline*. There is also a very concise and effective discussion of them in Russo and Schoemaker's *Decision Traps*. The most detailed treatment of scenarios, however, is in Peter Schwartz, *The Long View*. The material in these few paragraphs is based primarily on Schwartz.

94. Rosow and Zager, p. 229.

95. Leonard, *Mastery*, p. 37.

96. Womack, Jones, and Roos, *The Machine That Changed the World,* has an in-depth discussion of these differences.

See the Bibliography for more detailed information on the publications listed in this section.

Bibliography

These are some of the books and articles I consulted while preparing this book. As is the case with most bibliographies, the entries range from fairly good to absolutely superb. A few fall into this latter group. I have asterisked them; if you get the chance to read them, you'll learn a great deal more about smart training in a few pages.

American Society for Training and Development. "Basics of Instructional Systems Development" (pamphlet in Info-Line series). Alexandria, Va.: ASTD, March 1988.

*————. "How to Produce Great Job Aids" (pamphlet in Info-Line series). Alexandria, Va.: ASTD, April 1989.

Bandura, Albert. *Social Foundations of Thought and Action: A Social Cognitive Theory.* Englewood Cliffs, N.J.: Prentice Hall, 1986.

Boothman, Terry, and Harvey Feldstein. "The Principle of Engagement," *Information Center,* April 1990, pp. 13–19.

Bowsher, Jack E. *Educating America: Lessons Learned in the Nation's Corporations.* New York: Wiley, 1989.

Brandt, Richard H. *Videodisc Training: A Cost Analysis.* Falls Church, Va.: Future Systems, 1987.

Brinkerhoff, Robert O. *Achieving Results from Training.* San Francisco: Jossey-Bass, 1987.

Brown, John Seely. "Research That Reinvests the Corporation," *Harvard Business Review,* January-February 1991, pp. 102–111.

Brown, Mark Graham, and Kathleen Chartier. "Improving Financial Service Quality," *Performance & Instruction,* October 1989, pp. 17–22.

Carnevale, Anthony Patrick. *America and the New Economy: How New Competitive Standards Are Radically Changing America's Workplaces.* San Francisco: Jossey-Bass, 1991.

Carnevale, Anthony P., Leila J. Gainer, and Janice Villet. *Training in America: The Organization and Strategic Role of Training.* San Francisco: Jossey-Bass, 1990.

Carr, Clay. "Expert Systems: What Do They Mean for Training?" *Training,* December 1989, pp. 41–48.

————. "Expert Support Environments," *Personnel Journal,* April 1989, pp. 87–104.

————. *Front-Line Customer Service.* New York: Wiley, 1989.

———. "Should We Train—And Was It Successful?" *Performance & Instruction*, August 1989, pp. 33–36.

———. "Skilling America: The Potential of Intelligent Job Aids," *Educational Technology*, April 1988, pp. 22–25.

———. *Teampower.* Englewood Cliffs, N.J.: Prentice Hall, 1992.

———. "Total Quality Training," *Training*, November 1990, pp. 59–65.

Casner-Lotto, Jill, and Associates. *Successful Training Strategies.* San Francisco: Jossey-Bass, 1988.

Chalofsky, Neal E., and Carlene Reinhart. *Effective Human Resource Development.* San Francisco: Jossey-Bass, 1988.

Chevalier, Roger D. "Improving Efficiency and Effectiveness of Training," *Performance & Instruction*, May/June 1990, pp. 21–23.

"Corning's Object Lesson on Competitiveness," *Business Week*, May 13, 1991.

Craig, Robert L. (ed.). *Training and Development Handbook*, 3rd ed. New York: McGraw-Hill, 1987.

Fairbairn, Ursula F. "Lessons in Education at IBM," *Personnel*, April 1989.

Feigenbaum, Edward, Pamela McCorduck, and H. Penny Nii. *The Rise of the Expert Company: How Visionary Companies Are Using Artificial Intelligence to Achieve Higher Productivity and Profits.* New York: Times Books, 1988.

Garson, Barbara. *The Electronic Sweatshop: How Computers Are Transforming the Office of the Future into the Factory of the Past.* New York: Simon and Schuster, 1988.

Gery, Gloria. *Making CBT Happen: Prescriptions for Successful Implementation of Computer-Based Training in Your Organization.* Boston: Weingarten, 1987.

———. *Electronic Performance Support Systems.* Boston: Weingarten, 1991.

Gilbert, Thomas. *Human Competence.* New York: McGraw-Hill, 1977.

*Gordon, Jack. "Measuring the 'Goodness' of Training," *Training*, August 1991, pp. 19–25.

Gwynne, S. C., "The Right Stuff," *Time*, October 29, 1990, pp. 74–84.

Hamel, Gary, and C. K. Prahalad. "Corporate Imagination and Expeditionary Marketing," *Harvard Business Review*, July-August 1991, pp. 81–92.

Hampden-Turner, Charles. *Charting the Corporate Mind: Graphic Solutions to Business Conflicts.* New York: The Free Press, 1990.

Hampton, William J. "GM Bets an Arm and a Leg on a People-Free Plant," *Business Week*, September 12, 1988, pp. 72–73.

Hawthorne, Elizabeth M. *Evaluating Employee Training Programs: A Research-Based Guide for Human Resources Managers.* New York: Quorum Books, 1987.

Heiman, Marcia, and Joshua Slomianko. *Learning to Learn on the Job.* Alexandria, Va.: American Society for Training and Development, 1989.

Hequet, Marc. "Selling In-House Training Outside," *Training*, September 1991, pp. 51–56.

Hoerr, John. "Sharpening Minds for a Competitive Edge," *Business Week*, December 17, 1990, pp. 72–78.

Honold, Linda. "The Power of Learning at Johnsonville Foods," *Training*, April 1991.

Kanter, Rosabeth Moss. "Change: Where to Begin," *Harvard Business Review*, July-August 1991.

Kearsley, Greg. The CBT Analyst (MS-DOS computer program). San Diego, Calif.: Park Row Software, 1986.

———. Cost/Benefits Disk (MS-DOS computer program). San Diego, Calif.: Park Row Software, 1986.

———. Problem Analysis (MS-DOS computer program). San Diego, Calif.: Park Row Software, 1987.

Knowles, Malcolm S. *The Adult Learner: A Neglected Species* (rev. ed.). Houston, Tex.: Gulf Publishing, 1984.

Korzeniowski, George. "To Clone the Contented," *Human Resource Executive,* June 1991.

Krohn, Nico. "Users Aren't Embracing Multimedia," *Infoworld,* August 26, 1991.

Levering, Robert. *A Great Place to Work: What Makes Some Employers So Good (and Most So Bad).* New York: Random House, 1988.

Levering, Robert, Milton Moskowitz, and Michael Katz. *The 100 Best Companies to Work for in America.* Reading, Mass.: Addison-Wesley, 1984 (2nd ed. 1987).

Levine, Jonathan B. "Philips' Big Gamble," *Business Week,* August 5, 1991.

Lund, Robert T., and John A. Hansen. *Keeping America at Work: Strategies for Employing the New Technologies.* New York: Wiley, 1986.

Mager, Robert, and Peter Pipe. *Analyzing Performance Problems.* Belmont, Calif.: Fearon, 1970. (There are also more recent editions, but the content is unchanged.)

Mahoney, Michael J., and Carl E. Thoresen. *Self-Control: Power to the Person.* Monterey, Calif.: Brooks/Cole Publishing, 1974.

Morgan, Gareth. *Images of Organization.* Newbury Park, Calif.: Sage, 1986.

———. *Riding the Waves of Change: Developing Managerial Competencies for a Turbulent World.* San Francisco: Jossey-Bass, 1988.

Morrison, Roy. *We Build the Road as We Travel.* Philadelphia: New Society Press, 1991.

Mullen, Jim. "Owners Need Not Apply," *Inc.,* August 1990, pp. 76–78.

National Center on Education and the Economy. *America's Choice: High Skills or Low Wages!* Rochester, N.Y.: 1990.

Nilson, Carolyn. *Training for Non-Trainers: A Do-It-Yourself Guide for Managers.* New York: AMACOM, 1990.

Norman, Donald A. *The Psychology of Everyday Things.* New York: Basic Books, 1986. (The paperback version of this book is entitled *The Design of Everyday Things.*)

Paquet, Basil, Elizabeth Kasl, Laurence Weinstein, and William Waite. "The Bottom Line," *Training and Development Journal,* May 1987, pp. 27–34.

Pearlstein, Gloria. "Preston Trucking Shifts to Performance Management," *Performance and Instruction,* August 1989, pp. 1–5.

Peters, Tom. *Thriving on Chaos: Handbook for a Management Revolution.* New York: Knopf, 1986.

Phillips, Jack J. *Handbook of Training Evaluation and Measurement Methods: Results-Oriented Methods for Evaluating Any HRD Program and Showing Its Profitability.* San Diego, Calif.: University Associates, 1983.

Pollock, Michael A. "Business Is Dragging Its Feet on Retraining," *Business Week,* September 29, 1986.

Posner, Bruce G. "My Favorite Company," *Inc.,* April 1989.

*Prahalad, C. K., and Gary Hamel. "The Core Competence of the Corporation," *Harvard Business Review,* May-June 1990, pp. 79–91.

*Reich, Robert B. "Who Is Us?" *Harvard Business Review,* January-February 1990, pp. 53–64.

————. *The Work of Nations.* New York: Knopf, 1991.

Rogoff, Rosalind L. *The Training Wheel: A Simple Model for Instructional Design.* New York: Wiley, 1987.

Rosow, Jerome M., and Robert Zager. *Training—The Competitive Edge.* San Francisco: Jossey-Bass, 1988.

Rossett, Allison, and Jeanette Gautier-Downes. *A Handbook of Job Aids.* San Diego, Calif.: Pfeiffer & Co., 1991.

Rothschild, Michael. *Bionomics: The Inevitability of Capitalism.* New York: Henry Holt, 1990.

Russo, J. Edward, and Paul J. H. Schoemaker. *Decision Traps: The Ten Barriers to Brilliant Decision-Making and How to Overcome Them.* New York: Doubleday Currency, 1989.

Sanders, Walter L. "Cost-Effective CBT at Federal Express," *Instruction Delivery Systems,* July/August 1991.

Schaffer, Robert H. *The Breakthrough Strategy: Using Short-Term Successes to Build the High Performance Organization.* Cambridge, Mass.: Ballinger, 1988.

Schwartz, Peter. *The Art of the Long View: Planning for the Future in an Uncertain World.* New York: Doubleday Currency, 1991.

Senge, Peter. *The Fifth Discipline: The Art and Practice of the Learning Organization.* New York: Doubleday Currency, 1990.

Sheedy, James L. "Retooling Your Workers along with Your Machines," in David Asman (ed.). *The Wall Street Journal on Managing.* New York: Doubleday, 1990.

Silberman, Mel (assisted by Carol Auerbach). *Active Training: A Handbook of Techniques, Designs, Case Examples, and Tips.* Lexington, Mass.: Lexington Books (D. C. Heath), 1990.

Smith, Barry J., and Brian L. Delahaye. *How to Be an Effective Trainer: Skills for Managers and New Trainers.* New York: Wiley, 1987.

Stern, Sam. "The Use of Technology for Training in Japan," *Performance & Instruction,* July 1990.

Stewart, Thomas A. "Brainpower," *Fortune,* June 3, 1991, pp. 44–60.

*————. "GE Keeps Those Ideas Coming," *Fortune,* August 12, 1991, pp. 41–49.

Stolovich, Harold D., and Mike Lane. "Multicultural Training: Designing for Affective Results," *Performance & Instruction,* July 1989, pp. 10–15.

Taylor, Frederick W. *Principles of Scientific Management.* Easton, Penn.: Hive Publishing, 1985 (originally published 1911).

Various authors. Topical issue on "Emerging Technologies," *T.H.E. (Technical Horizons in Education) Journal,* August 1991.

*Walton, Richard E. "From Control to Commitment in the Workplace," *Harvard Business Review,* March-April 1985, pp. 77–84.

Walton, Richard E., and Gerald I. Susman. "People Policies for the New Machines," *Harvard Business Review,* March-April 1989.

*Wiggenhorn, William. "Motorola U: When Training Becomes an Education," *Harvard Business Review,* July-August 1990, pp. 71–83.

Womack, James P., Daniel T. Jones, and Daniel Roos. *The Machine That Changed the World.* New York: Rawson Associates (Macmillan), 1990.

Zeichick, Alan L. "Virtual Editorial," *AI Expert,* August 1991.

Zemke, Ron. "Shell Scores with Interactive Video," *Training,* September 1991, pp. 34–38.

Zuboff, Shoshana. *In the Age of the Smart Machine: The Future of Work and Power.* New York: Basic Books, 1988.

Index

About the Author

Clay Carr manages an organization that provides training design, development, and delivery worldwide for the Defense Logistics Agency. The organization combines high training competence with a fanatical focus on meeting the needs of its customers. Although it charges for its services—a first in the Department of Defense—it constantly has more requests for work than it can meet.

Mr. Carr's previous books include *The New Manager's Survival Manual, Front-Line Customer Service, The Manager's Troubleshooter,* and *Teampower.*